Cure the Procrastination Puzzle with The Power of Habits

Declutter Your Mind with Over 7 Highly Effective Atomic Mindset Tricks and Start Mastering Difficult Tasks with Mini Success Lifestyle Changes

Werner Brendon Marcus

© Copyright 2019 - All rights reserved.

The content contained within this book may not be reproduced, duplicated or transmitted without direct written permission from the author or the publisher.

Under no circumstances will any blame or legal responsibility be held against the publisher, or author, for any damages, reparation, or monetary loss due to the information contained within this book. Either directly or indirectly.

Legal Notice

This book is copyright protected. This book is only for personal use. You cannot amend, distribute, sell, use, quote or paraphrase any part, or the content within this book, without the consent of the author or publisher.

Disclaimer Notice

Please note the information contained within this document is for educational and entertainment purposes only. All effort has been executed to present accurate, up to date, and reliable, complete information. No warranties of any kind are declared or implied. Readers acknowledge that the author is not engaging in the rendering of legal, financial, medical or professional advice. The content within this book has been derived from various sources. Please consult a licensed professional before attempting any techniques outlined in this book.

By reading this document, the reader agrees that under no circumstances is the author responsible for any losses, direct or indirect, which are incurred as a result of the use of information contained within this document, including, but not limited to, — errors, omissions, or inaccuracies.

Contents

The Simple Yet Effective Methods to Cure Procrastination ___ 1

Chapter 1: The Science Behind Why You Procrastinate ___ 2

Chapter 2: 5 Steps to Stop Procrastinating ___ 13

Chapter 3: How to Stop Wasting Time ___ 22

Chapter 4: Get Organized and Productive Even with a Hectic Schedule ___ 36

Chapter 5: The Secret to Become Motivated ___ 49

Chapter 6: Guaranteed Tricks to Make Habits Stick ___ 61

Chapter 7: The 5 Non-Obvious Things That Kill Your Productivity ___ 71

Chapter 8: How to Set REAL Goals You Will Stick To ___ 79

Chapter 9: How to Stop Being Tired All the Time ___ 86

Chapter 10: The Secret to Work with Intense Focus ___ 97

Chapter 11: Essential Apps that FORCE You to Be More Productive ___ 101

Chapter 12: Wake Up Motivated Every Day Hack ___ 113

My Final Words ___ 115

Unstoppable Day ___ 117

Introduction ___ 118

Chapter 1: The Foundation of Success ___ 122

Chapter 2: Fundamental Key to Daily Self-Discipline ___ 131

Chapter 3: Habits of the Disciplined ___ 143

Chapter 4: Surprising Mind Tricks to Master Self-Discipline _____ 151

Chapter 5: The Secrets to Resist Temptation _____ 159

Chapter 6: Break the Cycle Holding You Back _____ 167

Chapter 7: Getting Work Done Even if You're Lazy _____ 175

Chapter 8: Why You Need a Long-Term Morning Routine_____ 183

Chapter 9: How to Multiply Your Time_____ 191

Chapter 10: The Science Behind Why You Procrastinate _____ 196

Chapter 11: Defeat Procrastinating with Your Mind _____ 204

Chapter 12: The Growth Mindset Think Long-Term _____ 208

Chapter 13: Shape Your Future _____ 214

Chapter 14: Eat Something You Hate _____ 218

Conclusion _____ 222

Relentless Mental Toughness and Optimism _____ 224

Chapter 1: There are Physical Limits but None for the Mind _____ 225

Chapter 2: Mindset is Everything_____ 232

Chapter 3: The Mind of a Navy SEAL _____ 241

Chapter 4: Daily Habits that Strengthen the Mind_____ 249

Chapter 5: Fragile Mind to Unbeatable Mind _____ 257

Chapter 6: Must Know the 40% Rule _____ 266

Chapter 7: Develop the Confidence to Lead _____ 273

Chapter 8: Techniques from Navy SEALs _____ 280

Chapter 9: Mental Training of the Top 1%_____ 289

Chapter 10: How to Actually Break Bad Habits _____ 297

Chapter 11: The Difference between Winners and Losers_____ 305

Chapter 12: Guaranteed Strategies to Build Mental Toughness _____ 313

Conclusion _____ 322

The Simple Yet Effective Methods to Cure Procrastination

Blueprint to Solving the Time Management Puzzle and Develop Highly Atomic Habits Boosting Your Productivity with Over 7 Concise Strategies

Chapter 1:
The Science Behind Why You Procrastinate

Procrastination is you delaying or avoiding doing a task that has vital importance. It is common in most humans. It may be noticeable in some instances and difficult to identify in others.

Procrastination and Laziness

A common error that people make is to confuse procrastination for laziness. These are two different concepts. To procrastinate, an individual will opt for a task that appears to be easy, less strenuous, and less urgent in favor of more pressing work that seems to be difficult. You are postponing a task to do another task that is more pleasurable but usually has less significance. Laziness, on the other hand, is the act of remaining idle instead of performing a task. In this case, you don't carry out any other task during the time but choose to be inactive for that period. There is no motivation to do the work at hand, but you motivate yourself to avoid putting the effort required. A significant similarity between a procrastinator and a lazy individual is the lack of motivation to perform a task. The huge difference, in this case, is that while the lazy individual has no apparent intention of completing the task in question, a procrastinator will finish it later.

Why Do We Procrastinate?

As an individual, you must have had a reason to procrastinate at one time or the other. Although it is more noticeable in some individuals, it is often negligible in others. It is easy to remember certain cases where you have put things off just because you felt you had enough time. You may also not forget other instances in which you were looking for the best way to start a project, so you had to delay.

Most people tend to underestimate the work and effort required to complete a task. As a result, they wait until the last minute to complete the task. The wait for the 'right time' or proper motivation to perform a task also plays a role. There are lots of reasons why people procrastinate. Understanding the reason why you procrastinate is often the first step to eliminating procrastination. Below are some of the prominent reasons why procrastinators do what they do:

No Sense of Urgency in The Task
Most of the time, it is easier to pay attention to a task that appears to be urgent. It is the same principle we apply when prioritizing activities for the day.

There are things that we don't create time to do just because it doesn't seem urgent now. Although it may be on your To-Do list for months or years, you may never create time to complete these tasks. It is easier to feed a crying baby than it is to visit a cousin in another State.

You Don't Know Where to Start
How do I start? What is the first step to take? These are questions that often lead to procrastination. It is easy to get confused, become disorganized, or feel overwhelmed when you are unsure of the first step to take. When this feeling comes into play, it becomes difficult to get yourself to do a task. It is a unique

type of procrastination which is caused by negative emotions and not avoidance. Negative emotions often result in feelings of incompetence. An individual will prefer to play a video game instead of attempting a task that makes them develop feelings of self-doubt.

You Have A Fear of Failure

As individuals, we often set high-standards that we need to match when performing a task. In other cases, these standards are put in place by society. The fear of receiving harsh judgment due to a task you complete can lead to procrastination. If you think you won't be able to meet the societal standards or those you have set, it becomes easy to put off work. If you don't do anything, no-one will judge you. It is an easy escape from what you fear the most. Through this act, you eliminate the option of failing. It is a method that works for as long as you can delay.

An individual that has a fear of failure will find comfort in procrastination. If given the opportunity to make a choice, people will pick a subjective failure over actual failure. Subjective failure implies that you fail at a task since you don't perform the task. Actual failure suggests that you put effort into the task but produced undesirable results.

The Excuse of Working Better Under Pressure

Sometimes it is easier to refer to this as crisis-making. It is a situation where an individual believes that they do their best work when there is a lot of pressure on them. Have you ever gone over an entire course outline two days to the exam? If you achieve success, in this case, it is easy to believe that you can work under pressure. You often love the adrenaline rush that comes with the pressure. It is also a way for you to escape the boredom you are feeling.

You Don't Want to Do Your Work

There are specific tasks that you don't want to do. It is much more fun to play video games than to do the dishes or arrange your room. If the tasks before you are boring, an opportunity for a more enjoyable task is the obvious choice. Once a task makes you feel bored, it becomes difficult to do it.

Distractions

Sometimes, you may be willing to complete the task at hand. The main problem is you get distracted very easily. It means you always find something that seems better than the task at hand. Distractions often result in instant gratification. Completing a task will usually result in satisfaction, but it takes more time. There are lots of activities that serve as distractions. To some individuals, it may be access to the internet or social media sites. To other individuals, it may be video games. It is common for people to have multiple distractions.

You Worry Too Much

When you worry too much, it becomes difficult to achieve anything. You become anxious due to worry. Things often appear to carry excess risk to an individual that worries. It may also seem like an unnecessary task. As a result, they prefer to avoid putting up with the challenges that come with the task. Worrying often results in self-doubt. It develops the feeling of incompetence. To avoid self-doubt and incompetence, it is usually more palatable to remain in a position where you are comfortable.

The Need for Perfection

A large percentage of procrastinators are perfectionists. It means that they want a task to be perfect on completion. It often results in delays. As a perfectionist, the goals you set for a task can be unrealistic and overwhelming.

Completing the task then becomes very difficult since what you hope to achieve is seemingly impossible. Trying to get time to put in the right details will often lead to procrastination.

Low Energy

Your energy level usually determines how much work you get done. A low energy level implies that you will be unable to do much. It indirectly leads to procrastination.

A low energy level is common in individuals that have an unhealthy lifestyle. It may be a poor diet or low quality of sleep that results in sluggishness or tiredness. The cause of low energy levels will differ for every individual so learning your reason for low energy is essential. To provide the necessary energy boost for a day, a lot of people perform exercises. Individuals that perform exercises in the morning will be motivated for work during the day through the energy boost it provides. Recognizing that you have a low energy level is quite easy. It may show a lack of physical energy to perform important tasks. You often find it easier to sit on a couch and watch television.

Finding Reasons to Delay

Delaying means you are simply putting off various tasks for certain reasons. The delay of a task is often not dependent on its urgency or difficulty in this case. Sometimes the reasons may be valid while at other times they may not. Some of these reasons include business and fatigue. When an individual claim to be busy, it may be a valid reason. Nonetheless, business may often result from an inability to say no when necessary. As a result, you receive so many tasks that it becomes overwhelming. Fatigue may also result from having too much to do.

Creating Too Many Lists

Making lists is a meaningful way to organize your tasks as well as your thoughts. So, what happens when you make excessive lists? Too many lists often result in too many things to consider. You pay attention to the smallest details of a project. In most cases, you are unable to get any actual work done during the time you spend creating a comprehensive list.

You Lack Vision

In some cases, individuals often procrastinate when they have no idea of the end goal behind a task or its importance. The absence of a bigger picture commonly causes procrastination. The bigger picture is often the end goal or the vision of a project. A vision is a guide to a long-term goal. Without a guide, it is much more reasonable to focus on the things that will have an impact on the present. Through an excellent vision, it is easy to act towards a goal.

Acting in Defiance Toward Authority

There are times when things may seem to be unfair in a work environment. It may be a simple situation where you are given more tasks than your colleagues. It can also be due to being under the supervision of someone you don't get along with. In a bid to prove your individuality, it is easy to postpone tasks given in such situations. It may simply be to prove a point. As a result, you end up procrastinating simply because the task is from a person that you don't respect.

How Does Procrastination Negatively Impact You?

Procrastination affects individuals in more ways than they are willing to admit. It is noticeable when procrastination becomes the lifestyle of an individual. A chronic procrastinator will often get a fine due to late tax payments. It is also

The Simple Yet Effective Methods to Cure Procrastination

common for others to do their share of a project at work to avoid missing deadlines. It is also common to notice higher stress levels in procrastinators since they end up doing a large portion of work in a very short time.

Social relationship is another aspect of life that is negatively impacted by procrastination. A lot of people stop depending on you because you consistently let them down. You may fail at a relationship because you have a habit of changing plans at the last minute. There are other negative effects of procrastination in life. Below, you will find some of the impacts which are steadily dragging you backward in life:

You Miss Important Opportunities
Opportunities in life often come and go. How you handle these opportunities when they come your way is important. Do you take opportunities as soon as they open? Or do you assume it will be available until you are ready? Opportunities are often once-in-a-lifetime events. If you miss it the first time, there is no guarantee of a second time. For this reason, you need to take immediate action when they arrive.

Procrastination will often prevent you from making that split-second decision that would have changed your life for the better. It could be an opening for a scholarship. You may fail to grab this opportunity if you procrastinate on writing an application for the scholarship. Scholarships usually have a closing date for applications with conditions that may make it impossible to apply due to age restrictions.

It Lowers Your Self-Esteem
Low-self-esteem is a leading cause of procrastination in most individuals. Also, procrastination also lowers your self-esteem. It means that there is a cycle

that keeps on going when you procrastinate. By keeping the cycle going, you are not only missing opportunities and ruining your career – you are also steadily destroying yourself.

Various self-destructive tendencies result from low self-esteem. It becomes easy to doubt yourself, and you also believe that you don't deserve certain achievements. You hold yourself from taking a step towards progress, and then the frequent question becomes, "Why can't I just take a step forward?" Although it happens slowly over a period, procrastination feeds on your confidence.

Inability to Meet Your Goals

The things you set out to achieve or those you intend to change usually develop into your goals. It is easy to motivate yourself when coming up with the goals you want to meet.

Procrastination will often prevent you from meeting these goals. It may lead to a delay in acting or taking the first step towards the goal. It can easily overshadow your strong desire to make these changes or achieve something new. You may think to yourself, "I want it so bad so I will get it." Procrastination is a stronger resistance. Goals often turn our lives around for the better. The inability to achieve these goals means that there will be no noticeable progress in life.

Health Challenges

Anxiety and stress are some of the mental health challenges that have a close relationship with procrastination. Depression may often result from actions of procrastination. As time goes by, other areas of your life will be affected by the negative impact of depression. The anxiety and stress are often the results of

The Simple Yet Effective Methods to Cure Procrastination

procrastinating on a task excessively. It becomes visible if there are other individuals involved in the task.

Delaying or postponing your visit or appointment with the doctor or dentist is a much clearer picture of how procrastination affects your health. You may also postpone exercises that are meant to get your body in proper shape. In both cases, the effect of procrastination can be a lot worse than what you imagine.

You Could Put Your Career in Jeopardy

When building your career, your achievements, results, and how your work has a direct effect on your growth. There are various ways procrastination can affect this growth. Procrastination may result in an inability to meet your monthly targets while also affecting your ability to meet deadlines.

If you consistently miss deadlines or monthly targets, you may lose clients and miss opportunities for promotions. The worst-case scenario is that you will be out of the job in a short time. Short-term procrastination may be easy to cover up. Long-term procrastination will expose you to ruin. It is often a common cause of crashes on the path to career growth.

You Waste Valuable Time

Procrastination is often a time-wasting activity. It is more noticeable when you procrastinate on a task that has a direct influence on your life.

Determining the time, you waste procrastinating is not as easy as it sounds. Nonetheless, it is easy to notice that it has been three years after graduation without any step towards progress in your career. Now you start thinking about how you didn't apply for any professional course or add a new qualification to your CV during these years. In some cases, it may be failing to put in the necessary effort to pass a course. When you fail at an educational course, you often must wait until the next year to have a second chance.

Since you can't go back in time to make the necessary changes, you are left with regrets that are often very terrible feelings. Regrets appear when you start thinking about how you could have done things differently, how you could have tried, or how you shouldn't have given up. Depending on how important the task is to your life, you may have to create more time to achieve the goal.

Poor Decision-Making

Procrastinating on important tasks is one thing but making decisions while doing this always has a negative impact. The decisions you make will always be poor. But how does procrastination affect my decision making?

It is simple. Procrastination creates a new set of conditions that will not be present if you already completed a task. Making decisions based on the new conditions will often lead to poor decisions. One such condition is the pressure that builds up when your deadline is getting close. You begin to make hasty decisions without thinking them through. Emotions like, "How you would feel bad if you are labeled incompetent" also start to creep into your decision-making process. The results you produce in life often depend on the decisions you make, either good decisions or poor decisions.

It Has a Negative Influence on Your Reputation

If you keep making promises you can't keep, no-one will be willing to work with you. It means that you have a reputation for letting people down. It is one of the effects of procrastination.

The Simple Yet Effective Methods to Cure Procrastination

It happens when you promise to help others with a task and fail to deliver on the promise by the deadline. As soon as you understand that you already have a reputation for missing deadlines, you also make it easy to procrastinate. No-one is surprised by your behavior, and neither are you. One of the problems that come with a damaged reputation includes the unwillingness of other people to depend on you. It can result in missed opportunities down the line. Your friends and co-workers don't want to be stuck cleaning up your mess after you fail to deliver.

Chapter 2:
5 Steps to Stop Procrastinating

Stopping procrastination will be impossible if you don't take any action. In acting, the right move is also significant. In this chapter, I will be discussing the best steps to take in stopping procrastination.

Forgive Yourself for Procrastinating

The infusion of negative emotions into your life is much easier when you engage in self-criticism. It generates emotions like depression, fear of failure, and anxiety. These are emotions that distract you from your goals, prevent you from taking actions, and disrupt your focus. You cannot create an environment that promotes your best performance through self-criticism. Failure is often a good way to learn your weaknesses and improve on them. If you don't take any action, you don't have the opportunity to fail or learn from your failures.

Why You Should Forgive Yourself

When you can forgive yourself for your failure, it becomes easy to go after a new goal quickly. You are more focused on growth and avoid dwelling on the past. Your desire to grow and learn outweighs your focus on performance-based goals. Since you don't have a fear of failure, you are less likely to take actions that result in procrastination. It becomes easier to create plans that will lead you towards a specific goal.

The Simple Yet Effective Methods to Cure Procrastination

Another significant benefit of forgiving yourself is the improvement in health. You are less prone to depression, anxiety, or stress. It will also follow through on health-related goals like weight-loss. Admitting mistakes, recognizing parts of your life that need enhancement, and being accountable for your actions is also possible if you can forgive yourself. Forgiving yourself when you procrastinate is a three-step process. It includes the following steps:

- Understanding and accepting that you are procrastinating. Allowing your body experience regrets, guilt, and the feelings that follow.

- Forgiving yourself for these feelings.

Understanding and Accepting That You Are Procrastinating

Sometimes, shifting a task to a later time may not be procrastination. In such situations, there is usually a legitimate reason why this task must be done later. It is what we refer to as re-prioritizing.

When you start evading tasks for an indefinite period without any genuine reason, then you are probably procrastinating. There are other signs of procrastination you should look out for. These include the following:

- Having a recurring item with significant importance on your To-Do list without taking any action.

- Stopping mid-way through a high-priority task to get a cup of coffee or respond to social media messages.

- Having a schedule filled with tasks of low-priority.

- Delaying until the 'right time' or 'right mood' to start a task. Failure to make decisions despite going through your emails over and over.

- Delaying your high-priority tasks while completing low-priority tasks that other people have assigned to you.

Experiencing Regrets and Guilt

The only way you will have the opportunity to forgive yourself is by experiencing certain negative emotions. If you fail to meet a deadline as a result of procrastination, it may often lead to self-criticism. It means you feel guilty for missing the deadline.

The first step is to understand that feelings of self-criticism are a natural response that is acceptable. As a human being, it is part of you. It is the same way a lot of your friends or colleagues experience fear, sadness, and anger. Negative emotions are like the rough times and difficulties in life; they will always be present. At one point, they will have to leave. It is crucial you don't judge yourself during the period these emotions are present.

Forgiving Yourself for These Feelings

The temptation to criticize your actions will always creep up. It is crucial you are vigilant any time these temptations become strong. Instead of throwing yourself under the bus, respond to these negative emotions in a more positive, compassionate manner. The secret to forgiving yourself is to recognize when you are harboring feelings of suffering, failure, and sorrow. Responding with kindness and positivity will complete the process of forgiveness.

Having a Game Plan for Achieving Goals

The Simple Yet Effective Methods to Cure Procrastination

How you go about creating your goals can often be a reason why you procrastinate. A lot of goals we set are often as a result of our excitement at that time. Once the target is set, you have no direction, so you move towards a less stressful path. That is not how goals work. Heading in any direction that seems the best will often leave you feeling lost with thoughts that you will never reach your goal. At this point, procrastination sets in. You start making excuses like, "It is too difficult," or "I'll try again next week."

There is no way you will achieve a goal on your To-Do list without making attempts. Waiting for the best to happen without putting in the work is why a lot of people are still over-weight and why others have still not started their business. To achieve your goals, you must be ready to self-manage these goals. It is a process that involves you getting in the driver's seat and steering yourself to the best position to achieve the goal.

Developing the Plan

A goal planner is vital if you are to make any real attempt at achieving your goals. A plan is a momentum that keeps throwing you towards the goal you intend to accomplish. Your plan should include the steps that you will take from the moment you set your mind on the goal until the moment you achieve the goal. A good plan will make it difficult to procrastinate. You will only procrastinate if you don't know how to get to the next point.

Your goal planner should also include a schedule. The schedule should show a specific date when you will take the first step towards your goal. Since you have listed steps, these are small tasks within the overall project. It means that each step should have a date and a deadline. To complete each step, you must commit to the step. As you progress through each step, there should be a milestone. The milestone is a point where you will celebrate your progress so far. It is also a form of motivation that eliminates any feeling of procrastination. The momentum you gain from the small steps you complete is usually the motivation that drives you to the end of the goal.

Reviewing Regularly

You can't learn a lot in life if all your focus is solely on what lies ahead. Sometimes, you need to look at how you got to your current position. It is also a way of checking for any other opportunity that is available. You can also improve your plan or re-evaluate some of the strategies within the plan. It is also a time when you re-evaluate yourself to determine if you still have the same strong feelings for the goal.

Through a review process, you will be able to identify achievements that are worth celebrating and failures that can teach you something new. You can also look at the future and the strategies for the future. Has there been any change in your circumstances to render these strategies obsolete? If a strategy is obsolete and you are unable to make changes in time, you will end up getting stuck at that point. This is when it becomes effortless to procrastinate. Your thoughts may run towards, "I've gotten quite far. I can take some time off to fix this strategy."

You also need to reflect deeply on your desires. It is acceptable for your desires towards the goal to change as your circumstances also change. The primary purpose of a review and reflection is to determine where you stand. It is also helpful in making sure you can adjust to changes in the direction that leads to your goal.

Avoid Perfectionism

The Simple Yet Effective Methods to Cure Procrastination

Perfectionism is an unrealistic ideal that usually promotes failure and procrastination. Unrealistic expectations and perfectionism can overwhelm us and set us up for failure. When you try to be perfect, you are likely going to develop feelings of anxiousness. It may sometimes prevent you from doing the task. Finding a way to avoid perfectionism is an excellent solution to the problem of procrastination. Perfectionism is noticeable in various instances. If your thoughts are filled with phrases like, "I need this project to be perfect" or, "I don't have the right tools to do justice to this project," then you are a perfectionist.

Imagine a task where you must design a logo. If you have an unrealistic expectation of your design skills, you may worry about creating a logo that isn't perfect. It will lead you to avoid making any attempt at designing the logo. Procrastination then comes as an option to prevent coming to terms with the fact that your design isn't perfect.

Your Right to Imperfection

If you accept that you can be imperfect, then you will be able to get around to doing any task without procrastination. No-one will be able to see if you are a great logo designer if you don't design any logos. It is why you need to understand that completing a task is much better than being perfect.

Perfectionism doesn't apply to everyone. Regardless, a lot of people also procrastinate because they don't want to be judged as incompetent by others. If you find yourself in this situation often, then you there are certain steps you can take.

Simple Steps to Avoid Perfectionism

Step 1
Get a clear understanding of why you are delaying a task. Do you have unrealistic expectations for your skills?

Step 2
Come to terms with the fact that your quest for perfection is preventing you from moving forward. Recall all the instances that perfection caused you to fail at a project.

Step 3
Accept that it is okay to be imperfect. Realize that it is better to be done with a task than to seek perfection and not make any progress. There will always be opportunities to improve on a project once it is complete.

Step 4
When you are procrastinating, take note of your thoughts. Are you having perfectionist thoughts? Counter these thoughts with logical reasoning.

Break Down a Project into Small Tasks and Remove Distractions

A Smaller Task Is More Straightforward to Tackle
If you find a task overwhelming, it becomes easier to procrastinate. Dividing your larger tasks into smaller bits is a helpful way to simplify the task. Once you separate it into these smaller bits, it becomes possible to focus on each bit. If a task still looks overwhelming after breaking it down, you can simplify it further. Breaking down a task into its simplest form will make it possible to

The Simple Yet Effective Methods to Cure Procrastination

finish a small part within a short time. As you complete the smaller portions, you can make rapid progress towards the finished project.

Let your focus be on each small task so you can produce the best results. As soon as you complete a small part, you can go on to the next part. Having deadlines for each small task is equally important. A single deadline for a project can often cause individuals to procrastinate until there is no time left. Creating specific deadlines also helps when breaking down a larger task.

Since your project will have an overall deadline, you can use this as a guide when creating specific deadlines for your smaller tasks. There should be a sense of urgency when creating deadlines. In this way, you will understand that you can ruin your plans if you fail to meet any deadline.

Removing Distractions

Sometimes, we procrastinate because we run out of energy for useful work. What is the easiest way to run out of energy in the workplace? It is by having to resist distractions around you. Imagine how difficult it is to resist visiting your Facebook page if it is open in a browser tab with notifications coming in. It may be easy at first, but you are likely going to give in later. As you start scrolling through your timeline, you end up procrastinating on important tasks. You will procrastinate more if you take actions that make procrastination seem like an easy option. Using site-blocking apps can help to block any site that can be a potential distraction. It is an option that is more suitable than deleting your profile entirely.

Have Someone Hold You Accountable

Move with People That Inspire You

Being around certain individuals can influence the way you behave. If you are lucky to spend some time with Elon Musk, you are going to have the inspiration to work harder. You won't get that opportunity as frequently as you require.

Nonetheless, this simple strategy remains effective. There are lots of hard workers and go-getters that you will interact with daily. These individuals can be your colleagues at work or your friends. Spending more time with these individuals will have a positive effect on you. It becomes easy to adopt the spirit and drive they put into all their activities.

Form A Team with A Close Friend

A close friend or companion to work with makes the work process easy to cope with and fun. Any person you choose as your buddy should also have goals that he/she is looking to achieve. Each person will be answerable for their actions as regards these goals. Although it is a lot better if you and your buddy have the same goals, it is not a necessity.

Goals that are similar make It possible to learn from one another. On a much larger scale, you can also inform more friends, acquaintances, and colleagues about new projects you are working on. People will like to talk about these projects to learn about new developments.

Is There Anyone That Has Accomplished a Similar Goal?

Do you have a goal? What is the goal you want to achieve? Do you know anyone that has reached a similar goal? Connecting with people who have achieved a similar goal is very helpful. They serve as proof that the goal in your sight is achievable. It is the most suitable trigger to get you to act towards the goal.

Chapter 3:
How to Stop Wasting Time

Time-wasting is often due to the irrelevant actions that we take. A great example of an irrelevant action is this introductory paragraph for a chapter heading that is self-explanatory. Straight to business:

Are You Intentionally Procrastinating?
There are certain cases where you knowingly delay a project. A lot of people usually say they are waiting for the 'right time.' Others say they want to get 'in the mood.'

Whatever your excuse, these are instances where you delay your projects on purpose. In other situations, it may be your willingness to complete tasks for other people rather than face your tasks. Although you may be helpful to these people, you are doing it at a cost.

In cases where you avoid your tasks, it is common for individuals to panic when the deadline starts getting close. Your state of panic is because you haven't done anything regarding the task. As a result, the job becomes an immediate emergency you must deal with. If you can identify these situations and accept that you are procrastinating, it becomes easy to overcome procrastination. Without proper identification of the reason for your procrastination, you cannot devise a suitable course of action to take in solving the problem.

The step to overcoming these time-wasting traits is to understand that you cannot wait for conditions that suit you before working on a project. You need to act immediately. Immediate action will also serve as motivation and prompt you to achieve more.

Avoid Multi-tasking

A lot of people may consider multi-tasking as a useful skill. When multi-tasking, an individual usually attempts to complete different tasks at the same time. It means they will have to continue shifting focus between various tasks until the tasks are complete. In truth, multi-tasking is usually effective when handling small tasks. For a more complex task, it is challenging to multi-task. In the end, it will take more time to complete the tasks.

If you attempt to divide your attention among various tasks, not only will you waste a reasonable amount of time, but you will also reduce your overall productivity. It is due to the unnecessary change in context that you will need to adapt to each time you move to a different task. Just because you appear to be very busy doesn't imply that you are making any reasonable progress in your task. Keep things simple. Focus on one task at a time. It will improve the quality of your output and productivity.

Take Immediate Action

If there is a task that you need to attend to, why not act as soon as you receive the task? Putting the task aside for a later date easily leads to procrastination.

Addressing small tasks and minor issues as they crop up will prevent you from dealing with a large complex task in the future. It also becomes difficult to achieve your immediate goals if you still have tasks from the past that require your attention. A lot of individuals often use these tasks as an excuse not to handle their present tasks. You are more likely to complete a task once you start working on it. Therefore, you should avoid setting aside a task for another time. If you find a task that requires your attention, address it as soon as possible.

Remove Distractions That Are Around You

There are lots of things that can serve as distractions when working on a task. The most common form of distraction nowadays is your phone. Your computer can also be a huge distraction if you are not careful. Creating a unique workplace can also help to avoid distractions. When setting up this workplace, you need to eliminate all forms of distractions. It is also vital you identify anything that serves as a personal distraction to you.

A common distraction can be a window through which you can enjoy an outdoor view. It can also be a desk that is cluttered. If there is a window with an excellent view in your workplace, then turn your desk away from the window. If a cluttered desk can distract you, then clean up the desk and tidy up the area around to eliminate distractions. Since phones and computers can be a huge source of distraction, there are various steps you can take. You can choose to turn off Wi-Fi access on your phone and computer if the internet is a distraction. You can also disable notifications on both devices when working on a project.

If internet access is necessary for your work, then use software that can block access to social media sites or other web pages that can serve as distractions. To avoid completing a task, distractions are usually the best options. Once you can identify your personal distractions, it becomes easy to remove these distractions.

Develop Better Strategies for Handling Your Email

The most effective way to manage your email is to ensure that you organize and clean your inbox. Answering emails can be a significant time-waster if you don't adopt the right method to handle it effectively. Without a proper plan, you will become a slave to the notification bell that goes off as soon as you get a new message. Regardless of the task at hand, you will instinctively switch to the email before returning to the task at hand.

As a result, you lose focus, motivation, and momentum towards the task. Below are the specific steps you can take to handle emails effectively.

Respond to All Your Emails Together

The same way you will handle tasks that are similar at the same time, you can also respond to your emails at the same time. You need to avoid responding to emails as they come in. By responding to emails at the same time, you can reduce your time spent on responding to each message.

Create Folders for Emails

It is possible to use a single account to manage various email addresses. It can be challenging to identify emails from each account without a label. To identify personal emails or business emails, you can use a filter and label on each address you manage on the account. To save time, you can attend to the business emails now and then go through your personal emails during your free time.

Short Emails Are Better

An email can be your work tool which you keep professional. To make it appear professional, you should make your email simple and straight to the point. Since you spend less time constructing your messages, you will have more time to spend going through other messages.

Allocate a Specific Time to Check Emails

Allocating a specific time to manage your email can be very beneficial. You can choose to check your email twice a day. The first time can be in the morning. During this period, you can respond to new messages that may have come in the previous day or earlier in the day. The second time can be after lunch. Having an automatic response can also help save time when responding to emails.

Prioritize

Prioritizing is an important step you take after breaking down a project into smaller tasks. It depends on how important each task on the list is to the overall project. As a result, you will be listing the items in descending order of importance. Using a color-coding system or a letter system can serve as a visual cue when prioritizing your tasks. Below are steps you can take when prioritizing:

- Create a list of all your activities the previous night.

- Identify the most important tasks on the list.

- What tasks are my personal tasks and what tasks are requests from others?

- What is the most difficult task on the list?

- What is the deadline for each task?

- How much effort do I require for each task?

As soon as you take these steps, it becomes easier to arrange your tasks by priority. There are a few things you should also do when prioritizing. You need to be flexible and avoid putting off personal goals.

Using the Eisenhower Matrix to Prioritize

When prioritizing your tasks for the day, the Eisenhower Matrix can be very beneficial. It is also helpful in making quick decisions. It is a decision-making strategy introduced by Dwight Eisenhower. It is a principle that is suitable for addressing your tasks in order of importance and urgency.

There is a need for this principle since unexpected changes are bound to happen during your day. These changes may affect your plans for the day. The strategy is a simple way to deal with these random disruptions and minor emergencies. There are four quadrants in the Eisenhower Matrix, and each quadrant needs a unique strategy and approach to address it. The arrangement of tasks into each quadrant is based on the urgency of the task. Tasks that you should not include in your lists and those that you should delegate to others will also become easy to identify.

Quadrant 1 (Q1): Urgent and Important Tasks

The tasks that fall within the Q1 are those that you should address first. These are the tasks that have a significant impact on your career or life. They need to be completed immediately. Completing a project that is due by the end of the workday is a Q1 task. It may also be a reply to a time-sensitive message from a client.

Quadrant 2 (Q2): Important Tasks but Not Urgent

The tasks that fall within the Q2 are the tasks that are important but do not require immediate action. These are tasks that have a significant impact on the long-term goals you intend to achieve.

A professional course that will get a certificate you need to enhance your career will fall in this category. Taking the course is important to your career, but there is no deadline to achieve this goal. Overlooking the tasks in the Q2 is easy.

Quadrant 3 (Q3): Urgent Tasks but Not Important
When you say yes to all requests you get, it is easy to pile up some tasks that are urgent but not important to you. These are tasks that have no significant benefit to you. Tasks in the Q3 are easy to delegate to other individuals. It is important you delegate these tasks carefully. Distractions are the main reason why you end up thinking that a task is urgent. Giving immediate responses, using your phone, or reading emails are some common distractions that can get you here.

Quadrant 4 (Q4): Unimportant Without Urgency
The main time-wasting tasks that you need to avoid at all cost make up the Q4 of the matrix. Since you are looking for options to create more time, eliminating Q4 tasks is your best option. You can then reinvest the time you get from eliminating these tasks into more beneficial quadrants. It is important you understand that certain Q4 activities are necessary for your life. It is often a way to balance your work life with your professional life. Some Q4 tasks include scrolling through the internet, watching TV, and spending time with your family. Spending time with your family is a task that you should perform to balance

your professional life. Watching TV may look like a good form of relaxation, but there is no significant benefit.

Time Management with a To-Do List

Create a To-Do List for Each Day of the Week
Planning is one of the most efficient ways to increase performance and productivity. Nonetheless, there are very few people who plan their day. With a To-Do list, you can simply plan your day with a paper and pen. Using technology, you can also incorporate time management apps to plan your activities every day.

Make It A Habit
When you repeat an action continuously, it slowly becomes a habit. The same applies to the use of a To-Do list. Always follow the activities on the list. You should also include any new activity that comes up to the list. A good step is to make your list the previous night or at the close of the day. The activities on the list that you are unable to achieve should come first on the list for the new day.

Create Your List the Previous Night
Sitting up the night before to create your lists is a sure way to improve your productivity. It is a way of planning. Your competence is a measure of how effectively you can make plans.

It is easier to rise above procrastination if you can develop excellent plans. You will also prepare yourself mentally for your goals. As you sleep, you will subconsciously go over the list, think of the best ways to achieve each goal, and wake up with new ideas on how to go about it. You will be able to work faster and more effectively.

Put A Check on Completed Tasks
As you progress each day, you will be completing the items on your list. Tick off each item to give a visual representation of your progress. It serves as motivation as you look at your success for the day. Visible progress improves your self-esteem and drives you to achieve more. It is an easy way to overcome procrastination.

Types of To-Do Lists
Depending on the purpose, there are variations of a To-Do list. The first type you will consider is a master list. It is a list that contains all the activities, tasks, and ideas that you have for the future.

The second type of list is your monthly list. It is a list that contains the activities for a new month. It is the list that you develop when sorting the master list. The weekly list is the third list. Here, you create plans for the week ahead. There may be changes that you will make to this list as the list progresses. The final list is the daily list. It consists of activities that you will be performing on a specific day. Items from your weekly and monthly lists usually make up your daily lists.

The Importance of Saying No
Performing tasks for other people is a leading cause of time wasting. It is usually a result of saying YES to every request you get. In the end, you may end up stretching yourself too thin. If you can say NO to certain requests, you can get your time back. Now you have time to focus on things that are more important. It is also a way to avoid making promises that you cannot keep.

If you are the type that cannot say NO, there are certain things that you have accepted that don't give room for things that are important. It is why your schedule is usually full. It also makes you feel overwhelmed when other things crop up. You can save a lot of time by merely saying NO. It also saves you money when you learn to say no to that gym subscription you don't use.

What Can You Say No To?

There are lots of things that you can say NO to. It becomes easier to identify these things if you prioritize them. When looking to manage your time effectively, priorities play a vital role.

What are the things that you love doing? What are those things that matter most? What will be the effect if you don't do this task? As you begin to answer these questions, things become a lot easier. The items that are left on the list after answering these questions are your priorities. The others are not necessary. All you need to understand is that you need to give up certain things to achieve others. If you notice that your music lessons are preventing you from performing tasks relating to your job, you need to ask yourself a simple question – do you love your job? If the answer is yes, then you should give up music lessons for now so you can focus on the job.

The same also applies to what you do during your free time. Are you spending more time playing games than with your girlfriend? Do you love your girlfriend? If you don't want to lose her, you should be ready to reduce your gaming time to have more time with her. Since there are a limited number of hours in a day, you need to make some weighty decisions to make the most of these hours. Identify how you are spending your day and make changes. You can say no to almost anything as long as you have your priorities. Your priorities are the things that are important. Once you can focus on these priorities, you can say no to the things that don't matter.

The Simple Yet Effective Methods to Cure Procrastination

Best Ways to Say NO

Avoid Giving an Instant Answer

Giving an instant answer will often lead to poor decisions. An immediate answer is usually a common response to any request you get when you are busy or distracted. Another easy way to identify an instant answer is to take note of requests you accept and then you instantly regret making that decision.

How does it waste your time? We often spend a lot of time wishing we didn't accept a request. It is also common to waste some of our time trying to re-schedule or backtrack on decisions. These are common methods of time wasting. Understanding when you are about to give an instant answer is important. Make sure you STOP before taking such decisions.

There are a few steps you can take to avoid making decisions in haste. First, you need to think about the request. Do you have time for the request? Do you really want to accept it? Answering these questions may require a pause but the time it takes is far less than what you spend backtracking.

Delay Your Reply

Buying yourself a bit of time before deciding can be very helpful. A simple response like, "Let me get back to you" is an excellent way to create time to think. It is much better than the regret that comes with an instant reply. Now, you have the time to check your schedule. Do you have time for this request? What time will be more convenient?

There is usually no rush with the response in this case. The other party will understand that you need to check with another individual or go through your schedule. There is also no specific time by which you need to decide. It gives you the time to think through your decision.

Avoid Digital Distractions

Social media, emails, and smart phones are the common digital distractions that often make it difficult to say no. How?

Once you appear to be online, people will assume you have some free time. Since this assumption implies that it is convenient for you, there will be more room for unnecessary distractions. Turning off your internet access is an easy way to lock out digital distractions. It is an excellent way to say no to interruptions. This is because you also make it difficult for people to get in touch with you while working.

Would You Do It Tomorrow?

Another easy way to say no to a request is to determine if it is a task you will want to do another day. Is it something you are passionate about? What does this imply?

Any task that you will be happy to work on tomorrow is a task that you are eager to work on. Then it is okay to say yes to such requests. If you feel you won't want to do this task tomorrow, then your best option will be to say no. Since there is no enthusiasm to do the task another day, it will become difficult to motivate yourself to perform the task. It is the reason you have the same task on your schedule for four weeks straight.

Move it to a More Convenient Time

There are certain situations where you may have an interest in the task before you, but you don't have enough time now. Then the proper line of action is to shift to a convenient time. To avoid commitment, don't accept the request but give the person a specific date to check with you again. In this case, you can avoid overloading your schedule while the other person will have this task on their To-Do list.

Don't Get in a Match with Time-Wasters

There are lots of people who know how to waste a lot of time on tasks. It can be on a complex task or a straightforward task. Time has no value to such individuals. These are the type of people that get a NO as an answer. If you avoid working with such individuals, you have the opportunity of saving your time and avoid stress.

So how do you identify a time waster? A common habit of most time wasters is to set up a meeting or call and then wait until the last minute to cancel the plans. The time you spend preparing for the meeting, adjusting your schedule to create room, or in some cases, the time taken to get to the meeting venue is already time wasted. Nonetheless, they still want you to make new plans.

Any person who sends unnecessarily long emails or anyone that agrees to a document being set it at a time and then fails is also a time waster. You should learn to say NO to such people. It gives you the opportunity to use your time for other valuable ventures.

Why You Are Always Exhausted

Freelancers and entrepreneurs are typical examples of people who experience burnout when they always say YES. It is often due to accepting any project from all clients. They usually have a fear that there will be no new work available.

In truth, if you don't say no to projects now and then, it can lead to exhaustion. You will also have to do a lot of work that you don't enjoy. It can be quite tricky to turn down projects as a freelancer. The same applies when turning down clients as an entrepreneur. You can start by saying NO to certain projects that you don't enjoy doing. As a result, there will be more time to fit in tasks and projects that you are passionate about.

Polite Ways to Say NO
One of the primary reasons why it is difficult for people to say no is the thought of offending others. If this is your main concern, then you can learn some polite ways to turn down people.

If you want to shift the task to the next week, you can reply with, "I simply haven't got time this week." It is also useful if you would like it after a month. You can also say:

- "It is a no I'm afraid. But thanks for asking me."

- "I simply haven't got the time right now."

- "I'd love to, but I've got other family commitments right now."

Chapter 4:
Get Organized and Productive Even with a Hectic Schedule

It can be tough to remain organized and productive when your schedule isn't giving you room to breathe. In such situations, you need to learn how to utilize the little time you have effectively. The two areas I will be discussing in this chapter are the time-boxing method and the use of digital tools. In the digital tools section, you will learn about some of the most important areas that require organization and how you can use technology for the best results.

Time-Boxing

What is Time-boxing?
It is a productivity technique that is useful in managing your time more effectively. The technique involves apportioning a specific time to an activity. You then complete the activity within the allotted timeframe. It is a technique that is simple on paper but can be very difficult to implement. Here we will be taking an in-depth look at the time-boxing technique. Below are some basic things you need to understand to apply the method effectively:

Types of Time-boxes
The time-boxing technique consists of soft time-boxes and hard time-boxes. Time-boxes are separated into these categories depending on the process required to handle it:

- The end of a soft time-box usually gives room for people to conclude and complete their current activities, tasks, or discussions.

- The end of a hard time-box requires people to stop immediately, go on a break, and then begin the event that comes next.

During a soft time-box, hearing the timer alarm implies that it is time to bring the task to a conclusive end. As it should, it notifies everyone that the time allotted to this task has been exhausted. Regardless, there is still room to keep working on the task or keep the discussion going. The soft box method is applicable in situations where the idea of time-boxing is just being introduced. It provides room for the necessary adjustments to take place.

The hard time-box is a much more iron-handed approach. It is also applicable in a situation where the idea is just being introduced, but it does not give room for an extension. In most cases, people will usually find out that they are unable to produce any meaningful result before the allotted time elapses. After experiencing a similar event a few times, it becomes easier to adjust work patterns. It also becomes a lot easier to work with the time allotted to a task. You must understand the type of time-box you will be applying and the reason.

Making Your Plan
Planning is an essential aspect of time-boxing. The plan should be laid out at an earlier time. It will make the technique more effective. How much time do you need for an activity? Certain activities and discussions can go on for a very long time if there is no limit to the time allotted. Failure to clearly state the duration of an activity will often lead to misplaced priorities. It is often the reason why some people fail to achieve the essential goals of the day. They spend too much time dwelling on the least important topics. By setting the time

for a topic or activity in advance, you can avoid these issues. Using the time/value ratio can also be helpful in these situations. Sometimes, an impromptu meeting may come up in your workplace. These are meetings that usually don't have an agenda. It is essential you take a short time to come up with a clear agenda, with duration for each activity or topic on the agenda. Communication is also vital. If you have a speaker, you need to let them know the time duration for their session.

Making Your Time Visible

The time for each activity should be apparent to every member of the team. It means you need to use a timer app on your smart phone or a simple kitchen timer. To ensure that everyone knows the amount of time left, a countdown timer is more beneficial.

Avoid timers that utilize simple numbers to indicate the time left. Instead, opt for timers that offer a visual representation of the time. Although there is usually a moderator to monitor the time for each activity, a visual indicator of the time makes it possible for everyone on the team to function as a moderator. You will notice some people motioning towards the timer to get other members to focus. Since it is visible to everyone, it becomes easy for anyone to silence any chit-chat during an activity authoritatively.

What is the Maximum Length of a Time-Box?

An important question that people often ask when using the technique is the maximum length for an activity. What is the maximum length for a time-box? A maximum of forty-five minutes is suitable for an activity on the time-box. There are reasons for this choice. One such reason is that forty-five minutes aligns with the biological rhythm of the body. It is a fact that psychology also supports.

It is the same reason why schools limit each period to forty-five minutes. When developing your time-box, you should not exceed the maximum of forty-five minutes. You should also include short breaks that can vary from five – fifteen minutes. If you have a topic that will require more than forty-five minutes, then using multiple time-boxes will be necessary.

Taking Breaks

To also support the maximum length of each activity, there should be a short break after this time duration. You can set a five-minute break after forty-five minutes or a fifteen-minute break after ninety minutes.

Another easy way to make plans is to set a fifteen minute-break after a forty-five-minute activity. Since the action and the break sum up to sixty minutes, it becomes easy to use a full hour for your activity planning. Avoid remaining on your seat during your break. It is an excellent time to get around, enjoy the sights, and get some fresh air. Do not indulge in activities like going through social media sites or checking your email. These will often make you remain on your chair.

It is also vital you make a clear announcement of the time the break will end. Stating that there is a five-minute break is not as specific as saying that the break will last till 2:50 pm. Most individuals don't look at their watch at the start of a break. Instead, they are more likely to check how much time they have left. Therefore, knowing the time, the break will end is more effective.

What is the Right Action When the Time is Exhausted?

Standing your ground when the time is up is important for the effectiveness of the time-boxing technique. Frustrations and panic are common reactions you can expect if a person is unable to complete a task within the allotted time. It may be tough to deal with early on, but you will learn to appreciate it over time.

When working with others, providing a warning is important. Letting others know two or three minutes before the time up offers ample time to conclude their work. A visual timer can also be of help, either a kitchen timer or a smart phone app. As soon as the time for an activity or task is up, you need to decide on the right step to take. The options available are to either create a new time-box for the current activity or go on to the next action. It all depends on you.

Do remember, it is necessary you avoid focusing on what may appear to be important. According to your time-boxing schedule, you have already made definite plans based on the importance of each activity. Stick to these plans. It may also be worth taking a few minutes to carefully consider if it is worth creating a new time-box for the activity. Your decision should be purely based on the strategic goals you intend to achieve.

Advantages of Time-boxing
There are lots of benefits to the use of this productivity technique. They include the following:

- It promotes the inclusion of regular breaks.

- The technique encourages people to come up with results.

- It helps in maintaining a focus on priorities.

- The development of results makes it possible to measure progress.

- It becomes possible to predict when the next activity will begin since you know when the current activity will end.

- Anyone has the power to end un-necessary discussions during work regardless of position.

- It is an excellent technique to improve productivity.

Downsides to The Use of Time-Boxing

Although time-boxing is important and beneficial to a lot of people, there are others who may not find it as appealing. It may often be due to certain jobs that require the best quality. These are tasks that you need to perform regardless of the amount of time it takes to complete. Using time-boxing in such situations can lower the quality of the output. Another clear case is the need to stop an activity and switch to the next as soon as the time is up. It can be challenging to do this if you are in the zone and fully immersed in the task. No-one will be willing to give up that momentum which usually makes it easy to come up with great ideas.

Following a strict schedule may often be very difficult for some individuals. It is usually due to interruptions in the form of a colleague walking up to your desk, phone calls, or other distractions.

Setting the right length of time for an activity can also be very difficult. An activity with excess time will often make it very easy to procrastinate. On the other hand, if the time is too short it reduces your chances of accomplishing any meaningful result. It is important you assess your speed on various types of tasks before creating a time-boxing schedule. You can then organize your

Using Digital Tools to Get Organized

activities accordingly. As powerful a tool as time-boxing is, it is only effective when used under the right set of conditions.

Technology currently has a massive impact on how we perform different activities. The way you utilize technology can have a huge impact on your productivity. Learning about digital tools at your disposal can be very helpful. In this section, I will be discussing some very important productivity apps that you can easily use to organize your day and improve your productivity. To make things simpler, I have taken an extra step by creating different categories with similar apps.

Focus Apps

Focusing on your important tasks during the day can be very difficult with internet connectivity. That is why you need focus apps. These apps usually help in blocking some of the time-wasting sites you visit regularly. Apps in this category are suitable for people who prefer to be on social media sites like Instagram or Facebook instead of doing actual work. One of the excellent apps that you can use is:

StayFocusd

If you want to improve your discipline and focus, then you can try out the StayFocusd app. It functions as an extension on Google Chrome that limits the duration of your access to a site. There is a time allotted to a site for a day. You will be unable to access that specific site for the remainder of the day once you use up the allotted time. The blocking feature extends to specific pages, sites, in-page content like games, and subdomains. It promotes positive focus habits while blocking sites that waste your time during the day. Since there is a limit to how long you can use a website, it is suitable for individuals who like to keep some sites open in a browser tab. Other apps include:

- Freedom

- Focus

- Forest

Scheduling and Time Management Apps

The personality of individuals is often very different. Some people enjoy making plans and organizing their lives. For others, a little assistance will do a lot of good. In both cases, having an app that can help with scheduling and time management will be beneficial. They are suitable for making both short-term and long-term plans. Here is an app that falls within this category:

Todoist

This app allows users to take down notes like creating a text message quickly. The app then recognizes this message and creates a task by interpreting the text you input. Using a hashtag on the app makes it possible to group tasks into categories.

In a case where you have a text input that reads, "Visit the store for new games at seven p.m. tomorrow #gaming," the Todoist app will create a 7 p.m. reminder for the next day under the gaming category. There are also other additional features on the app including an option to integrate with more than sixty different apps. These include Slack, Dropbox, Amazon Alexa, and more. You can also choose to assign various tasks to people in a group using the app. Other similar apps in this category include:

The Simple Yet Effective Methods to Cure Procrastination

- Taskful
- Blink
- Google Calendar
- Things

Personal Apps

When your own life gets stressful, messy, and disorganized, turning to a personal productivity app is your best option. These apps provide reminders of the essential things you need to do. They remind you of your errands, upcoming birthdays, and what you have on your grocery list. If you have a goal you want to achieve, you can also set it up on any of these apps. Some are available in the form of meditation apps that ensure that your stress levels remain in check. An app you can try out in this category is the popular Strides app.

Strides

Strides is an excellent option for achieving some essential life goals. It may be a good habit you are trying to develop or a bad habit you want to eliminate. It also allows users to set up routines that they would like to follow. To ensure that you are held accountable for your actions, the app features a SMART tracker. If you love visual representations, then you would enjoy the charts, red and green pace line system, as well as the reminders that the app offers.

If you want reminders of your daily routine in detail, Strides is a great option. Another great feature is that the app is free. Others that offer similar functions include:

- Google Keep

- Mindfulness

- Kiwake

Workplace Apps

Your workplace is supposed to be the place where you get a lot of work done. It is one of the easiest places to get distracted. Due to these distractions, you may be piling up a lot of work. The chances that you will lose focus and have low productivity usually increase when you have access to a computer throughout your work period.

Apps that promote productivity in the workplace help with team management, files and documents organization, communication with team members, and tracking your tasks. The apps in this category vary in terms of function, but I will be discussing the communication app – Slack.

Slack

Slack is an effective communication app that is suitable for team communications. Connecting with team members on Slack is easy. The app helps users build and connect with over 1,000 team members. You can build a channel for communication on the app. There is also a feature to give the channel a name based on the topic of discussion or team.

The channel you set up on the app may only include a select number of individuals or can be a company-wide channel. In addition to the channel messages, you can also send a direct message to any member on the channel. It is much faster than using email. The app also supports videos, photos, documents, and GIFs sharing. It is possible to integrate this app with Twitter, Dropbox, Google

Drive, and lots of other apps you may use in the workplace. Other apps you can use include:

- Trello
- LastPass
- Quip

Writing Apps

Writing apps are useful for taking quick notes to ensure you can recollect important information later. In addition to notes, you can also use these apps in creating To-Do lists. There is an increase in the efficiency of the note-taking, and information recording features these apps offer. You will often find exporting, editing, annotation, sharing, and organizing options on these apps. Evernote is a popular writing app available.

Evernote

The Evernote app is a hybrid of a planner and a notepad. It is an excellent option for creating a To-Do list and make short notes. The functions available on the app include document sharing, sketching, writing, and dictating notes. You can choose to create a checklist or plan an agenda. There are premium features that you can access by paying a monthly subscription. Nonetheless, it still offers excellent functionalities on the free version. The writing apps have a lot of features that are common, but there are also some with unique features. I would advise you also check these alternatives:

- Hemingway Editor
- Notability

- Bear

Meeting Apps

The meeting apps are those that help when you are trying to schedule a meet. It may be a workplace meeting, event planning, or social media event planning. It helps to eliminate back and forth during the scheduling process to makes things much more manageable.

Doodle

A major problem with scheduling a meeting is finding the time when everyone will be free. It often results in multiple emails going back and forth to fix a suitable date. In addition to being time-consuming, this process can be very inefficient. By making use of the Doodle app, you have the option of selecting some dates that will be preferable for the meeting. The invitees can then choose from the list of suggestions you send to them. By functioning through Whatsapp, iMessage, email, Facebook, and other options, the invitees don't need the Doodle app to select. To ensure that everyone is on the same page regarding the date, the app supports integration with a calendar.

Email Apps

One area where a lot of people have difficulties is in effectively managing their email. There are lots of new emails that come in every day. It may be a personal email, work-related email, special offer emails, or spam. To minimize the time and effort it takes to read through your emails and properly organize them; you can use any of the numerous email productivity apps available. Below are some of the apps available:

Trove

The Simple Yet Effective Methods to Cure Procrastination

Trove is an email productivity app that provides functionalities that make it easy to organize your emails. It allows you to indicate what email requires your immediate attention and those that can wait till another time for a response. Users can categorize emails as Connect, Radar, or Nudge using flags. The flags serve as reminders indicating how you should deal with an email. Trove is an excellent option for individuals who get a lot of emails daily. There are other email apps you can try out if necessary, including:

- Newton

- Astro

Voice-to-Text Apps

As the name implies, these are apps that assist in transcribing audio. It is a great feature that helps when you must go to a lecture. It is quite common to find a few lecturers that don't give you enough time to keep up when handwriting.

Otter

As a student or a journalist, you can't underestimate the benefits of this note-taking app. It functions through the combination of transcription, audio, and speaker identification. It is a good app for days when you would rather listen than take notes. Using voice identification, it can identify the various speakers if there is more than one. The transcription option is also designed for the long lecture and conversations in the long-form. There is a free account that offers 600 minutes of free transcription while the premium account offers a recording time of 6,000 minutes.

Chapter 5:
The Secret to Become Motivated

Motivation is the set of needs and desires that drive an individual to take a particular action. Motivation can be intrinsic or extrinsic. The importance of motivation is to strengthen your behavior towards achieving a specific goal. There are different ways to get motivated. Read on to find out how.

Discover Your Passion
One of the easiest ways to get motivated is to do something you are passionate about. In most cases, you do things you are passionate about not for what you can gain, but for the meaning it brings to your life. It is easy to lose motivation when you are performing a task for the money involved. Setting your sights on only what you can gain will make you lose sight of why it is crucial.

Regardless of what you are doing, there will be days when you are feeling low. You may be low on energy, ideas, or inspiration. It doesn't matter if it is something you are passionate about or not. Doing things, you are passionate about will make it easy to persevere through these low periods.

Willpower
The ability of an individual to complete a task is what I refer to as willpower. It is the ease with which you can perform a task. Like the muscles of the body, willpower is a thing that you can relax and flex when necessary. You lose the

The Simple Yet Effective Methods to Cure Procrastination

ability to make the most of it when you fail to use it often. You can also make it more powerful through practice and training. It is also possible to weaken your willpower when you depend on it excessively during your daily work periods. There are two significant steps you can take to improve the way you utilize your willpower. They include the following:

Increasing Your Willpower

Similar to how you strengthen muscles, you can also strengthen your willpower. To push your willpower to its limits, you need to discipline your mind. It is also important you take proper care of your health. As a result, your willpower becomes stronger and higher.

Minimize Your Dependence on Willpower

Just because you have enough doesn't mean you should waste it. There are other easier ways to make it more effective. It is also like how we avoid overworking the muscles. Although you may be strong enough to carry all your purchases at a grocery store, a trolley can ease this task. With willpower, certain tricks help to minimize the amount of willpower you require to perform specific tasks.

How to Increase Your Willpower

The problem with a lot of individuals is that they don't understand that they have weak willpower. If you don't believe it, then try studying without responding to a social media message. Changing your career, starting an exercise routine, visiting the gym more often, or simply learning a new skill are some arduous tasks that often expose a weak-willed individual. It is the reason you need to develop strong willpower.

When this is all said, how do you develop strong willpower? It is important to understand that willpower is not something physical. As a result, you will be applying some methods that may seem somewhat unconventional. Since it depends mainly on your physical and mental health, using the tricks below will help in developing strong willpower.

Performing Exercise

Inactivity of the body will also lead to the inactivity of the brain. It means that the brain will shut down as the musculature shuts down during prolonged periods of inactivity. A musculature that remains active will provide the necessary support that the brain needs to function efficiently. The support is in the form of efficient blood flow to the brain. In offices, a new strategy to ensure that the body remains active is using standing desks.

If you don't have access to a standing desk, taking shorts breaks during which you move around can be very beneficial. To exercise the body doesn't necessarily mean you need to perform strenuous activities. All you need is for the body to be active. Tweaking your daily schedule to include an activity is an easy way to meet this requirement. There are easy activities you can include in your schedule. It may be standing in certain situations where you usually sit or using the stairs instead of an elevator. Getting a minimum of 10,000 steps in a day can also be very helpful.

Any activity you enjoy that will engage the entire body is suitable for this process. It is the easiest way to replenish and increase your willpower for the day. A walk is one of the easiest activities you can perform. It is also the best option when you are trying to get work done, but you feel completely exhausted. A simple five-minute walk around the office will have you feeling a lot better.

The Simple Yet Effective Methods to Cure Procrastination

Maintaining Good Health and Diet

There are various downsides to having an unhealthy body. One of them is an unhealthy brain. The brain is not only the most important organ of the body; it is also the most complex. It requires a lot of attention. When the brain is in a poor health condition, the impulse control of the body also becomes weaker.

The feeling of sluggishness you may be experiencing may be as a result of blood sugar fluctuations. The fluctuations are often an effect of being overweight or having a high Body Mass Index. These are both noticeable signs of an unhealthy body.

Sluggishness usually makes it more difficult to start a task, as well as see it through to the end. In addition to weight, a lack of micronutrients such as Vitamin D also affects the willpower of an individual. In this case, cognitive performance is usually the target. Keeping the body in a healthy condition will provide the necessary increase in willpower that you desire.

Getting Adequate Sleep

Sleep is crucial when topping off your willpower or increasing the limit. Its effects become noticeable when you apply it in combination with exercise and a good diet. Getting less than the recommended seven-eight hours of sleep per night is referred to as sleep deprivation. It is a situation which results in a lack of willpower. In more understandable terms, your mental functions will operate at a level like that of a drunken individual. There will be a negative impact on your willpower by just a single day of sleep deprivation. If you can get the full seven-eight hours rest per night, you can replenish your willpower to its peak levels. Besides, you also improve your productivity during the day.

Learn the Techniques of Meditation

Another popular method of increasing your willpower is through meditation. The importance of willpower is to help improve your focus and avoid distractions. When you meditate, it is a way of training the mind to focus. You train it to be able to maintain concentration on a small part of your life. It may be focusing on a mantra, your breath, or a point in the body.

Learning to focus on intangible things like your breath makes it easier to use your willpower to focus on the task directly in front of you. Another benefit of meditation is the complete control of your emotions. Temptation, anger, and frustration are some of your emotions that hinder your focus. When you meditate, you can allow these emotions to pass freely and then redirect your focus to what is important.

Stay Hydrated

Water intake is very important to us as human beings. A lot of us only understand its importance in keeping the body function. Water is also very valuable in maintaining your willpower. The cognitive functions of an individual can be negatively affected when dehydration sets in. Daily, you should consume at least eight glasses of water. It is equivalent to two liters.

Aim directly for your target, and you may come up short. The same applies in this case. It is better to aim for one gallon per day so you will be able to get past the minimum. In addition to increasing and maintaining your willpower, staying hydrated also helps in maintaining your weight by reducing hunger and improves the appearance of the skin.

Practice More

Your willpower is something that can be improved through practice. Repeatedly testing your limits will provide the necessary improvements you desire. There are lots of minor activities that can help in testing your willpower. Once you can complete these activities, you will observe improvements in your willpower.

Activities you can perform include resisting the urge to use your smart phone during a meal, going to bed early instead of watching another episode of your favorite series, drinking water in the morning instead of coffee, etc. Simple activities that are contrary to your bad habits are the best when it comes to strengthening your willpower.

Reducing Your Willpower Requirement

Like all important resources in the world, you must be careful about how you make use of your willpower. Just because your storage is full doesn't mean it won't go empty. To avoid using up your willpower quickly, you need to learn how to manage it throughout the day. There are different ways to avoid using up too much willpower on a single task. The strategies below will help in using only the necessary amount of willpower so you have enough for other tasks that may come up.

Split Larger Processes into Smaller Inputs

Intimidation is often an easy way to lose willpower. It is easy to become intimidated when you look at a project or task you are about to undertake, and the scope is more comprehensive than you imagine. It is like how it seems impossible to upload one blog post every week.

Simply split the larger task into smaller parts. For example, you can decide to write a 300-word paragraph of your blog post every day. At the end of 5 days, you will have a blog post with 1,500 words. As a result, the overall task becomes easier to tackle. You will require a ton of willpower to start a project or task that appears to be intimidating. When you break it down into smaller parts, you drastically reduce the amount of willpower you require.

Develop a Habit

What makes habits so important? They are activities you engage in sub-consciously. A sub-conscious activity doesn't require you to decide. Your body automatically knows that it is the right action to take at that time. A good habit you can develop is to make your bed as soon as you wake up in the morning, head to the bathroom, and wash your mouth. Once these activities become a habit, you require less effort to complete them every day. It also provides the opportunity to think about other things. Developing good habits is an easy way to conserve your willpower for the rest of the day.

Consider your commute to work every day. You may decide to develop the habit of reading the morning news before getting to work. If you can repeat this activity for a week, it becomes a habit, and you don't require any willpower to read the news on your way to work.

When creating a habit that will conserve your willpower, always consider your most demanding tasks. You can decide to develop a habit of completing the most challenging task of the day as soon as you get to the office. You may also add a condition that you can only go through your mail once the job is complete.

Committing to a habit can be very difficult during the initial stages. To make it easier to commit, you should learn to use commitment apps like Stickk and Beeminder. It is also important to remember that you can also develop bad habits. These may have an adverse effect of reducing your willpower.

How Is Your Environment?

The Simple Yet Effective Methods to Cure Procrastination

An easy way to maximize your willpower is to create an environment that minimizes its need. You will have more willpower if you don't need to use it frequently. What does it mean to create an environment to support your willpower? It is quite simple. A pull-up bar at the entrance of your office will reduce the willpower you require to perform a pull-up. In the same regard, you will use up a lot of willpower trying to resist using your phone if it is on your office desk and you keep hearing the notifications beep. If technology is a significant hindrance to your work, you can use certain apps to create a suitable environment. Apps like Freedom and RescueTime can help block certain sites to prevent access while working. Using Time-boxing techniques can also assist when you need to focus on a task.

Removing anything that may act as a distraction like your phone, your candy bars, or magazines can be very helpful. It is easier to forget about some things when they are not visible.

Using the If-Then Technique

When using this technique, you use an activity to serve as a trigger for another activity. It is also another excellent way to reduce the amount of willpower you require for a task. In this case, you create certain conditions like, "If I complete my first task at the office, then I can go through my emails." It is a simple condition that reduces the amount of willpower you require to focus on the present task. You understand that the only way you can check your emails is by completing the first task of the day.

As humans, we like to stay true to our words. Sometimes, having two contradictory ideas can be quite difficult. It is the reason why you are inclined to follow the conditions you have set. It is in a bid to prevent cognitive dissonance according to psychology. This technique implies that you can quickly begin a difficult task by creating a trigger using a much simpler task.

Understanding the Body Rhythms

At what time do you do your best work? At what time does your body need to take a break? How long can you go without using your phone? What is your circadian rhythm?

Understanding these types of questions is an easy way to become self-aware. According to the circadian rhythm, a lot of people lose some of their energy at about 2 p.m. while they experience the most fatigue at around 2 a.m. By learning what your circadian rhythm is, you can avoid excessive use of willpower during these periods. You can also reduce the amount of willpower you need for a task by learning about your ultradian rhythm. The ultradian rhythm regulates peak alertness and low alertness over a 90-minute cycle. Picking the peak periods to complete a task will reduce the willpower requirements for the task.

Don't Get Dragged into Hearing Bad News

The state of your mind can directly affect your willpower. An unhealthy state of mind is often a result of an unhealthy body. Other things that may result in an unhealthy state of mind include stress, sadness, and other negative emotions. Stress and sadness can often result from the type of information you consume. Information is available from various sources. It may be from a colleague, newspapers, social media sites, blogs, and other platforms.

Information that contains details on a downward trend in the markets, homicides in your neighborhood, or a bombing in a well-known city will often lower your willpower. Another easy way to lower your willpower is to go through the Instagram profile of a friend that is more successful. You may find pictures of exotic cars or a vacation to a Caribbean island. In truth, a lot of us are guilty of this action.

Learning to avoid these sources of bad news can be very helpful. The bad news you are getting in these situations have no direct impact on the decisions you will be making during the day. The information you need to learn about as a Forex trader includes the market movement. Any information relating to the life of a celebrity is irrelevant.

Develop a Personal Mantra

Having a personal mantra can be very helpful to motivate yourself to complete a task. It is an inspiration to be the best you can be and an affirmation of your great qualities. In general, a personal mantra is a statement or phrase that positively affirms the direction you want in life. When finding a way to achieve a goal, a personal mantra can encourage and motivate you to focus.

A personal mantra is only beneficial when it is visible and audible. Your mantra can also serve as a guide for your thoughts. If you are trying to lose weight but are currently thinking of taking junk food, an excellent personal mantra can be, "I am on the path to fitness, and my healthy body is my pride." To create a personal mantra, you need to do some thinking. It should be based on philosophy. Attaching a quote that you create or a quote from someone else is also important. The quote should be short and serve as a representation of the philosophy you have chosen.

Write down the mantra on a piece of paper that you will be able to see every day. You should also set aside a time each day when you read the mantra and make it a part of you. You should be reminded of your feelings every time you read your mantra. It should also reaffirm your beliefs in a case where you are slowly beginning to self-doubt.

Have a Hunger That Is Insatiable

What is the difference between a person that violently goes after a goal and another that gives up on a goal as soon as things become difficult? This is a question that applies to goal-getting as well as completing a task. It is something that you notice when you take the time to study human behavior in different situations.

A lot of successful individuals have an insatiable hunger. It is this hunger that keeps driving them when things get difficult. It is what serves as their motivation in tough times. Regardless of the setbacks and failures that some people face, they usually remain focused on achieving their goals. The ability to learn from failures, rise, and keep going is what makes them unique.

There are various things that you will get from an insatiable hunger. It will feed you images and thoughts of your success. It will also help in the elimination of self-doubt. Developing an insatiable hunger is like creating an inner conviction you follow. You can build this conviction based on people who have achieved a similar feat.

You keep asking yourself questions like; "What are the changes I want that I can get from achieving this goal?", "What kind of person will I become after attaining it?", "Why is it so important to achieve it?" Every time you answer this question, it motivates you to push forward towards the goal.

To build an insatiable hunger that will serve as motivation, you must be willing to adapt. Learn the best way to go from the challenges of life. Your motivation

The Simple Yet Effective Methods to Cure Procrastination

will usually come from your devotion to your goal. To remain motivated by your goal, it must provide meaning and purpose to your life. When a goal can provide these qualities, you will always have the motivation to achieve it.

Chapter 6:
Guaranteed Tricks to Make Habits Stick

Making a habit stick is a critical task. There are easy ways to make a habit but how do you make it stick? The steps below will lead you to that goal. They are all smaller parts of the more extensive process that you need to follow.

Start Small

When you are trying to make a habit that will stick, it is best to start very small. The mistake a lot of people make is trying to produce a huge change rapidly. Trying to achieve something large too fast will make it easy to give up on your goal.

Using the Seinfeld Calendar Strategy

It is difficult to stop doing an activity when you notice you have invested a lot of resources into the project. It can be a new blog post, a video mash-up, or a computer code. The same applies to your habits. If you can visualize the effort you have put into developing this habit, it becomes more difficult to break.

A simple strategy that applies to this situation is the 'don't break the chain' strategy that Jerry Seinfeld uses. In his description, he was trying to become a better comic by creating a joke each day. Once he achieved the goal for the day, he made a large 'X' on that day on the calendar. From this description, we can visualize two clear concepts. The first is a visual representation of your achievements. The second is a chain that is formed by crossing consecutive days with an 'X.'

You can use this strategy for any new habit you want to stick. As it becomes visible that you are on a roll from your calendar, you will be struggling to keep it that way. As a result, it becomes more difficult to break that habit. Every day you wake up without motivation to repeat any activity you set, the large crosses on the calendar serve as a reminder. It reminds you of the time and effort you put in to get so many crosses on the calendar. As a result, you will be motivated to repeat the activity. The longer your chain grows on the calendar, the easier it becomes to perform the activity. Repetition of the same activity over time will result in a habit that is difficult to break.

Use Implementation Intention

Implementation intention refers to the use of 'if-then' statements in developing your habits. It is an advantageous strategy since it doesn't depend on willpower to achieve results. The implementation intention will require you to create a link between the habit you want to develop and the activity you do regularly. By attaching a developing habit to an already established routine, it becomes easier to trigger your action.

Develop Keystone Habits with Goals Attached

It is easier to give up on a habit if there is no goal behind the habit. What is the long-term benefit of the habit? Is there a goal you will be able to achieve once you can form the habit? Setting goals in your mind is not the same as writing out your goals. By writing out your goals, you are creating a physical manifestation of the things you want to achieve. If they remain in the abstract world, it becomes easier to change them without any consequence.

When writing out your goals, be clear in the intent. What do you want to achieve? When do you want to achieve it? How do you want to achieve it? Why do you want to achieve it? Now you know the goals you have in mind. What are the habits that can help in achieving these goals? You should look for keystone habits that will help you achieve your goal at a much faster speed.

A keystone habit is merely a habit that produces a reaction that leads to the formation of other positive habits. Developing many keystone habits will produce other good habits in the long-run. It will also help in eliminating some of your current negative habits.

An example of a keystone habit is saving money. By saving money, you also develop the habit of spending on things that matter. It is because you know that your savings are only for emergencies and not for your daily spending.

You also learn to live within your means. Since you will be managing the little that is left after removing your savings, it becomes easy to live a life without borrowing. Although keystone habits usually have far more benefits, they do not require any additional effort to develop.

The first step is to list out the keystone habits that can help in achieving the goals you have set. The next step is to pay more attention to these habits during the early stages. In time, you will be able to reap more benefits from these habits.

Supportive People Should Be Around You

The way you behave is often a result of the people around you. If you have a friend that spends a lot of time studying, you will also find it easy to study. Distance is usually not a limitation to the support you get from friends. It is also common to choose goals that are like those of the people that are around you the most. So, if you want to be successful at a habit, you need people working on the same habits around.

For people who have friends with undesirable habits, it is crucial you find new friends with the habits you desire. The same applies to friends who are pessimistic. The negative comments from these individuals will have an adverse effect on your progress. Be selective of the five closest people around you. They usually have a significant impact on your behavior. Create a support group consisting of individuals that will serve as an inspiration and help you get back on your feet when you fall.

Pre-Commitment Is Necessary

By pre-committing to a habit, you are cutting off your escape routes. It means you have no option but to perform the habit or there will be consequences. A good example will be going jogging with a friend. If you agree to meet at 7:00 am, it becomes difficult to cancel your jog at the last minute. A lot of people wake up and change plans to their benefits once they start over-thinking. In truth, the lack of consequences for changing plans makes it very easy.

It is the same way you end up arriving late to a meeting after hitting the snooze button multiple times. "I'm feeling very tired. I still have enough time to rest for five more minutes. This will be the last time I hit the snooze button." In this case, if you have a friend that you agreed to meet at the bus stop at a specific time, it becomes easier to get up, so you don't delay.

In some cases, people pre-commit through a payment that they forfeit every time they fail to perform an activity. What better way to motivate yourself than to put some money on the one? Publicly announcing your daily targets is also a form of pre-commitment. Now you are accountable to your family and friends. To avoid making up excuses when people ask questions, you will want to perform these habits. It quickly becomes effortless to perform these tasks once you apply one or all these pre-commitment strategies.

Make Changes to the Environment

Your environment often determines how you behave. Designing your environment to promote the desired habit can be very helpful. A simple example is developing a habit of doing pull-ups. What do you think is the best method through which your environment can help you develop this habit? In this case, simply installing a pull-up bar at the entrance of your office will serve as your motivation.

It is a simple process that works in the same way as eating food simply because it is set in front of you. Understanding that your environment is the best tool to support your habit and using it to your advantage will help you effectively develop the habit. Taking deliberate steps to develop these habits will improve your chances of rapidly developing the desired habit.

Activation energy is also an important term you need to understand. It implies that there is a specific amount of energy that is necessary to perform a habit. A habit that requires high activation energy is usually more difficult to achieve. Reducing the activation energy is usually very important. For example, when learning to do pull-ups, you may find it easy to ignore the bar when stepping into your office space. The following steps can help:

- Reduce the activation energy by installing a pull-up bar at the entrance of your office space.

- Lock your office door before leaving.

- Place the key on the pull-up bar (to reduce the activation energy to reach for the pull-up bar).

It is an easy way to shift your attention towards the pull-up bar at the entrance of your office.

Negative Thoughts Should Be Eliminated

Negative self-talk is one way to derail your progress. It also causes the mind to develop a defeatist mindset. You start having more than a thousand thoughts that overshadow your goals, dreams, and hopes. Canceling all forms of negative self-talk is an essential step to take when developing habits that will stick. Questions that start with, "I don't think I can..." or "What if I can't..." are common forms of negative talk.

It is common to consider yourself to be unworthy of certain achievements. These include career, money, weight loss, and relationships. It may simply be thoughts that you do not deserve the things that you currently have. This is a flaw that is common to all humans. It is an imperfection that is inherent to us as individuals. Your primary objective is to be happy with the things you are doing and those you can achieve.

A simple way to get over your negative thoughts is to write them down. As soon as you write them down, you can re-phrase these thoughts into positive scripts. You should also give reasons why these negative thoughts don't apply to you. If a situation should arise where you find yourself getting overwhelmed with negative thoughts, take out your positive scripts. Repeat the sayings on the script to eliminate the negative thoughts.

What Is Your Inspiration?
Having other people to inspire you is a great way to make habits stick. What serves as the source of your motivation for this habit? Do you have any individual that encourages you? Is there anything that motivates you? Develop a vision around the answers to these questions. You should also create a board where you can place your vision. The board will serve as a reminder.

The board should be in a place where you can easily notice it every day. Attaching images to the board along with quotes can also serve as excellent reminders. Compiling visual aids that relate to your vision will also play a vital role in the impact of the visuals. The visuals may be images of places, things, or people.

Since you will see it daily, it will serve as your constant reminder of the reason behind a habit. It becomes possible to subconsciously think about what you intend to achieve and the steps you will take to achieve these goals. The only way you can keep working towards developing a habit is to have something always to remind you about that habit.

Develop One Habit at a Time
A habit is often key to personal development. Sticking to a habit is often vital for anyone that is looking to make progress in life. Selecting one habit to change at a time is usually a better option if you intend to make progress when developing a habit.

Consider a situation where you are looking to start going to the gym, making changes to your diet, and maintaining your weight. These are three new habits you intend to develop. Trying to do these three things at the same time can prove to be overwhelming. On the other hand, you can create a list of the habits you intend to develop. After making your list, you can then pick one habit to focus on developing. It becomes easier to plan and then work towards that habit. In the situation we are considering, your first step will be to make changes to your diet. Developing this habit will make it easy to feed your body correctly with healthy foods. Eating healthy will make it possible to lose weight. As a result, you will have the motivation to start going to the gym to maintain the weight you have worked hard to achieve.

Reward Yourself

It is common to find a lot of people who consider rewarding themselves anytime they make a meaningful achievement. It is a useful tip, but most of these individuals use it in a wrong manner. When developing a habit, proper use of rewards is a sure way to make such habits stick.

If you decide to give yourself a large reward for your progress, it can be harmful. It is also better you avoid rewards that come at the end of the week or month. Examples of large rewards include a vacation, a new gaming console, or new clothes. These are harmful to the development of habits that stick. Why? Using large rewards makes it easy for you to translate this reward into a prize. A prize is something you set out to win when performing an activity. A reward, on the other hand, is not the focus of developing the habit. An individual that is trying to develop a habit to gain the reward has a higher chance of quitting. Habits in most cases are difficult to create. What if an individual measure the reward in comparison to the stress that it takes to develop the habit? – It is easy to conclude that it is not worth the effort.

Taking steps to develop a habit for the reward also implies that you won't be willing to perform the next step if there is no reward. Regardless of the passion you have for an activity, it is easy to lose motivation when rewards are put into the equation. When selecting a good reward for your progress, there are certain things to consider. Below are some features of good rewards:

- They are small.
- They relate to the activity.
- You receive them immediately you complete the activity.

They Are Small
Having a larger reward always appeals to us as humans. A larger reward is often a great motivation to carry out a task or perform an activity. That is what makes it a problem when developing a habit that will stick. As a motivation for performing an activity, it means that without the reward you won't be inclined to repeat the activity. Your thoughts will align with phrases like, "I am doing it for the reward."

They Relate to the Activity
The reward for any action done should have a direct relationship to the action. In simpler terms, the reward should only be available if you can complete a particular action.

You Receive Them Immediately You Complete the Activity
One significant importance of a reward is to reinforce a behavior. For this reason, it is important you receive the reward immediately after the behavior. If you decide to wait till the end of the day to give the reward, it becomes difficult to identify the behavior you want to reinforce.

By receiving a reward immediately after an action, you will feel good about these actions. It promotes immediate recognition of an accomplishment. The

The Simple Yet Effective Methods to Cure Procrastination

functioning of the brain also makes an immediate reward important. The response of the brain to a reward is instantaneous. To make a habit that will stick, you want the brain to associate this reward to the activity you have completed at that instant.

Chapter 7:
The 5 Non-Obvious Things That Kill Your Productivity

Most of the things that kill our productivity are buried right under our noses. They have become an integral part of our daily lives, so it is difficult to notice them. In this chapter, I will be exposing some of these things that reduce your productivity without you noticing.

Your Bad Habits
One of the non-obvious things that kill productivity is habits. The many bad habits you have developed are steadily killing your productivity. They remain unnoticeable because these habits have become a vital part of your daily life. There are different ways through which your bad habits can reduce productivity. Here are some you may be experiencing.

Your Bad Habit of Not Making Lists
There are numerous benefits of a list in the workplace and the home. It helps you to remember the essential things that need to be done. It is also vital if you need to prioritize your tasks. Your reluctance to create lists of your daily tasks will often result in you forgetting some of the most critical tasks of the day. Have you ever gone to the grocery store and missed a few vital items?

Your Bad Habit of Being Overly Independent

Being independent is not a bad thing. It only becomes a problem when you are unable to meet up with urgent deadlines. In the workplace, working in a team is often very important. It provides the opportunity to delegate different aspects of a project to different people. It makes it easy to meet targets faster and meet deadlines. An easy way to avoid this bad habit is by starting to rely more on friends, family, employees, and co-workers.

Frugality as a Bad Habit

Frugality is one F the few habits you may have developed that may not seem like a problem. It can be a serious issue if you take it too far. If you decide to be frugal and avoid upgrading your work computer or programs, you end up with obsolete work tools. When your work tools become outdated, you start to lose a lot of time either from the slow boot-up of the computer or the slow response of the programs.

Not Getting Enough Sleep

Nowadays, the amount of sleep you get usually has a significant impact on your level of productivity. To create more time to work, a lot of people often sacrifice their long hours of sleep. As a result, they are killing their productivity without noticing. Just a single day of sleep deprivation can have damaging effects. These effects include poor judgment and an inability to retain information. If sleep deprivation becomes a consistent part of your life, there are other effects such as cardiovascular diseases, diabetes, and obesity.

Sometimes you may know about the importance of getting enough sleep but find it difficult to go to bed early. You must create a habit. Through the development of this habit, you will be able to go to bed as soon as the time is right.

The necessary performance boost you have been searching for is usually hidden beneath a good night's rest.

Poor Health Diet

ANOTHER NON-OBVIOUS killer of productivity is your diet. Certain foods are killing your productivity that you don't know about. Below, I will be discussing these foods so you can get a better understanding of why you need to avoid them. Things you should avoid include:

- Eating in excess.

- Too much processed and frozen foods.

- Intake of fluid in an improper manner.

- Consuming too much caffeine in the morning.

- Failure to take snacks between meals.

- Excess junk food items.

Access to Technology

Technology is currently affecting our daily lives in lots of different ways. You have a computer, smart phones, internet, and many more. As helpful as technology is, it may sometimes be a subtle killer of your productivity. Here are different ways it results in lower productivity:

Your Computer

A computer can kill your productivity with its slow performance. It results in downtime while you wait for data transfers to be complete. It will also delay you and prevent work from being done when trying to open a program. The non-obvious ways it kills your productivity is noticeable in the shift in focus while waiting. Now you are concentrated on the discussion you are having with a colleague or the messages you need to reply on your smart phone. It is now necessary for you to think before you can know the next step to take.

Sometimes, the systems you use may be getting outdated or running older versions of important software. If there is no plan for a replacement or an upgrade, a sudden failure will result in downtime. The time it takes to fix this sudden breakdown is often more than the time spent when it is planned. It is important that software for business purposes should be updated. It is also necessary to plan for replacements of computers in the workplace. Using the expected life of the unit is an easy way to determine when replacements are due.

How You Use Your Smartphone

Hands down, smart phones are easily one of the best inventions in the world. Nonetheless, if they are not handled properly, they can also be very destructive. In the workplace, smart phones offer the easiest form of distraction. Using your smart phone when you are supposed to be working is bound to have an adverse effect on your productivity.

It may be to check a personal email, visit a social media page, or reply to messages. Regardless of the reason, smart phones usually make it easy to lose focus. To solve this problem, you should keep your smart phone in a place that is difficult to see. If it is out of sight, it becomes out of mind. Your productivity at your work should be a priority. Using a smart phone will change this priority.

Distractions from Emails

If you get distracted easily, then you will have gone to your email to refresh it at one point. It is quite common with individuals who don't have a specific time for checking emails. It is one of the most subtle killers of productivity at work. Why? It has the appearance that you are performing a productive activity. It is a reasonable misinterpretation since you might be expecting a reply from a client. To deal with this problem, turning off your internet connection may not be the best solution since you may need it to work. Instead, create time on your schedule during which you check your emails. You should also close the email tab and disable notifications to avoid distractions.

Social Media
Connecting with people is a great way to create social relationships. That is the primary function of social media. It also helps to grow your network for business purposes. Although it has its benefits, social media is also a productivity killer at work. A notification pop-up on your screen will often take your attention away from your work. Falling for this trap and opening the social media site will also have its effects. It wastes time since you will end up scrolling down the timeline to find out what is new. Friends on social media sites also find it convenient to send messages when you appear online.

To avoid this non-obvious productivity killer at work, you can use site blocking apps to prevent access to social media sites during work sessions. You should also have a time that you will visit these sites.

Clutter
Clutter in your workplace and the home hurts your productivity. Your ability to work, mood, and resilience usually suffer from the effects of clutter. It is also possible to develop high-stress levels from the disorderliness that clutter creates. Mental and emotional distresses are common effects of clutter in the home environment. An individual may feel that he/she has no control over their

lives due to the clutter around them. Distraction is one of the few effects clutter has on you. It also impedes the ability to process new information by the brain. As a result, you are unable to perform efficiently. It is difficult to fight all the distractions that are present due to a cluttered environment. It depletes your mental energy, reduces physical energy, and causes frustration. When you are frustrated, you end up being unproductive.

If you fail to find a solution to the clutter around you, you may end up lowering your self-esteem. It often causes both emotional and mental discomfort. In most cases, addressing the clutter around may require a ton of energy. It is effortless to avoid it as a result. The clutter may end up spiraling out of control if you are unable to find a solution early. Below are some of the areas where you need to focus on when addressing clutter:

Clutter Can Be in Digital Form

Digital clutter is usually present on your phone, tablet, or computer. A digital clutter may be notifications or files that require your immediate attention. Your productivity when using your computer or smart phone depends on how easy it is to use and its functionality. Having many files on these devices can make it difficult to locate important files when you need them. Having too many files to check through will often reduce the effectiveness of the brain. It leads to a poor job and a reduction in your productivity levels.

Your Home

The home is the place where you start your day. Having an uncluttered home can help with the enhancement of your mental and emotional health. Removing clutter from the home may seem overwhelming. In truth, it is much easier if you break the task into smaller parts. You may decide to clear the clutter room by room. You may also choose to address it according to categories from your cutlery to laundry and so on. A much faster way to ensure that items causing clutter don't find their way back into the home is to throw out a few, sell some, and give away the rest. You should also look for options that allow you to recycle some of these items. Selling items, you don't need is always an easy way to make extra cash for more important things.

Your Workspace

Your workspace is where you perform your important tasks for the day. It may be your home office or your desk in an office building. Clutter in your workplace consists of all those unnecessary items taking up space on your desk. As a source of distraction, your brain will have to expend more energy to ignore these distractions. It makes you exhausted a lot faster with a direct impact on your productivity. To clear the clutter on your desk, you will need to create time. You may have to pick a few days during which you won't be going out for lunch. You will be spending this time organizing your desk and workspace.

Some items that you should clear out from your desk include old magazines, outdated files, and books that you enjoy reading often. Other items that are now irrelevant should also be cleared out. In addition to improving your productivity, a desk that is free from clutter will also have an attractive appearance and provide motivation.

Your Mind

We have discussed digital and physical clutter but what about clutter in your mind? Clutter in the mind may often be due to unnecessary information that you are storing but have no use for. Learning ways to get rid of this information will do you a lot of good.

The Simple Yet Effective Methods to Cure Procrastination

Clearing your physical clutter without resolving it can often be the cause of clutter in the mind. It is often a result of not having a To-Do list for your activities. A To-Do list will prioritize the activities you have for the day. Using a To-Do list will also show you in clear terms that you cannot complete all your tasks in one day. As a result, your mind will focus on the things that are currently of importance. Clutter will always be present in our daily lives. It may be in its digital or physical form when it appears. Although it is impossible to eliminate, there are always options to control clutter. Setting aside time for this process is necessary to increase your productivity level.

Chapter 8:
How to Set REAL Goals You Will Stick To

Creating goals is the first step to achieving success. Following through and achieving the goal is the most crucial part. It is also the most difficult. Learning some methods that can help in creating goals that you will follow is very important. Let us look at these rather simple methods

Create Goals from Your Vision

Having a vision is an integral part of creating a goal. There should also be a purpose behind any vision you have for your life. Once you are clear on these two aspects, it becomes easy to create a goal. At this stage, you may have multiple goals that you can develop from your vision. It is not a problem. Simply take time to write out these goals on paper, notebook, or journal. It should be a place that you can easily find it – some people prefer printing a Word document.

Visual aids are also useful when listing your goals. Creating goals requires commitment and seriousness. Goals that remain in an abstract form show that you are not willing to commit to these goals. Some key aspects to remember about creating goals include the following:

- You should have both short-term and long-term goals.
- There should be a time-frame for achieving goals.

- Making it appear on paper makes it tangible.

- Be specific.

- Determine a means of measuring the goals.

- A goal should align with your passion. Aligning goals with passion makes it more exciting for you.

Start with Just One Goal

Trying to achieve too many things at once is an express route to failure. It is a common mistake that everyone makes. Although it is great you want to turn your life around, you can't make a long list of changes in one go.

To change a single aspect of your life, you require willpower. The amount of willpower will vary depending on what aspect of your life you intend to change. Too many aspects at once will need a ton of willpower which is why it is usually overwhelming. To put things in a way you can control, set a single achievable goal that you will focus on at a time. As you progress, you begin to get a handle on things. Later, you can add another goal.

Set SMART Goals

The SMART acronym is a rule that most people know about. Knowing in any context doesn't imply that it is being applied. Are you using the SMART principle in your daily life? If you want to set goals that are sure to achieve and which will also have a significant impact on your life, then it should be a SMART goal. Here is a breakdown of what the SMART acronym defines goals to be:

- Specific

- Measurable

- Achievable

- Relevant

- Time-bound

Setting Goals That Are Specific

A goal that is specific is well defined, clear, and easy to understand. It is not easy to identify your direction if your goal is generalized or vague. Your goals need to point in the direction you should take.

Having a specific destination will help in finding the right direction. A simple example will be setting a goal to build up your savings. You won't make any reasonable progress with a goal like 'save some money as soon as you get paid.' On the other hand, 'save $1,500 as soon as you get paid' will yield much better results.

Setting Goals That Are Measurable

A measurable goal is one that you can quickly assess for progress. It is a goal that includes amounts and dates with which you can make comparisons. Using our previous example, 'build-up savings' is a good goal but not a measurable goal. A measurable goal will be to 'build up my savings to $10,000 by the 1st of April.' With this goal, you can assess your progress on the 1st of March to see how much you have saved and how much to go.

Setting Goals That Are Achievable

Whatever goal you set should be a goal that you can achieve. Setting goals that are far beyond your reach will have negative impacts on you as an individual.

The Simple Yet Effective Methods to Cure Procrastination

Such goals will eat away at your confidence and work against your motivation. In the same regard, you may not get a reasonable sense of fulfillment if the goals you set are too easy to achieve. The low sense of fulfillment is because you don't need to put in a lot of effort. Your goals should be realistic and challenging.

Still working with our goal to build-up savings, a goal to 'save $1,500 as soon as you get paid' will be impossible if you make just $1,600. A more realistic and achievable goal will be to save the amount on a payment of $2,500. It is a more realistic goal which will come with lots of challenges. By setting this goal, you are telling yourself that you need to live with less than what you earn. If you find that you can survive on what is left, this goal can develop into a long-term strategy.

Setting Goals That Are Relevant
When setting a goal, ensure it is relevant to your development. It should be beneficial to your life or your career. As a result, it will be easier to focus on what you hope to achieve. When building up your savings, you can do so to register for a professional course. You may also do so to pay the college tuition for your child. Since these goals directly affect you, it becomes easy to focus on achieving them.

Setting Goals That Are Time-Bound
Adding a deadline to your goals is essential to measure your success. There is also a sense of urgency that you develop when you know you must meet a deadline. Just like in our example, our deadline was set to the 1st of April. If you can meet the target before this date, it will create room for celebration.

Set Short Term Milestones

Just because you set a single goal doesn't mean it will be straightforward to achieve. Sometimes, it becomes even simpler to procrastinate on these goals. A goal is usually a long-term destination. Having a short-term milestone is also important. A short-term milestone is an easy way to track your progress and manage your goal. You will be able to identify the progress you have made. It also provides opportunities to make changes when necessary. Create bite-sized pieces of your SMART goals and define actionable steps that will lead to achieving these goals.

What Does Your Subconscious Mind Know About Your Goals?
A LOT OF PEOPLE often wonder why they fail to achieve their goals. It is easy to think that you will achieve a goal you have set due to the initial motivation that pushes you to set these goals. In truth, motivation doesn't last forever. Once the motivation fades away, interest in a goal quickly follows.

So how do you solve this problem?
The only solution is to burn your goal into your subconscious mind. By doing this, the actions you take become a habit. A habit is one of the most challenging things to break as an individual. Relying only on your motivation to achieve a goal will not yield the desired result you expect. Motivation is an excellent tool that you may be able to harness now but will be unavailable in the future. When you depend on habits, on the other hand, you can always leverage the positive influence.

- Create habits from your goals by programming them into your subconscious mind.
- Now, how do you burn your goals into your subconscious mind? Here are steps you can take to achieve this:

- Make sure you can see these goals every day by using a visual board.
- Regularly visualize a future where you have achieved your goals.
- Review your goals regularly.
- Repeat your goals daily to reaffirm these goals.

Inform Others about Your Goals

Your chances of success often become a lot higher when you share your goals with others. Your chances go up when you put your money on the line to achieve a goal. There are various people you can decide to tell about a goal you intend to achieve. It may be your boss, friend, or family. Once you tell someone else about your goal, it becomes more than just a dream. Anyone you tell will take it as their duty to monitor your progress. Try to give regular updates on your goal to anyone you tell about it.

Take Time to Review Your Goals

Just because you have a goal doesn't mean you are making any meaningful progress toward your goal. You may gradually be forgetting about these goals if you are not taking the right steps. You need to take the time to assess your progress.

If you fail to review your goals continuously, it is easy to get lost within the rush of your daily activities. It will shift your focus from the targets you have set to the targets directly in front of you. As a result, you will steadily forget about these personal targets. An easy way to maintain focus is to review the goal. By reviewing a goal, you will be able to get an insight into your progress and know if you are on a path that leads to your goal or one that deviates from the goal.

Do You Need Improvement?

As you make progress towards your goals, it is essential you also evolve your strategy. During the initial goal-setting phase, you will have come up with a plan as well as the actions to take in achieving a goal. It is also important you understand that things won't always go according to plan. Regardless of the setbacks you experience along the line; you need to keep pushing forward. Failures and mistakes are a huge part of the learning process.

Through your review, you will be able to understand the things that didn't work and why. The failures and mistakes translate to feedback. Learning from these feedbacks and making the necessary changes is the best way to reach your goals. Don't lose sight of your goals. Keep improving until you get a method that works effectively.

Chapter 9:
How to Stop Being Tired All the Time

If you feel you are tired all the time, there are a lot of other people with the same feeling. There are lots of individuals who struggle with the feeling of exhaustion all through the day. As a result, more individuals consume coffee and energy drinks to boost their mental alertness during the day. The real question – why do you always feel tired all the time?

Why Do You Feel Tired?

Various factors may result in a feeling of tiredness and fatigue. It doesn't matter if you are getting the recommended amount of sleep. If you still have no idea about the common causes of tiredness, here are some likely reasons why you feel this way:

Poor Quality Sleep

When determining the quality of your sleep, you need to check the amount of time you spend sleeping. Depending on your age, the recommended number of sleeping hours will vary. For adults, it is between seven – eight hours.

If you assess your sleep duration and determine you are getting enough sleeping hours, then you should consult a doctor. A doctor can help determine if you are struggling with a medical condition that you don't know about. It is a common cause of poor quality of sleep. Various factors determine a high quality of sleep. These include the following:

- Waking up a maximum of once every night.
- The ability to fall asleep within thirty minutes.
- Spending a larger portion of your time on the bed asleep.

There are also external factors that may reduce the quality of your sleep. These include excess light in the room while sleeping, an irregular sleep routine, consuming alcohol or coffee before bed, leaving the TV on while sleeping, and other factors.

Stress

Irritation is a regular outcome of stress, but fatigue is also another common effect. In addition to causing fatigue, it also becomes difficult to get a good quality sleep when you are stressed out. Stressful situations may result from relationship issues, work pressure, or financial worries. There are lots of stressful situations you will have to face daily. There can be severe distortions to your sleep patterns when you are stressed. Since stress can result from worries, your worries may also be keeping you up all through the night.

When the body is under stress, chemicals like cortisol and adrenaline are produced. These are flight or fight chemicals. It is the process through which the body prepares for emergencies. As a result, the body subconsciously makes it harder to fall asleep when it is under stress.

Living on An Unhealthy Diet

The Simple Yet Effective Methods to Cure Procrastination

The type of nutrients that you receive from your diet can affect the body. A diet that is unable to supply the necessary nutrients will lead to fatigue. It may include deficiency of vitamins and minerals like vitamin D, vitamin B12, iron, omega-3 fatty acids, and more. A low nutrient diet may result in the deficiencies of essential nutrients while you also may be losing energy when you follow a diet that is rich in added sugars and unhealthy fats. Consumption of processed foods may also add to the problem. The synthesis of sleep regulation neurotransmitters in the body requires these various minerals and vitamins. Consuming more vegetables and fruits can aid this process.

It is important you avoid junk food, candy, caffeine, and alcohol. The caffeine and alcohol can have adverse effects on your sleep pattern if taken before bed. The energy you get from junk foods, and candy only lasts for a short time which means the feeling of fatigue will return in a short time.

Dehydration

A significant cause of dry-mouth and fatigue is dehydration. It is also important that you understand that dehydration isn't necessarily due to low water consumption. Vomiting, diarrhea, and excessive sweating can also lead to dehydration.

So, what is the simplest way to fight dehydration? Drink water to remain hydrated. It will also help to reduce the chances of sleepiness during the day time. Having a water bottle within an arm's length can help in this situation. In this case, water is the primary source to remain hydrated. Don't rely on alcohol. There is a fatigue-inducing and dehydrating effect that results from alcohol consumption. Other steps you can take include washing your face regularly, taking a shower regularly, and taking a glass of water before a meal.

A Sedentary Lifestyle

A common belief that we have is that sitting down will help to conserve our energy levels. Moving around is a more effective way to overcome fatigue. Spending too much time sedentary will deplete your energy much faster.

Having a proper balance between rest and activity is more beneficial. The body will also be more tired if you decide to perform excess physical activities. Nonetheless, exercising every day is important. When exercising or working out, you can aim for a single session of twenty minutes. It will be more beneficial than having multiple hours of gruesome workout. Please note working out in the evenings is not advisable. It will often make it more difficult for the body to fall asleep as you lay on the bed later at night.

A Medical Condition May Be the Problem

A lot of people attribute fatigue to their type of lifestyle. So, what happens when you make positive changes to your lifestyle without improvements? Then it is time to make an appointment with your doctor. There are various possibilities when considering medical conditions that lead to fatigue. Below are some of the common conditions that may be resulting in fatigue:

- Depression

- Sleep apnea

- Anemia

- Diabetes

- Thyroid disease

- Chronic Fatigue Syndrome

In some cases, certain medications may result in fatigue. It can be both an over-the-counter medication as well as a prescription medication.

How to Eliminate Exhaustion

To assist in eliminating tiredness, you can use any of these strategies. The strategies listed are natural and work for the various causes.

Consistency in Your Sleep Routine

The consistency in this situation applies even on weekends. To eliminate fatigue, the most important first step is to improve the quality of your sleep. Follow the checklist below to encourage a high-quality sleep:

- You should have a bedtime that you follow both during workdays and on weekends.

- A combination of relaxing activities that form a bedtime ritual can be very helpful.

- Healthy habits like regular exercise, low caffeine consumption, no alcohol before bed, and avoiding tobacco can be beneficial.

- A room with a cold temperature without any lights or noise is essential to promote a good night's rest.

- Go outside and take a walk, visit your favorite park, and enjoy nature.

- Perform activities that reduce stress daily.

The duration of your sleep is also important. Getting less than seven hours of sleep at night may also lead to some health challenges such as:

- Depression.

- Mood, memory, and thinking impairment.

- Higher chances of heart problems and diabetes.

- Reduction in immunity.

Although the leading cause of exhaustion is a short duration of sleep, you may be risking certain health challenges if you are sleeping over nine hours every night. The challenges include headaches, obesity, and diabetes. Therefore, seven to eight hours of sleep is recommended for adults. Hitting the snooze button on your alarm may also be affecting your energy levels when you wake. The snooze time is often enough to doze off, but it is not enough to get restorative sleep. For this reason, it is better to avoid the snooze button.

Engage in Regular Physical Activities

Avoiding the temptation to lie on your couch when you are feeling tired is the best way to eliminate fatigue. Getting some exercise is your best option in this situation. Regularly performing physical activities can reduce fatigue and provide high levels of energy. It is also helpful in improving your mood and lowering anxiety. These are also other known causes of tiredness and fatigue. The physical activity you choose should be one you enjoy performing. The exercise also promote metabolism, and a twenty-minute jog can have significant benefits to the body.

Calm Your Mind

The Simple Yet Effective Methods to Cure Procrastination

Some of the most significant energy drainers in the body are depression, negativity, and stress. Sometimes, seeking professional help may be the only way to rid all these negative feelings from your body. On the other hand, there are some more manageable steps you can take to free your mind from negative feelings and thoughts. You can start by meditating daily. There are lots of benefits you can gain from meditating for just five minutes every day. It can help improve your alertness and awareness while also calming the mind. Volunteering to help others is also another way to boost your energy levels and improve your mood. It also helps in making you feel good about yourself. Sometimes, we are often the cause of most of our problems. You may be harboring negative thoughts in the form of resentment, grudges, anger, or self-pity. Learning to let go of these emotions and forgive is one of the simplest ways to free your mind from the burden.

Another beneficial feeling that a lot of people tend to overlook is gratitude. Showing signs of gratitude and appreciating the things you have can help eliminate feelings of stress. Simply writing down all the things you are thankful for before going to bed can make you happy and remove negative thoughts that may keep you up all night.

Find A Way to Deal with Stress

As an adult, it is common to deal with stress in one form or the other. Trying to address this stress is the only solution. When you are selecting a method to de-stress, it should be something consistent since your stress may also come up consistently. Taking a walk is one of the common ways to de-stress. You can take a walk around the neighborhood or walk up and down the stairs at work. It is also important you have a good view of your surroundings or an audio book that can take your mind away from the stressful thoughts. The release of endorphins is excellent for eliminating stress hormones.

Changing your view on a situation can also be very helpful. Create a positive outlook for a somewhat stressful situation. As an individual, you may find it stressful to take a longer route to work due to road construction. If you take it as more time for you to listen to a podcast, it can take the stress out of the process. Having fun is another method that is self-explanatory. There are different ways to have fun. What's more, a lot of them are free.

You can start by looking for activities that make you laugh. Laughter is one of the immediate cures for stress. You can get it by reading a comedy novel, watching funny movies, watching stand-up comedy, or simply listening to a friend that makes you laugh. There are other fun activities you can enjoy. Simply engaging in an activity that you are passionate about will provide a fun time. Trying out a new sport, visiting the new restaurant down the road, and making changes to your routine can also be very helpful.

Another easy way to unwind and relax is to be around plants. In a much broader perspective, being in tune with nature will help reduce stress and calm the brain. Taking a break during which, you can visit the local park or tend to your garden can help reduce any stress that has built up.

Eat Healthily

Your health is significantly influenced by the food we eat and those we avoid. The circadian rhythm of the body is also affected by the food we eat. For this reason, it is necessary to watch the food you consume. Making a few adjustments to the diet you consume can have a significant impact on the quality of your sleep. You can start by including cherries to your diet. It is an excellent

The Simple Yet Effective Methods to Cure Procrastination

natural source of melatonin. Melatonin is a hormone that is responsible for the control of the body clock. Staying away from alcohol is also important. All kinds of alcohol will have a negative impact on your sleep if consumed a short time before you go to bed.

Eating peanuts is also beneficial to individuals who find it hard to fall asleep. The peanuts promote the release of serotonin that makes us feel sleepy. Natural peanut butter will also produce the same effect. Another thing you can include in your diet is dark chocolate. It is a lot different from milk chocolate. Tyrosine is present in milk chocolate, and it functions as a stimulant by converting into dopamine. When starting your day, it is common for most people to avoid taking breakfast. Others may decide to load their stomach with lots of carbohydrates in the form of cereals, muffins, or donuts.

A large amount of carbohydrates will usually result in a rapid rise in blood sugar. As the blood sugar level returns to its normal level later in the day, you start craving junk food from the vending machine. Instead, it is important you add proteins to your meal to balance the carbohydrates. During breakfast, you can make scrambled eggs, take a protein bar, a protein-enriched smoothie, fruit with a bowl of yogurt, or simply spread peanut butter over your toast. By preventing rapid changes in blood sugar level, proteins can help keep you alert and awake.

Say No to Caffeine
CAFFEINE HAS BECOME an excellent option for individuals looking to mask their fatigue. It can provide a short-term energy boost, stimulate the nervous system, and make you feel awake. Nonetheless, various side effects come with the consumption of caffeine. They include the following:

- Insomnia

- Anxiety

- Abnormal or rapid heart rhythm

- Dehydration

- Restlessness

- Dizziness

- Dependency

- Headaches

The dependency, in this case, is the need to consume more caffeine over time in order to maintain your alertness. The side effects that everyone will notice may differ from those of another individual. There are also many energy drinks and coffees that contain a large amount of sugar. These can lead to exhaustion at a much faster rate. Besides, the caffeine may also disrupt your standard body clock.

If you decide to stop your caffeine consumption, you can expect a few caffeine withdrawal symptoms. One such sign is an increase in drowsiness. In place of caffeine, you can choose to drink a lot of water all through the day. It is a natural way to make the body energized and alert. You should also eat foods like blueberries, oranges, spinach, almonds, and salmon that are energy-boosting foods.

Gain Vitamins from The Sun

The Simple Yet Effective Methods to Cure Procrastination

Some essential nutrients assist in your fight against fatigue. Vitamin B and vitamin D are two such nutrients. It is also important to note that the sun can provide the body with these nutrients. A deficiency of vitamin D in the body is usually indicated by a feeling of moodiness, tiredness, or stress. If you spend just about fifteen minutes under natural light, you can help promote the production of these vitamins in the body. It can help maintain the energy levels of the body.

Take A Nap for An Energy Boost

The benefits of a nap are often understated. This short time of rest can produce improvements in memory, alertness, performance, and learning. The napping process also must be appropriately planned. A nap that exceeds twenty minutes can often have an adverse effect when you wake. Be sure to set an alarm before taking your nap. If you doubt the benefits of a power nap, then do you have a better answer to the reason why The Huffington Post and Google have designated zones for sleeping in the office?

Switch Off

Various devices like your television and smart phones usually have a significant effect on your sleep. In addition to leaving your smart phone on overnight, it is also possible that it doubles as your alarm clock. There have been conclusive results from research which show the effect of using your smart phone before bed. The bright light that emits usually tampers with your sleep patterns. It often makes it difficult to fall asleep. To avoid these situations, you should set a time at which you stop using these devices. You can then switch to a book or listen to music before bedtime. It is also important you get an alarm clock rather than using your smart phone for this function. It will also help prevent any interruption during sleep if you forget to disable an alarm at an earlier time.

Chapter 10:
The Secret to Work with Intense Focus

Focus is a valuable tool that determines how well you will be able to perform a task. If you lack focus, you will be giving in to distractions which will limit your ability to get work done. In our world of technology, a single click is all it takes to get to your distractions. Luckily, there are a few methods that can help in maintaining focus when you want to get work done. Some of these methods may require practice but offer massive rewards. Let's look at some of these methods below.

Work as an Individual

You may be aware of this to an extent, but you don't want to admit it. The people you work with are often the reason why you find it difficult to focus on the task at hand. Sometimes, it may not be intentional. When working with others, conversations may come up and you will want to be a part of these conversations. As the conversation progresses, you slowly lose focus on your task and turn your attention to the ongoing discussion. It is one of the reasons why some individuals tend to be less productive when their colleagues come over to their cubicle.

In other cases, it is simply having someone working on another task that is different from yours which may affect your ability to maintain focus. It may be as a result of you visualizing what it will be like to perform the task the other person is currently working on. It may also simply be you taking an interest in the task to see how it ends. If you decide to work as an individual, you are separating yourself from others. When working far from other people, there is no opportunity to become a part of the conversation. It also improves your concentration on your task since there is no other person around whose task might seem more interesting. Working alone can also help you work with intense focus since you know you are the only one working on a task. You don't need to serve as a moderator to make other team members complete their part of the task.

Improve Your Focus by Taming Random Thoughts

Random thoughts are just that, random. These thoughts develop at an unexpected time within your head. It is a form of distraction that comes from within the body. It is commonly noticeable as the voice in your head speaking to you. It is an interruption that you are inevitably going to respond to if you don't have proper mental blocks. The following are some of the thoughts you may have:

- "Have I already sent the document?"

- "I do not remember locking my door before leaving home today."

- "Will I be able to get the loan from the bank?"

If these questions follow the same structure as those you usually have, then you need to learn how to curb these random thoughts. There are different methods you can use in curbing your random thoughts. These strategies are listed below:

- Use journals to write down thoughts.

- Use your breathing as a means of returning your focus to the task.

- Become adept at mindfulness.

Effectively Managing Stress

Developing a system that you can use in managing stress is vital if you hope to maintain focus. In your daily life, it is almost impossible to avoid stress. For this reason, you should prepare yourself to tackle this issue. Various activities help with stress reduction. Learning what activities work for your personality is also important. You should be considering activities like healthy eating, meditation, yoga, walking, running, etc.

Mindfulness

Another effective way to maintain focus is through mindfulness. This is a topic that should interest you at this moment. Mindfulness is a method of increasing your awareness of the task you are doing and where you are. When you practice mindfulness, it will make it possible for you to focus on the work that is directly in front of you. It also improves your concentration on a conversation or your ability to notice the environment when taking a walk. There are different ways to engage in mindfulness including the following:

- Mindful Movement such as Yoga.

- Meditation.

- Mindfulness-based stress reduction.

Being in the Present

A common reason why you may be losing focus is due to your worry about the future or reminiscence of the past. If you often get consumed by these

The Simple Yet Effective Methods to Cure Procrastination

thoughts, then it will be difficult to focus on the present. You are entirely out of sync with what is happening in the present.

Understanding that you cannot change the past and learning that you will never be able to predict the future is essential. You can only learn from the mistakes of the past and make changes to avoid a repeat of these mistakes. Taking full control of your thoughts and living in the present will provide a lot of benefits to your mental focus. You can remain sharp by paying attention to the task at hand. Most times, using your smart phone can often take your mind away from the present. You may find an old picture that brings back memories on your phone. It is why you need to clear all these distractions. Many other methods have been discussed in previous chapters. They include the following:

- Focusing on one task at a time.
- Eliminating potential distractions.
- Pre-committing to a task.
- Taking breaks.

Chapter 11:
Essential Apps that FORCE You to Be More Productive

Most of the apps that force you to commit to a task or goal are popularly known as commitment apps. These apps require you to make a commitment to achieve a goal. The commitment is necessary to prompt you into action. Some apps require commitments in the form of money you put on the line or your reputation. Others may limit your access to things you find enjoyable but unproductive. Below are some of the popular apps you should be using:

Beeminder
Beeminder is a platform that helps to keep you on track to achieving your goals. It creates a yellow brick road that you need to always remain on. The platform automatically creates the yellow brick road as soon as you input your goal. It allows users to input a goal that they want to achieve and quantify these goals. In a quantifiable term, you can add a data point (+1) every time you take a positive step towards your goal. Data points that fall on the yellow brick zone mean that you are safe and on the course. Any data point that doesn't fall on the yellow brick road indicates that you are off course. When a data point goes off course, you lose money.

Where Can I Use Beeminder?
The Beeminder website is available for use on your computer. For easy on-the-go access, you can also download the mobile app for Android and iOS devices.

The apps allow users to view their dashboard that shows their progress, sends reminders, and inputs new data. To create a new goal, adjust your yellow brick road, or make any other significant changes, you need to use the Beeminder website.

Setting Up A Goal and The Types of Goals Available on Beeminder

To set up a new goal, all you need to do is to click on the 'New Goal.' As soon as you click on this button, the platform will require you to select the type of goal you want to set up. Below are the different types of goals you can set up on Beeminder:

Do More Goals

The Do More goals are the most common types of goals on the platform. As the name implies, it helps increase how much you perform an activity. Goals that fall within this category include jogging and studying more. It is not the same as a goal you would like to do more frequently.

Weight Loss Goals

What is the hint you get from the name of this goal? Yes, it is that simple. It is a goal that assists with your weight loss process. If you need to lose ten pounds in the next five weeks, you only need to set up this goal and input your results daily. Weigh yourself and input your current weight. There are also other types of goals including the following:

- Do fewer goals- it is a type of goal for activities you want to do at a reduced rate.

- Odometer goals – this is a goal that adds up over time like how you keep getting to a higher page when reading a book.

The two goals listed above require the Infinibee premium plan.

What Can You Find on Your Graph?

There is a graph that will be displayed on the goal page. Above the graph, you can find a derailment countdown while there is an input space below the graph. The things that you find on the graph include the following:

- Yellow Brick Road

- Road Dial

- Akrasia Horizon.

How Do You Input Data on The Platform?

There are different options for data input on Beeminder. It can simply be using the data entry box that is below the graph. Other methods include sending a response to the bot emails, through text message, or using the mobile app. There is a specific format for inputting data on the platform.

Reminders

The reminders from Beeminder come in on emergency days. The default time to receive a reminder is around 9:30 am on these days. If the time is not convenient, you can change it in the goal settings menu. If you don't take any action, you will continue receiving these reminders at a higher frequency. Zeno polling – that is how Beeminder describes the reminders. It is also possible to turn it off when necessary.

Derailing

Derailing on this platform implies that there is a data point that doesn't fall on the yellow brick road. In this case, the data point will appear in the color red. It

The Simple Yet Effective Methods to Cure Procrastination

is what creates an emergency day. If at the end of the day you are unable to get the data point back on the yellow brick road, it leads to a derailment. The deadline for a derailment can be customized in the settings menu. To eliminate difficulty trying to catch-up after a derailment, the road adjusts to the current data point.

What are Legit Checks?

A legit check is an email that you receive from the platform any time you derail. Through the email, the platform will try to find out if you have derailed from your yellow brick road or you have simply failed to input the latest data. It is how the platform avoids making erroneous deductions. It is also more comfortable than having to refund money after deductions. If you feel this is just an easy way out of your commitments, then you can use the 'Weaselproof Me' option in the goal settings menu. By checking this option, you may need to send additional proof that it wasn't a legitimate derailment.

Pledges

Beeminder usually requires users to enter a credit card detail. The charges for your derailment are deducted from the credit card. You can start using the platform without a credit card. In this case, your first derailment will cause the platform to freeze your goal. At this point, there is no money on the line so no consequence for your derailment. To continue with your goal, it will be necessary to make a pledge at this point. The pledge is usually $5 that will be charged on the next derailment.

The charge for derailment increases as the number of derailments increases. It follows a progression that looks like, $5, $10, $30, $90, $270, $810. The charge will keep increasing until it reaches an amount you are not willing to lose. At this point, you will have the right motivation.

The Most Dangerous Writing App

It is a web app that is designed to prompt you to write by pushing you to your limits. As a writer, it is common to experience writer's block. It may be due to your fears of not being good or the inability to face criticism from your readers. Whatever the reason, it is crucial you find a way to overcome this problem. That is where the Most Dangerous Writing app is helpful.

How does this app push you to the limit? Simple – it deletes any progress you have made if you remain inactive for an extended period. To start using the app, you will need to start a session. The session can be as short as five minutes and can also span multiple hours. You must keep writing for as long as the session is active to avoid losing your progress. When it is about to delete your progress, there will be a countdown warning. You may not consider it as a serious writing app, but it can be an excellent way to eliminate feelings of self-doubt when writing. By blurring everything you have written you don't have the opportunity to over-analyze. It forces you to come up with new ideas.

Freedom

An essential app that helps in blocking distractions is Freedom. The app is excellent for preventing access to websites and sites that may distract you from important activities that you need to focus on. It is suitable for use on iPhone, iPad, or computer.

Freedom allows users to create a session and then select the things they would like to block. It may be your access to Facebook, Twitter, or the internet. The session may also be recurring for a specific period every day of the week. If you find it easy to get distracted even during a session, you can also use a Locked Mode. In this mode, it becomes impossible to change the settings of the app while a session is in progress.

Stickk

Stickk is a platform that assists you in achieving any goal you have set. It promotes your productivity by making you place something of value on the line. The consequence of failing to reach your goal is the loss of whatever you put on the line. You can decide to put money of reasonable value on the line or stake your reputation. If you fail to reach a goal, you will lose the money you have put on the line. In the same regard, if you decide to stake your reputation, the platform will notify your family and friends anytime you fail to achieve a goal. As a result, you slowly damage your reputation. By holding you accountable, the platform prompts you to act. The success of the platform is noticeable in the way it makes users commit to a goal.

The unique feature on the platform is how it forces you to pay up for your failure. Since you put the money on the line before making the commitment, there is no opportunity to go back on your goals. It is also sure that you will lose the money if you fail since it is not your family or friend that you can easily convince to refund the money.

A Brief Example on the Use of Stickk

A simple goal that you may want to achieve is building your savings up to $10,000 in the next ten weeks. This is a large goal, and the first step to take is to break it down into smaller parts (a simple strategy from lessons within this book). A breakdown of this goal will be to save $1,000 every week.

On the Stickk platform, there is a Commitment Contract available. To complete this contract, you can type in your goal to save $1,000 per week for the next ten weeks. You can then fund the Stickk escrow account with an amount that will be painful to lose. It can be $500 in this case. To ensure you don't lose your money, you will keep updating your progress every week. If you are unable to meet your $1,000 target for a week, you will lose $50. A lot of people may be wondering how Stickk will be able to determine if you are making progress. The platform usually allows users to add a referee. A referee is a person who will track your progress to determine if you are telling the truth or not. The site also uses the honor system.

You may be considering the design of the platform as a scheme to get rich by the developers. Why? Well, where is my money going? To avoid these issues, Stickk allows users to select an organization that gets the money you lose. It refers to these organizations as 'anti-charities.' The reason for this unique name is that any charity you select will be one that you don't like at all. As a way to prompt you to action, the platform makes donations to the cause that you don't believe in. Some of the anti-charities on the platform include:

- NRA Foundation
- William Jefferson Clinton Presidential Library
- Educational Fund to Stop Gun Violence
- Americans United for Life
- Nature Conservancy
- George W. Bush Presidential Library

The Simple Yet Effective Methods to Cure Procrastination

- NARAL Pro-Choice America Foundation.
- The option to pick a friend or random charity is also available.

Will It Work?

The reason why a lot of people give up on their goals is the lack of consequences for their actions. The lack of accountability also supports this behavior. You can use Stickk as a tool to prompt you into action.

RescueTime

RescueTime is a tracking application that is useful for recording the time spent visiting a site or using a specific program. It makes it possible for you to identify how you spend each minute of your day. Using the application, you will be able to identify areas where you are spending more time than necessary. Setting up the application for use is also easy. You may require about a week to tweak the system, but once it is complete, you are all set to boost your productivity.

Setting Up RescueTime

The first step is to install the program on your computer. It will be the only useful step you will be able to take for a while. Since you will need at least two days' worth of data, you will need to wait a bit to reorganize how you use your time. To get the installer, visit the RescueTime website. On the site, you will find a 'Get Started' button that you need to click. It then comes with the option to select an account type. There is a free account and a pro account available. Selecting the free account should offer the things you need to utilize your time efficiently. On the pro account, you get features like individual documents tracking within a program, website blocking, and alerts. It is possible to get some of these features by using other apps like Freedom for site blocking. You also get a fourteen-day trial during which you can test the unique features of the pro account to decide if it is worth getting.

You will need to create a username and password after selecting the account type. There will be a prompt to download the installer. During the installation, the wizard will require you to input activities that you consider as 'distractive' or 'productive.' You also have an option to skip this selection process. Now, you can install RescueTime on your computer and then run the program. It will run in the background until you decide to shut it off. It also has a pause option which can be for fifteen minutes, sixty minutes or pause till the next day.

Running the program may not be a suitable option for you. In this case, you can right-click on the icon to open a menu with the 'Dashboard' option available. On the dashboard, the right-hand corner has a settings link through which you can access the 'Monitoring' tab on the program. The 'Monitoring' tab allows you to choose the days and the time during which you want the program to run. It is better to make these settings on the days and times during which you work. There are other settings you can also adjust. After saving the settings, you need to let the program run for a few days to gather the necessary data.

How Long Should You Let It Run?

After running the program for two days, you can decide to make changes based on the data it has accumulated. The main question here is; is it an accurate reflection of your week? There will be days when your schedule is not as tight as other days. If you are only using data from two days out of a five-day work week, you will still need to make changes later. Instead, you can choose to wait about a week before heading to the RescueTime Dashboard to make the necessary changes. As a result, you won't need to return anytime soon to tweak the settings.

Analyzing the Data

Since you have been able to accumulate a reasonable amount of data, it is now time to analyze the data. On the RescueTime Dashboard, you will find charts and graphs that can tell you about your time usage during the week. On the right side of the screen, you will find tabs such as the 'Time Reports' tab. By clicking on this tab, it will provide access to graphs which are more detailed. The graphs available include:

The Overview Tab

Here, you will find a graph which shows your activities by grouping them into communication and entertainment activities. There is a color-coding on the graph with the red indicating an activity that is distracting while a blue color indicates productive activities.

Activities

The activities page displays the sites you visit and the programs you make use of on your computer. The time you spend on these programs or sites is also available in this section. Your productivity level is also indicated using the color-coding method.

Categories

The Categories tab is a more in-depth graph that splits your activities further into categories such as Calendars, Meetings, Social Networking, and News/Opinion.

Goals

What do you want to achieve? What can this application help you change? In the goals section, you can easily set goals within the application. It can be a simple goal or a more complex one depending on the changes you hope to achieve.

Efficiency

The Efficiency section contains a chart with just one bar. The bar indicates your percentage efficiency. It is the time spent on productive activities in a percentage. Sometimes, the efficiency may not be as useful as the information you get from the Activities section. The period for each graph can be adjusted to display reports in respect to day, week, month, or year depending on your preference.

Adjusting How the Application Categorizes Your Activities

There is also a 'Categorize Activities' link on the Activities screen that is more useful than you can imagine. Using social media sites will often be labeled as being a distraction if no-one knows your reason for visiting these sites. The same also applies to how RescueTime categorizes certain activities. In some cases, Instant Messaging may be labeled as a distracting activity. In truth, you may need it to communicate with colleagues during work periods. In the context of the job you are performing, it is an incorrect analysis. The 'Categorize Activities' page enables you to adjust such descriptions. Plus, and minus signs are present on the right side of a row which allows you to change the productivity level of activity.

Sometimes, when adjusting the productivity level of an activity, it may also be necessary to change the category. It is often due to the inability of RescueTime to deduce the function of an application. The option of changing the label of an entire category is also available from the settings. A lot of people need this useful feature if they require social networking sites to work. Since the default

The Simple Yet Effective Methods to Cure Procrastination

label is 'Distracting,' it is possible to change all social networking sites to 'Productive.'

It can either be by changing the productivity level of an entire category or simply creating a new category. The changes you make in the settings will reflect on your graphs instantly. Slowly and steadily, the graph will be becoming an excellent reflection of your daily activities. It will give better pointers to your productivity level, how you are spending time, and the various weaknesses you are struggling with. It is important to know what causes the most distraction during your work periods. Once you can take note of it, you will be motivated to avoid using the program or visiting the site.

Review Regularly

Regular review of the application is the only way to get the best results. Review of the application will become the next course of action as soon as you begin to get accurate results from your graphs. The review of the application should be about once or twice a week. Sometimes, at the end of a very unproductive day, it will be very beneficial to visit your dashboard. It can identify areas where you lost track of your essential tasks. Minimizing distracting activities is important when reviewing. It is essential you avoid eliminating such activities totally as it is often necessary to take breaks to replenish your energy levels. Nonetheless, if you find out that you are spending the most time on Facebook or Twitter, then you will need to cut back on time spent.

Chapter 12:
Wake Up Motivated Every Day Hack

Throughout this book, we have been discussing some of the most critical aspects of procrastination and how it can affect your life. Understanding how it differs from laziness has also been a real eye-opener. Time-wasting is one of the most significant causes of procrastination in life. Learning how to avoid this dream killer will also result in massive rewards as soon as you put what you have learned into action.

You schedule is not going to be as desirable as you want it to be. Some days, it can be so tight you have only a little time to take a break. Nonetheless, there is a valuable insight into how you can use technology to get the best results from a hectic schedule. If you think there is no powerful tool to motivate yourself intrinsically, I'm sure you have realized your error. Willpower is a tool no-one teaches you how to harness in school. It is something you must develop on your own. Learning to make the most of this vital tool is the key to success in achieving your goals.

Developing sticky habits is something we often overlook. We often misplace our priorities by performing an activity for short term rewards rather than long term benefits. Habits that stick usually require a different approach with a focus on the long-term benefits that I have thoroughly explained within this book.

The Simple Yet Effective Methods to Cure Procrastination

If you bought this eBook looking to reinforce your belief that procrastination is the only killer of your productivity, you should have realized your mistake at this point. There are subtle productivity killers that you are indulging daily. It is time to have a re-think and perform a complete check to determine where you are going wrong.

Tiredness is often the result of trying to achieve more in the day at the expense of your sleep. Other various factors may lead to this undesirable event. If you have been paying attention to the tips within this eBook, you should be noticing significant improvements in how you feel when you wake up. Focusing solely on the task at hand can be quite difficult. There are some traditional methods that I have put into this eBook, but I have taken a step further to tell you the best way to utilize technology. Using the various commitment apps, I have described earlier, you will not only be improving your focus but also your productivity.

Werner Brendon Marcus

My Final Words

As my reward to you for getting this far, I will be giving you a tip you can apply to automatically motivate yourself to work as soon as you wake up. The first step is to develop a cue that serves as a trigger for your habits. It is also possible for a cue to trigger a mindset in you. It is the crucial quality I want you to remember.

Every time you get new shoes from your favorite designer, you always become more confident when walking around the streets. You haven't particularly done anything spectacular – except changing the shoes on your feet. It is you associating the new shoes to your confidence. Wearing new shoes is your way of gaining a confidence boost for the day. It blocks out all the negative comments that would pull you down on any other day. It is a cue that puts you in the right mindset.

Having new shoes as your cue is not a great choice. Find something that is easy to repeat daily. It can be shaving every day or tying your hair in a ponytail. A common cue with most individuals who work in an office is wearing a tie on a shirt. Once they dress this way, their mindset automatically switches to the hard work ahead.

Different things might serve as your cue. These are things you do on the days you achieve a lot. Finding the unique thing you do on such days will help determine your cue. Remember, it might be a simple, insignificant activity like making

The Simple Yet Effective Methods to Cure Procrastination

your bed before leaving. In addition to motivation, using a cue will also result in more willpower.

Unstoppable Day

The Morning Routine to Eliminate Procrastination and Boost Productivity. No Miracles Just Pure Self-Discipline. See the Effects In 3 Days

Werner Brendon Marcus

Introduction

Self-transformation is a hell of a mouthful in this generation where everything is ruled over by technology. We wake up in the morning and our first activity is to check our Facebook page for any updates. Next, we tweet about the first thing that comes into our minds such as, "Dreamed about having a house party. Want to make it a reality?" As if it ends there, we post an Instagram update of an early selfie with a caption, "Woke up Like This" and have our friends like it. At eleven, instead of cooking a fully-cooked meal, we prefer to order take out and post a Facebook update that says, "Brunch from McDonald's be like" and have our followers fawning over burger and fries.

In the afternoon, we would sulk on our couches watching Netflix until 5 pm, where our nightlife starts. We call our friends about plans and gimmicks at the club and meet there at around 7 pm. From there, we dance our feet off, chugging cases of beers, and drinking cocktails until midnight. We would spend the whole night having fun, telling stories, and just hanging out. Only to wake up and repeat the cycle the next day.

See, I think there is nothing wrong with that routine. I believe it actually is fun to be with friends whom we call "family." It maintains our youthful existence. It keeps the hype up in our lives. That's what people call "Living Life to the Fullest." Who would not want to experience such a thing?

Unstoppable Day

Personally, I believe that it is a healthy lifestyle IF YOU WANT TO REMAIN UNSUCCESSFUL IN LIFE. Yes, partying and procrastinating is a good way to preserve youth and happiness, but for how long? I hate to be blunt, but money is a temporary commodity unless it is used in a productive way. So, what if your parents have loads of money? So, what if you are the heir of a big company? That does not mean you can do whatever you can with your assets. Think of it this way, what if your so-called company went bankrupt and your parents cannot support you anymore? What will you do by then? Sulk in your couch the whole day, waiting for apples to fall into your mouth? Even apple trees die if not taken care of properly.

Unsuccessful people look at prestigious individuals saying, "That is no big deal. They had lots of money to start their business. It is no surprise their company would grow like that. Besides, they had someone on the inside. They have it all figured out." Just like you, they might have been someone's successor as well. But even so, their journey to becoming successful was not easy. It took them years of hard work to even deserve to be a successor.

There are others out there who literally started from rags to riches. They grew up in a third-world country where houses are made of boxes and scrap materials. Some of them started as garbage men and steel collectors. They did not have the resources to reach high school. Nevertheless, that did not stop them. Most of them already have their own line of bag and dress designs. Some of them became celebrities, showcasing their talents all around the world. Those poor individuals who were bullied and discriminated have their own company, providing jobs to thousands of people in their country. What is their secret to prestige?

If you compare your status to that of the poor, aspiring people mentioned above, you are 100 steps ahead towards success. You have a stable roof over your head. They only have garbage bags as roofing. You eat three times a day, with an allowance that can buy you everything you want. The poor people out there only eat once. Sometimes, their meals barely even touch the linings of their stomach. You were able to study and acquire a college degree, they barely reached primary education. Despite all of that has been given to you, all you do is complain and ask for more. Out of the billions of people in this world, you are part of the lucky 20% who does not experience poverty. You have everything you need to reach success if you wanted to. So, what do they have that you do not?

Courage, Persistence, and Inspiration. These three words kept them going despite everything they do not have. These words kept them alive. It allowed them to rise from the line of poverty and reach their dreams as they moved forward. Because of these three words, they were able to send their nine siblings to college. These three words gave them the power to look past their differences and persevere towards success.

If you are wondering how these three words alone brought them success, it all goes back to the most important trait: SELF-DISCIPLINE. Those poor people could have chosen to procrastinate and remain stagnant. Instead, they thrived in the depths of poverty and seized every opportunity to survive. They could have chosen to feel helpless and sorry to be born and die in poverty, but no, they chose to change their lives. Simply put, it was all about mind over matter - A concept that 20% of the world seems to disregard.

Unstoppable Day

Controlling the mind can do wonders to your life. With self-discipline, you can survive your worst nightmares. You can thrive in the midst of your hardest battles. You can rise from the depths of the hell you are going through. All you need to do is keep in mind the three words that will bring you to success: COURAGE, PERSISTENCE, AND INSPIRATION. Not only will you transform into a powerful being, but also reach a paradise you once deemed impossible to achieve.

Chapter 1:
The Foundation of Success

We all know that "Determination is the key to success." And with determination come our three big words: Persistence, Courage, and Inspiration. Everyone has what it takes to develop these characteristics over time, yet only a few reaches their ultimate goal. Why is that? Simply because most people disregard the trait that roots all values. The one word that encompasses the definitive morale that leads to success – SELF-DISCIPLINE. It should not be "Determination" as the key to a prestigious life, but "Self-discipline" itself. Without it, persistence, courage, and inspiration -among other values- will cease to exist.

Self-discipline is the value of persistent self-control. It is the ability to stick to your decisions and goals, learning to say "no," and obtaining full command of your mind and body. Self-discipline entails focus, control, and restraint to overcome even the most enticing temptation in life. In other words, self-discipline is the power of mind-mastery. It is the ability to take control of your mind and not be a slave to it. Do you know why millions of people aspire, yet only a few of them succeed? Because people speak of self-discipline as if they know so much about it but, when it comes to its application, it is way easier said than done. People have a lot of perceptions as to what drives a person to succeed. Some say passion, others say hard work. Truth is, all of these values mean nothing without self-control. SELF-DISCIPLINE is the mother of all values. It magnifies the ability to elicit and emancipate the necessary values to succeed. In this chapter, we will dig deep on the qualities that drive a person to success, and explain why SELF-DISCIPLINE is the true foundation to success.

Every dreamer is like a painter. First, they envision their creation before they engage on the verge of artistry. On the road to success.

Motivation drives a person to move forward. It serves as the blank canvass where we visualize and craft our dreams and aspirations, giving us guidelines on what our future can look like. Motivation is the cognitive appraisal of a reward that feels like success. It gives us a reason to work hard and persevere against all adversities. Whether the reward is extrinsic -such as wealth and fame- or intrinsic -such as honor and happiness- a person's motivation provides inspiration to thrive despite hardships and challenges.

A lot of situations can deter us from our motivation. Sometimes, we get tired of putting so much effort into our dreams and we start to lose hope. We start to lose sight of what it means to succeed. We start to dissuade ourselves from ever moving forward because all we see in front of us is a dead end.

On the road to success, never expect to have few trials. In real life, we face a daily skirmish with our minds, our hearts, and our society. There is a never-ending search for goals and meaning. All you need to do is develop the art of not giving up. Developing a good sense of self-discipline will allow a person to look past the challenges and focus on the prize ahead. It keeps the vision straight and crystal clear. See, motivation is not only an impetus towards success, but it is also a conduit towards positive thinking. Self-discipline will push you to look past the negativities and have a more positive perception of everything.

Courage is the first step we take before our real trials begin. The journey begins once we discover our audacity to engage in different life battles. Trust me, life will beat you down and take a little bit of your soul every day. Courage allows you to walk past the pain and agony and learn from your mistakes. Life will test your bravery. It will make you face your deepest and darkest fears. At this stage, every step you take seems to lead into a pit where none of your dreams will survive.

But with self-discipline, you convince yourself: "No, I will not yield from your challenges. Should I fail, I will rise up and conquer all trials and live my dream to its fullest." We know for sure there are battles we cannot win. In turn, self-discipline teaches the mind to take it on anyway. It is not about overcoming challenges but learning from them instead. That is the key. courage should not be only at the beginning. We should muster bravery consistently even after we have reached our goals. There is no end in learning, which is why we should be brave enough to tackle every challenge and gain more wisdom as time goes by. Developing self-discipline helps you be bolder. You need to face all the trials in life. There is so much bravery in learning from your mistakes. It pushes you to keep your head up high no matter how hard life has beaten you down.

Determination means being purposeful to overcome all challenges in life. You stick to your plan and stay focused on your goal no matter what it costs. As you begin your journey towards success, trials will be inevitable. Some challenges will cause you to lose your sense of purpose, diminish your spirit, and break your intent towards your dreams. Without self-discipline, it is easy to give in to pressure.

Unstoppable Day

I once knew a person who wanted to be a successful psychologist. She wanted to build her own clinic and make a name for herself as a successful therapist. She wanted to provide a home for the mentally disabled and teach them practical habits of survival. For four years in college, she was determined to study hard to pass the board exams. This way, she would be one step closer to her dreams. When she graduated, it was difficult for her to find a job suitable for her course. Her parents disapproved of her career choice, so they kept convincing her to find another line of work. Her parents always wanted her to be an accountant because of the salary. One of her uncles was willing to send her back to finish an accountancy degree, but she was a very determined woman. That is what I admired about her. Despite the pressure her parents put upon her, she stuck to her goal and passed the Psychology Board Exams. Now, she is a well-known psychotherapist who has provided shelter to hundreds of mentally incapacitated people and given job opportunities to aspiring psychologists. She could not have done it without her rock-solid determination.

With a tiny bit of self-discipline, your determination will be unstoppable. None of those hindrances will be strong enough to break your meaning and purpose in life.

Commitment is vital to success as well. This pertains to a person's dedication to his or her goal. Commitment or dedication causes a person to uphold his responsibilities and duties no matter how difficult it is to accomplish them. On the road to success, life will test your commitment to your goals. For example, you want to build a business by investing in your skills. Being committed to your goal means facing any adversity to make your dreams happen. This includes holding yourself liable for any profit or loss incurred in during the process.

A lot of people out there are skeptical about starting a business. Sure, it is a good way to earn money, but people only see how risky it is. It entails a regular, in-depth analysis of both the market and economy. Starting a business is a trial-and-error method of which services or products to introduce. It involves strategic advertising and promotion to establish a name and gather customers. Business includes risking a huge amount of capital, hoping it can generate income, and not incur in a loss. The steps we take towards success are straight-up terrifying and dangerous. These challenges can and will test your commitment but, with self-discipline, no amount of fear can dissuade you from pursuing what you love. It commands you to keep moving forward despite the losses. It pushes you to keep trying until you succeed in your chosen line. With self-discipline, no amount of liability will make you lose sight of your goals. No amount of burden will derail you from being committed to your dreams.

Time Management is better known as self-management because it is the ability to organize -and carry out- your activities. It also refers to the establishment of sync between your mind and body. You are not actually managing the time of day. You are handling yourself to establish a productive body clock to accomplish your tasks as scheduled. Self-management refers to the balance between rest and effort without procrastinating. Without this coordination, no agenda will push through, leaving you in the depths of lethargy and stagnation.

The most notorious enemy of self-management is procrastination. When continuous effort causes burnout and fatigue, the mind and body start to wear off. When this happens, all you want to do is sleep all day and think of nothing else but relaxation. However, too much rest is detrimental to progress, since it leads to unproductiveness. Do not underestimate how tempting temporary idleness can be. Never listen to your mind when it tells you, "Fifteen minutes on

Facebook will not hurt." Minutes turn to hours. Hours (can) turn to days. When your mind and body start to procrastinate, it is a very difficult place to come back from, which is why self-discipline is a necessary trick against lazy days. It sets your body on alarm, preventing it from giving in to procrastination. If you plan to rest, set an alarm and condition your mind to rest for a few minutes before you get back to work.

Time-management is a major factor in leading a successful life. Even so, without self-discipline, your system and schedule will turn into a lost cause. Body and mind conditioning revert back to zero. Precious time is wasted. And all your efforts will soon be undone. To maintain a stable mindset towards success, always develop your sense of self-discipline. It commands your brain towards consistency. It allows you to defer from distractions and efficiently walk a straight line on the road to success.

Willpower. It allows for self-reliance and independence to flow on a person's veins. It teaches the mind there is nobody else to rely on but oneself. With the streak of independence coursing through your actions, your decisions are your command. Your actions are made out of your own will. No other person can tell you what to do or how to live your life.

However, there are challenges that can put your willpower to the test. Sometimes, we feel like things are getting out of control and we can no longer do anything about it. It may seem that fate is doing an intervention, telling us our dream is not meant to be. Don't despair. This so-called destiny is a mind-driven concept. Wherever you are now, it's a consequence of your past actions and decisions. If you decide to keep on living towards your dream, then *that* will be your destiny. No hardship or "signs" from the universe will tell you otherwise.

With willpower, you have the strength to break the hands of destiny and walk your own path. You should not burden yourself with common sayings such as "If it is meant to be, it will be" because if you really want something to work, you will do everything in your power to make sure it does. Not even destiny will be able to stop you.

Self-discipline plays a key role in your consistent will to reach your goals. Without self-discipline, your mind will start to doubt your dreams and you will give in to your fears. Your mind will be inclined to listen to criticism that will derail you off your tracks. If you really are determined to reach your dreams, focus on your decisions. Learn from your mistakes. Never let it detract your focus and lose sight of the prize.

Passion refers to the emotion you put into your work. It is your zeal, your emotion and your enthusiasm that leads to success. Passion brings fire into your life. It boosts up your fervor and magnifies your power. Passion is the love you have for your work; it is what drives you into doing whatever it takes to succeed. Without passion, your life would feel like an improvised prison. Success will feel more like a burden rather than an inspiration. Every accomplishment will seem more like an encumbrance rather than a blessing. On the road towards success, it is important to keep passion flowing. Not only does it spark confidence, but determination and persistence as well.

Of course, your passion will be challenged plenty of times, but you need to remember why you loved your work in the first place. Remind yourself how it makes you feel. Remember the great moments that brought learning and growth. In doing so, your passion will ignite a never-ending motivation, giving way to change in your life. Self-discipline -along with passion- will make you unstoppable in reaching your dreams. Self-discipline will train your mind not to lose hope despite any circumstances. It will show you how to maintain a burning love and zeal towards your line of work. With these two values combined, nothing can stop you from achieving the success you deserve.

Confidence and self-discipline form a very effective combination. People always tell you to "believe in yourself" in order to achieve your goals. Thing is, it's very difficult to follow that motto when in self-doubt. It is common knowledge that confidence refers to your belief that you can accomplish a task or a goal. It is your faith that YOU CAN DO IT! Self-confidence is your assurance of your own skill set and intellect. Confidence is an important way to master boldness and face your trials. However, too much of it can cause your timely undoing. As human beings, there is always room for improvement. We will always have weaknesses in line with our strengths, which is why there should be a balance between humility and confidence. Crossing the line into overconfidence can lead to great peril on your road to success. Overconfidence inhibits your ability to reflect in your abilities and acknowledge your mistakes. It gives way to greed and avarice, characteristics that have doomed millions of entrepreneurs to failure.

Confidence powered by self-discipline will allow you to keep track of your behavior. It prevents a lack of confidence and self-doubt. In turn, it inhibits your mind from being too arrogant and greedy when making decisions. It signals your mind not to enter the depths of overconfidence. It sends out an alarm saying, "Whoops, aren't you a bit out of your head? Humble yourself up a little and reflect on your real skills. Stop being so greedy." Self-discipline maintains the normal threshold of diffidence a person can have.

Integrity is one of the most important values of mankind. It means being trustworthy and honest to other people. It is about having a good moral compass or choosing the right way rather than the easy one. Integrity brings honor and decency to an individual. It pushes us to make noble and righteous decisions. To achieve pure happiness in life, a person must uphold his integrity over others. Success out of mischief and deceit never lasts long. Sure, it can get you out of problems, and probably get you more money, but those means of action will eventually come back to haunt you and drag you back to the depths of your own hell.

On the road to success, you will face issues that challenge your commitment to integrity. These problems will tear your willpower apart, doubt your existence, and influence your actions. Eventually, you will get tired of all the righteousness and morality you uphold in our decisions, but this should not stop you from doing the right thing. With self-discipline, you can withstand any temptation that goes your way. With a proper mindset, you can ward off any influence that dooms your decisions into treachery or any other forms of immorality. If you develop and maintain self-discipline, you can uplift your spirit into doing what's right. As long as you know your conscience is clean, you will find no setback that can pull you out of the road to success.

Chapter 2:
Fundamental Key to Daily Self-Discipline

"If you want to live a happy life, tie it to a goal, not to people or things."

Albert Einstein

I grew up in a society where beauty, health, and fitness matters. Social media has created a definition of what is attractive, sexy, and intelligent. In this modern world, beauty means being white and blemish-free. Sexiness is defined as having a Coca-Cola shaped figure. Intelligence means taking a course in engineering, accountancy, teaching, or architecture. The rest is subject to bullying and criticism. When my cousin Liddy was a teenager, her classmates and neighbors kept making fun of her because of her body. Ever since she was a kid, she had a very slow metabolism. No matter how much she engaged in weight-loss activities, nothing worked. Eventually, she just stopped trying and disappeared into a pit of helplessness. This made her a victim of body-shaming and bullying on campus. As she grew up, she became very desperate to lose weight and have a "sexy" figure. She was envious of the girls who seemed carefree in maintaining their weight and figure.

I watched her try every trick in the book, including carb cutting and workout, but nothing really worked. One Monday morning, I decided to keep her company at 5:30 to jog around the city. I was really excited to see our fellow fitness enthusiasts. To my surprise, at 5:30 in the morning, we saw businessmen walking to and from the streets. Liddy and I stared at each other in disbelief. Offices did not open for at least another 2 hours. How come people were already suited for work? As we jogged further, we overheard a fellow fitness enthusiast talking with a suited man, "Done with your routine?" he asked, and the suited man gave him a quick high-five and passed on. Could it be that at 6:00 in the morning these businessmen had already done their early morning workout and got ready for work? I mean, how do they do that? I can even barely wake up at 4 AM, much less finish working out at 5.

Could it be that these daily routines play a role in becoming a fit and successful entrepreneur?

For many years, I have observed and studied the habits of the successful. I have concocted my own surveys on how those entrepreneurs get to finish their workout at 5 AM and be on their business attires 30 minutes after that. After months of continuous learning, I have determined the most important value: SELF-DISCIPLINE. This time, not only will it lead to success, but overall life-transformation as well.

Over the course of my life, I have watched as my cousins tried different weight-loss activities and lose hope as time went by, going back to their old habits. Because of this, I realized that successful weight loss is not about diet or strenuous exercise, it is about commitment and faith laced with long-term self-discipline. My cousins never intended to follow a diet or training program after a month without improvements. This repressed their ability to keep pushing themselves to the limit. The process is the same when striving for prestige and success. It is not always about the decisions and actions you take, but the commitment and faith you put into your work. These two values lead a person towards a holistic life transformation, including physical, emotional, and psychological development.

Earlier, we discussed the relationship of commitment and confidence to self-discipline. In this chapter, I will talk about the five fundamental steps to a long-term self-transformation – the conduit towards goal achievement.

The Fundamental Steps to Self-Transformation

These five steps towards self-transformation will allow you to acquire a higher level of self-discipline. Soon thereafter, you will realize that every other value, such as commitment and confidence, will follow suit. These steps do wonders for your physical development and will start to hone your psychological and emotional strength as well.

But why should you need psychological and emotional strength if your only target is weight loss? Well, I personally believe that every person has the inclination to achieve self-actualization or the fulfillment of one's putential and finding the meaning of life. Everyone has the need to rise from the depths of being a 'nobody' to becoming the 'somebody' this world needs. Developing long-term self-discipline will allow you to do just that. Before you start following the steps below, you must know that self-transformation is not an overnight thing. Sometimes, it takes two to three years before it can be attained. Trust me when I tell you it will be worth the wait. The self-transformation you gain through commitment and self-confidence will emancipate you until your last breath. For this, I want you to promise yourself to stay committed to your goals and actions. I want you to believe in yourself, to believe that you can do it. Take courage to start and finish your milestones without having any kind of self-doubt.

Without further ado, here are the Fundamental Steps to a Successful Self-Transformation:

Establish a Vision

First, I want you to think about your body, career, relationship, family or financial goals. Or anything that matters in your life. Visualize what you want to happen. Describe it detail by detail. If it helps, you can jot those down on a piece of paper or a notebook and hold on to it for dear life. I want you to imagine what it would be like to have the sexy body you always dreamed of. Picture your dream partner reaching towards you. What is he like? What do you have in common? What about your career? What do you really want to do in life? Do you want to be stuck reading and shredding the same number of papers every day or do you want to achieve something greater? How huge do you want your salary or income to be? Do you want to stick to the low-grade salary you always get at the end of the month or do you want to raise your commission? Think about your family. If you have kids, think about their future. What do you want it to look like? What would your plans for your parents be by then? Where -or how- will you spend vacation with them in five to ten years' time?

See, this vision that I want you to develop is the motivation to keep going no matter happens. It is your drive, your prize, your inspiration to move forward through all adversities. I want you to write it all in a journal in deep detail. If it helps, you can sketch out your dream body, dream house, and dream car.

In the morning when you wake up, and at night before you go to bed, I want you to rethink your dreams and aspirations. Remind yourself why you want self-transformation. Visit your journal and reread what you want in life. To keep you focused on your goals later on, I want you to never lose sight of that promise you made to yourself. In a way of helping, you can create your own mantra and focus on it, such as, "I will achieve my dreams only if I will allow it," or "I can do anything as long as I believe." Small as these actions are, they help you become unstoppable.

Create A Plan of Action

Your plan of action is the long-term milestone you want to carry out. However, this can be very hard to accomplish without a stable sense of self-identity. SELF-IDENTITY or SELF-CONCEPT is a very important factor for a realistic goal-setting. It defines how much you know yourself, how you perceive yourself, and how you present yourself to challenges. Without a good sense of self-identity, establishing an attainable plan of action is impossible. Too much self-appraisal can cause depression, anxiety, and other mental health-related issues. Too little self-appreciation can diminish self-worth and repress your strength, all of which are crucial to establishing a life-long self-transformation goal.

Creating a plan of action requires knowing yourself from the inside and out. To set your short-term goals later on, you need to know your strengths, weaknesses, opportunities, and threats. You must analyze what you need and what you can provide. On the aspects you mentioned above, I want you to do a SWOT (Strengths, Weaknesses, Opportunities, and Threats) Analysis in relation to each one of them.

For example, on your journey to weight loss, you have an opportunity to join the gym and hire an instructor. However, the threat is that you own a pastry shop and it is hard to say no to the good stuff. In your career, you can indicate your skill set as your strengths, and identify your fear of giving up the position as a weakness. On your opportunities, indicate whether there is a chance for promotion or any other jobs offered with a greater salary. The only probable threat is, "What if I do not get the job, what will I do then?"

Deal with Adversities

Seeing your weaknesses on that SWOT Analysis table can be pretty devastating. It causes self-doubt and erodes your confidence. However, in this step, you will learn how to deal with various adversities, walk past the negativities, and regain your confidence once again.

Acknowledge your Weakness. Everyone has their own weaknesses, but this should not get in the way of leading a successful life. Before you feel dissuaded into pursuing your dream, remember, you do not have the worst weakness in the world. Other people cannot even get out of their houses because of Agoraphobia, or the irrational fear of being helpless in public places. But even these people do not get discouraged by their phobia. On their road to success, they put triple efforts on their recovery just to regain their functionality as a person. So, if you think you have the biggest issues, think again. Whatever situation you are in, there is always a fixture to keep you going. All you need to do is accept your weaknesses and acknowledge them as a part of you. Once you have embraced your weaknesses wholeheartedly, you will be more inclined to face the adversities that your weaknesses will give way to.

Remind yourself of its Temporariness. The most permanent thing in this world is change. Much like adversities, we solve a challenge for a day just to wake up and face another one, but as you walk along the road to success, you will realize that all adversities are temporary. You are faced with different problems each day. Some are more difficult than others, but still, they teach you different lessons. These life trials eventually pass, sometimes even on their own. What you

Unstoppable Day

need to do is have a little bit of confidence and courage to face each day with a burning passion and will. Remind yourself you have tackled worse problems than what you are confronting now. Think about the times when you almost broke down and turned your back on your goals but didn't because you believed in yourself. Look where it got you. See, these challenges are a normal part of life. Everyone experiences them to learn, grow, and develop. If you acknowledge problems as a part of life, nothing can dissuade you from aiming for that goal with all your strength.

Learn from Others. You do not have to be alone when dealing with adversities. Sometimes, we need other people's assistance to teach us how to overcome the challenges we face in the pursuit of our dreams. If you want to lose weight, join the gym and ask for an instructor. If you want to learn some skills, approach someone who can teach you. If you want to be a successful entrepreneur, learn from the actions of successful businessmen and imitate what they did to gain prestige.

Believe in Success. Our trials in life can keep us from reaching further. Sometimes, we feel hopeless, helpless, and desperate in our path to success. Time will come when we would eventually feel like all our actions are useless and all our dreams are impossible to fulfill. To keep your confidence burning under your skin, look for people who have successfully reached their life milestones. Read stories that can inspire you to keep pushing yourself to the limit. Remind yourself your dream is possible because, if they could do it, you just have to believe you can do it better.

Some people came from poor families but were able to transcend from that status and rise up to be successful entrepreneurs. They had literally nothing but commitment and confidence. Look at your current status: you have a roof over your head, a comfortable bed to sleep on and eat three times a day. You have everything you need to magnify your strength. If the only thing stopping you is self-doubt, take a look at the people who you admire the most. Where did they come from? Where did they start? Now, look at yourself in the mirror. You have clean clothes on your back and a penny in your pocket. That's when you realize you have more than what they started with.

Do you want to redefine the meaning of impossible? Think of them. Let their success stories be an inspiration to drive your confidence on the road to success.

Create a Collateral. If you are still hesitant to face the adversities of life, the simple thing to do is focus on your threats ahead of time and plan a collateral for them. If you really want to overcome the challenges you encounter when sprinting towards your goals, plan how to beat them with many days to spare. For example, if you want to lose weight and run a pastry shop at the same time, you must learn to say "No, thank you." The pastry is not your enemy. *You* are the impending threat. Your mind will tempt you to look at how delicious those goods are, but you need to be strong enough to commit to your diet and say *No*. Of course, the first days of 'abstinence' will be the hardest thing you will have to go through. Give it a week or two. Eventually, saying no becomes your forte. Not only will you avoid the goods in your pastry shop, but any other no-no food as well.

Another example is when you plan on applying for another job but are too afraid of resigning. Then don't. If you apply for another job, keep your old job as a collateral just in case you do not get it. At least, you tried your best and did not lose anything. However, this does not mean that you will stop trying. There will be other job opportunities out there that will certainly work wonders for your career, which is why you must never stop believing.

Generate Goals

The next step towards self-transformation is setting your short-term goals according to your plan. This is the stage where strict monitoring and commitment is required. Once again, generate your short-term goals for each of the life aspects you have listed above. This time, you will need to boost your commitment to every objective you constitute.

For example, if you aim to lose weight, you need to choose and start following a diet and a workout program. Commit yourself every day and monitor your improvements as a way of motivation. Remember, discipline is the key. To establish a successful self-transformation, you need to overcome any temptation that can get you off track, or your efforts will flush themselves down the drain.

In order to gain long-term self-discipline, you can start by going one week without breaking any of your goals. This is the hardest phase of the self-transformation project. For the first step, set an alarm and schedule your workout routine and create a list of the 'dos' and 'don'ts' on your diet. Follow this routine for one to two weeks without any glitches and everything will flow like a river. Whenever you feel lazy and tempted to break it –even for a minute-, look at yourself in the mirror and repeat your mantra at least ten times. Condition your mind into believing that breaking your habit will bring you back to where you started. Remember your motivation. Remember what inspires you. Never let yourself break character. Here are five tips to maintain your daily self-transformation streak:

Remove any Form of Temptation. Wherever you go, make sure to eliminate all sources of temptation. As in the case of weight loss, make sure to remove all unhealthy food in the fridge, and exchange those with veggies, fruits, and yogurt. If you want to work without any distractions, create a workstation in a separate room without any television or gadgets to tempt you into procrastination.

Changing does not always feel right. Self-transformation can cause positive change to look like an impending crisis. However, you should not let this stop you. Your body does not label change as something positive in the beginning. It will always feel like there is something missing. It will make you unhappy and doubt your decisions. On the road to self-transformation, you need to acknowledge the "It does not feel right" perception to avoid being misled by temptation. Keep your mind focused on your goals and never stop committing to them. Sooner or later, your body and mind will start to accept these changes and they will become a huge part of your personality.

Failure is a Part of Success. We are only human beings. We are prone to making mistakes and bad decisions. On the road to self-transformation, do not beat yourself up whenever you don't do well in a task or you do not get something right. Discipline takes practice, it cannot be mastered overnight. Whenever you fail, do not be dissuaded from moving forward. Consider all mistakes as a form of learning. Retrace your steps to what went wrong and grow from it, but never beat yourself up because of it, since it can lead to depression or anxiety, which in turn might be the cause of your dreams' demise. Learn to forgive yourself when you encounter a glitch in your way. As human beings, we fall down, all the more reason to rise back up higher.

Unstoppable Day

Focus on one day at a time. As you establish your milestones on the road to self-transformation, learn to focus on the present, not the past nor the future. Putting your attention on the past will only distract you from your current goals. It reminds you of your past failures and mistakes. Do not focus on tomorrow either, as it brings stress and apprehension. Thinking about tomorrow can detract your focus on what is in store for you today. To concentrate on getting through your tasks, focus on what you need to do right now and stick to it. Do not overthink your future plans. Learn to cross the bridge when you get there. For now, think about what you can do to improve yourself even more.

Use technology wisely. At this day and age, gadgets will most certainly distract us from accomplishing our objectives. Believe me, I know there are a lot of cool and interesting apps to try out, but in order to build a fully-transformed self, you need to utilize your gadgets in accordance with your plan. There are a lot of applications that can help you lose weight. There is the daily workout reminder app, drink water app, a routine for fitness app, and many more. If your goal is to target your cognitive aspect, you can download brain training apps, reading apps, and quiz bee apps that can help you sharpen your mind. If you lack motivation, there are apps that can help you meditate or provide helpful quotes and inspirational messages.

You can also put gadgets in a different light by using them as a 'time signal' for your workout routine. If you want to watch television, do it while working out. If you want to listen to music, use each playlist as a timeline for each set. If you want to play a game, download one that can make you sweat, such as Dance Central and other body simulation games.

Get Some Rest

Cheat days are important for keeping your head in the game. Schedule one day in a week where you can do whatever you want. You can break your diet and your exercise routines, procrastinate and give into temptation. We are only human, and as such we should not be deprived of the things we love. If we are, we become prone to untimely breaks of our self-transformation habits. To ensure the development of continuous self-discipline, a break from time to time can help a person stay motivated, stay on track. Cheat days are also known as reward days. Once the brain is accustomed to a reward at the end of every week, it will be conditioned to keep putting an effort into every routine. Do not be afraid to fall back into the abyss after the cheat day. Once you start your week with another routine, you will find your commitment and confidence to be stronger. Any other setback will seem like a walk in the park.

Now that you know everything necessary to have life-long self-discipline, the last thing to do is to maintain a strong sense of commitment and confidence. These two, laced with self-control, will lead you to become one of the most successful people on Earth. Who knows, you will probably be writing your own success story in a couple of years.

Chapter 3:
Habits of the Disciplined

"Whenever you want to achieve something, keep your eyes open, concentrate and make sure you know exactly what it is you want. No one can hit their target with their eyes closed."

Paulo Coelho

Successful minds have disciplined hearts. Not only do they have control over their thinking, but they also have mastery over their emotions. These two combined create an unstoppable personality that can withstand any adversity in life. The real reason for prestige is not only sweat and blood, but also self-command. It requires practice, training, and persistence to master. No matter how much you speak of it, if you don't know how to apply it, nothing good will ever come towards you. In order to achieve self-transformation, one needs to develop the habits of the disciplined. Once a person has fully mastered these tricks, nothing will ever come in their way towards success.

A habit is something that automates your routine and runs your behavior. It allows a higher-level thinking, unstoppable focus, and an unrelenting persistence towards a person's decisions. A habit is something that controls your mind and vibrates into your body. Once acquired, actions will flow easily and peacefully throughout your veins.

If you are wondering how successful people figured their lives out, it all started by developing important behavioral habits. As we discussed earlier, it is important to obtain commitment and self-confidence to execute these actions successfully. Start one day at a time, practicing each one as they come along. You do not have to rush yourself into mastering these abilities. With time and practice, you will be able to carry these out without even thinking about it. Once you do, congratulate yourself, for you have achieved the first milestone towards a self-actualized personality.

Below, I have constituted ten habits of the disciplined. As you adopt these behaviors, you will realize how strong they can impact your ability to cope, understand, think, and decide. Being successful means creating change in the world. These 10 habits are your primary stepping stones into changing old habits and gaining self-discipline.

Avoid Wasting Time. First and foremost, avoid idle time. It is important to always do something productive in your day-to-day routine. Instead of being a couch potato, watching movies the whole day, try reading inspirational books to keep you going or, if you want to watch a movie, why don't you work out while you do it? Use technology wisely. Do not let it sulk you into the depths of procrastination and unproductiveness.

Successful people are uncomfortable wasting time because it is the most expensive commodity that nobody can bring back. Once time has passed, the only things left are satisfaction or regret. A person is satisfied when he knows he has done something good with his time. On the other hand, all the lazy person has is regret. At least in the long run. Yes, for a while, he had some fun, but as

Unstoppable Day

he grows up, he will soon realize that he should have done something good while he was young.

This generation underestimates the allure of time. People only realize how precious it is once it has already gone by. Do not be like the rest, who spend all their time on social media and playing games when you can be out there establishing your business, investing on your skills, and trying your best to become successful in life.

Focus on the Present. There is always room for improvement in a person's personality. People who say, "This is who I am. You either accept or reject me" are somewhat immature and narcissist. A person will always have room for personality development, no matter how dark or crooked his background is. On the road to Self-Transformation, one's background is not of importance. In its place, the present takes the spotlight, as you prepare for the future. The society where you came from, the abuse you have experienced, the hardships you have overcome. All that brought you to where you are now. Instead of focusing on negativities, focus on what you can do now to furnish your personality on your way to success. The past is just a setback. It reminds you that you are worthless and undeserving of happiness and success. Do not listen to those voices inside your head. Grasp it, take a hold of it and do not let it control you ever again. Your past doesn't dictate your destiny. You are the captain of your own ship, and as such, you decide where to go and what to do.

Create a Formula. If you're wondering what famous scientists like Albert Einstein, Isaac Newton, and Rene Descartes did to achieve their success and fame, let me tell you: they created their own formula. You do not have to be a scientist to make your own. All you need is a little bit of wit and creativity. Try to apply a formula in everything you do. For example, in your expenses, for every X that you earn every month, you will only spend Y. For every calorie intake -X-, you need to burn an amount -Y-.

Some people think these formulas are just mere child's play, that they don't really work. There are a lot of possibilities that can challenge this concept, but on the road to self-discipline, challenges will not be a problem because of your persistence and control. If you stick to this formula, you can use it to gain control over your actions. Who knows, maybe you will even write about it one day.

Be one with the Community. If you're thinking about how being one with the community can help you transform, I have the answer: you cannot learn everything on your own. By interacting with different people, you can learn a lot of values, skills, and life lessons. Being one with the community does not mean pouring your time to socialization. It just means being supportive and trustworthy, especially in the face of calamity. On your way to success, don't expect to always walk through it alone. You will always find travel buddies and companions who will help you. Being one with the community through interaction teaches three of the most important values in a team: cooperation, understanding, and reliability. To be a good leader someday, you need to be a good follower. In order to be a good follower, you need to be an effective leader.

Make the habit of socializing with other people, even if you're not comfortable. Apart from the fact that you learn from their experiences, you also muster the confidence and self-esteem to become more open to the world and more assertive in your actions. Socialization can decrease self-doubt and increase your interpersonal intelligence. Therefore, it can help you develop a healthy emotional status. It has been proven that interacting with other people, especially friends and family can reduce the risk of depression, anxiety, and other mental disorders.

Eat Healthily. Our bodies are like machines. They need healthy fuel to function properly. Remember: you are what you eat. On the path to success, you need to start choosing what you take into your body. Avoid junk and fatty food as much as possible, given that these can make your body and mind sluggish, inhibiting your ability to think, decide, and criticize your actions. Ingesting a lot of junk food and artificial sugars can impair the balance of hormones that our glands secrete. In turn, it causes physical problems such as obesity, and heart and kidney failure. Moreover, junk food can also cause psychological disturbances. Eating unhealthy foods can cause an imbalance in a person's level of serotonin, dopamine, and endorphin, which are the necessary features to feel good and happy.

Eating more fruits and vegetables can boost up your mind and provide enduring energy for your body. Once you start eating power foods and stick to the diet, you will realize the wonders it can bring to your body when it comes to physical, emotional, and psychological wellness. Depressed individuals are advised to eat nutritious food groups and avoid skipping meals. When they follow the program effectively, changes in their mindset start to occur, and they become better individuals eventually.

At first, it would be difficult to adjust your body's eating schedule, which is why you might want to set an alarm when mealtime comes. Accustom your mind to eat three times a day. It could be at 8:00 AM, Noon, and 7 PM. Remove any temptation from your refrigerator, and exchange it with healthy food. Do this for a couple of weeks, and you will find yourself to be healthier than ever.

Maintain Healthy Sleep. Sleep is important to regulate the status of your body. After a long day's work, the body experiences a lot of stress, causing an imbalance in its chemical structure. This affects our physical and psychological health. Sleep reverts the body back to homeostasis, relaxes both the mind and the body, and 'recharges' you for another stressful day. If you look closely at the people who do not get enough sleep, they are more prone to depression, anxiety, and physical illnesses. They are prone to having heart diseases and other organ failures as a result of restlessness.

If you're not used to sleeping early, force yourself to get into bed at 8:00 or 9:00 PM. Tell your mind you need to sleep so you can wake up early in the morning. Do not let your mind take control of your body. Grab a hold of your mind and command it to sleep. The first few weeks will be the hardest, but once your mind has been conditioned to sleep at those hours, you will realize that falling asleep early will not be a problem anymore. It only takes commitment and persistence to master this craft.

Exercise Regularly. Exercising regularly is a very important tool when striving for success in self-transformation. Scientists have proven that exercise can increase the levels of endorphin or "feel-good" hormones in the body. This is a must to carry out your activities for the day. It hypes up your mood and enhances your energy to have a powered mind and body to get through the day. In the previous chapter, we discussed how to schedule yourself towards regular exercises. Now you know that working out is not only necessary for weight loss but also necessary towards a successful Self-Transformation. This will provide balance for your body and strengthen your mind in the face of certain adversities that life can send your way.

Unstoppable Day

Organize your Schedule. Managing your schedule will not make you a control freak. It just means you're strong enough to manage your time and accomplish goals for the day. Scheduling your tasks and objectives is key when going for success. It avoids idle time and reminds you of the things you need to do. Organizing your schedule means living on your body clock. To accomplish this, you will need self-control and commitment. For example, if you take long showers, you must reverse that habit by setting yourself on alarm. If you want to take a shower at about 8 o'clock in the evening, set a 15-minute timer. Once it goes off, you should get out of the bathroom and get dressed. Another example: if you take too long to eat, schedule you're eating period for about 15 minutes for every meal. In the morning, schedule your meal from 8:00 to 8:15, 12:00 to 12:15 at noon, and 7:00 to 7:15 in the evening. For TV, gaming, and social media enthusiasts out there, you can create your schedule to limit your use of all your gadgets as well. For example, to decrease the number usage hours, set your game time, TV time, or social media time for one hour. Once the timer goes off, move to more productive activities.

Maintain a clean environment. How can a clean environment help in self-transformation? Well, within this is a very important factor to boost the mind, body, and soul. Clutters and garbage can impede the mind from thinking smoothly. As the old saying goes, your actions imitate your thoughts. If your things are scattered, it could mean your mind is scattered as well. This could indicate a lack of focus and concentration on your plans and activities. Psychologists have linked the cleanliness of a workspace or work environment to optimal performance. Specialists have also found that uncleanliness is directly correlated to mental illnesses and physical diseases.

Now, if you were to ask me, "This is my personality. It is how I like my things to be. How can I change it?" As I explained earlier, every person has room for change. In this case, the first step to do is clean your house and organize your things. Maintain the habit of putting anything you use or displace back where it was. I know it is going to be hard for the first few weeks, but you can pass this test with flying colors if you're persistent and committed. As days go by and you grow accustomed to the tidiness of your place, you will realize how brighter and how comfortable your life will be.

Reward Progress. We have discussed that rewarding accomplishments conditions the mind into believing there's something to look forward to every time you make an effort. This is not only in the case of weight loss on the cheat day. It is also applicable if you plan to develop a useful habit towards Self-Transformation. Whenever you get something right, it is important to reward yourself. Buy anything you want. Eat anything you want. Or give yourself one day to just relax and do nothing. The cheat day is a necessity to keep discipline at its peak. Depriving the mind and the body of the things it wants does more harm than good. Trust me, starving the body of goodness slowly pulls the mind into discouragement, which may cause the total cessation of the process towards self-discipline and self-transformation. That is why it is important to give yourself a day off. It helps to forget about the stress, anxiety, and pressure your journey is putting upon you.

Chapter 4:
Surprising Mind Tricks to Master Self-Discipline

What is the secret of a magician? For starters, it is neither about the illusions nor the tricks up their sleeves. The real secret of a magician is the innocence of the naked eye. The reason why magicians never reveal their tricks is that when they do, it strips their illusions of their fun. Everybody would know how they do it. Nobody will be enticed to watch his show again.

I personally believe that everybody's a magician. They all have their way of doing things that other people cannot entirely understand. Some people have more self-discipline than others. Some took a shorter time to achieve Self-Transformation. Other people seem to make little effort to find success. What we don't realize is that there is a secret in everything these people do. To our innocent minds, it just seems to beat the impossible. It all seems like a magic show. Truth is, we don't know the extra efforts they put in their work. We don't know how they overcame their shortcomings. We have no idea how they acquired an unstoppable sense of self-discipline. As people with innocent eyes, we have no clue how they strived from the depths of their own hell. It is like watching Master Houdini escape from his chains of death.

Do not be discouraged if you feel like you have nothing to offer to the world. Each of us has a "magic" or skill that other people do not have. Every one of us has a forte that nobody else can beat. The trick to unleashing that power is by developing an amazing sense of self-discipline. Once you do, self-transformation will allow you to uncover your optimal potential to use it towards success. In this chapter, I will be showing you tricks to take control of your mind. These illusions will train the mind to unleash its full potential. As you see, these activities seem to be very common and easy to do, but what you do not know is it impacts the brain dramatically, training it to be better without even knowing. Are you ready to learn various magic techniques to trick your brain into self-discipline? Here are twelve mind tricks to get the most out of your brain.

Increase Intensity. If you have tried going to the gym, you might have noticed that once a person develops his resistance on a certain weight, he aims to add more intensity to his routine. Just like your brain, it needs an increasing amount of intensity to keep learning, to keep pushing, and to keep improving. If a person chooses to remain stagnant in his level of thinking, he will not make any improvement. Why does a person need to increase the threshold of his abilities? Simply put, as time passes by, challenges evolve along with it. As you push through the road to success, you will find your challenges harder each day. This is why you need to prepare yourself in various levels of adversity. It helps your mind adjust and cope easily, reducing your instances of breaking down.

Always look for an opportunity to grow. Do not be afraid to make mistakes because the lessons you learn from your experiences are timeless, and come in handy as you progress on each milestone. Do not be afraid to feel pain, once you've grown resistant to it, you will be stronger, bolder, and wiser every day.

Write it down. Did you know that writing your thoughts down can help you gain self-discipline? Unlike speaking, writing about your feelings can boost your

Unstoppable Day

concentration level and enhance your focusing skills. Pouring your feelings out using pen and paper not only grants mind control, but it can also help regulate a person's emotions. Psychologists have found that keeping a journal of your thoughts and feelings can help alleviate stress, sadness, and anxiety. Think of it as giving yourself a pep talk where you experience a lot of realizations and reflections to use later in life.

Keeping a journal is also effective in monitoring the progress of your self-transformation. You can write about how you feel about a task before, during, and after you accomplish it. This way, you will feel more motivated to keep pushing yourself into accomplishing more and more each day.

Share your Goals. Sharing your goals with your friends and family has been proven to bring wonders to your journey towards success. Apart from the fact you can learn from their suggestions, they can also push you to your limit by motivating you into working hard. Family and friends can help uplift your spirit, especially in times of hardships. It will be best to know there are people who support and love you for who you are.

Sharing your goals with your loved ones is also a form of socialization. It allows you to interact, speak up, and assert yourself. It helps you rehearse how to deal with some of the timely crises in life. Furthermore, this can also help you adjust yourself in social situations. This may come in handy if you are shy. Your friends and family can help you develop your interpersonal skills.

Learn from your Mistakes. A lot of people out there get dissuaded every time they make a mistake. Always remember: we are only human. We are prone to making bad decisions. We are prone to wrong our fellowmen. You are born to make mistakes. Life wouldn't be called that way if it was easy. That is why we need to acknowledge that mistakes really are a part of our journey. Once we realize this, we will never hesitate to take another stepping stone. The fear of committing mistakes hinders us from being assertive. It depletes our confidence and commitment to our line of work. It fills our mind with self-doubt, which is detrimental to the progress of our Self-Transformation.

One of the most common reasons why a person is afraid to make mistakes is the reputation he upholds in society. He does not want to be ostracized by society. Be that as it may, it should not stop you from being yourself in doing what you need to achieve success. Your neighbors, no matter how perfect their life seems, commit mistakes too. Who knows? Maybe they made even worse mistakes than you. All you need to remember is that as long as your conscience remains clear and you know you're not stepping on others' toes, as long as you know that you are not violating any other people's rights, then you have nothing to worry about. Keep on doing what you need to, and society will come to accept the new you. Remember: you are not doing this for anyone else but yourself. For your own development.

There is no Right Time. Why wait when you can do it now? Lots of people are very hesitant to act courageously and take their first step towards success. The reason they keep buried in their minds is 'the right timing'. Ask yourself what is the root of that doubt pertaining to the "Right timing." If you are not going to do it now, when? Is it because you are not ready? Or is it because you are too lazy to think about it? Earlier, we came to the conclusion that time is the most precious commodity. Once it has passed, you can never take it back. The only thing that is getting between you and the right timing is your mindset. You don't control time to be ready for success. You control your mind to be willing to make an effort towards success. The problem is not the right timing.

Unstoppable Day

The problem is a strong mindset towards readiness and commitment to hard work.

Self-Motivation. What motivates you the most? Is it your dream, the people pushing you towards that dream, or both? If it's both, then consider yourself lucky. Some people out there strive towards success without the support from their loved ones. Some tread in the dark world all alone without any care or love from their family and friends. If you're one of those people who do not rely on anyone but themselves, this mind trick is for you. You don't have to rely on other people to feel motivated. You can motivate yourself. All it takes is a little bit of commitment, confidence, and self-discipline. Whenever you feel the need to give up or break down, stop for a moment and think. Signal your mind to stop thinking about the negativities that life brings you. Instead, focus on positive things. Put yourself in a calm and comfortable space, and think about what went right instead of what went wrong. Self-motivation is the key to moving forward without any glitches or self-doubt. If the world is giving you trouble and no one is there to support you, support yourself simply because you can. If you can motivate yourself on your own, you will find endless numbers of inspiration to focus on. Nothing will derail you on your way to success.

Say Thank You more often. Gratitude is a very important value among mankind. It fosters happiness, contentment, and simplicity in life. It avoids greed, avarice, and boastfulness that can make a person hit rock bottom. Saying thank you more often leads to a peaceful life. Being thankful for what you have is better than pining over what you don't. It helps you avoid any temptation that makes you lose focus on your goals.

If it helps, you can include a list of people to thank in your journal. Write a short message about their regards, their help, even the small tokens of support. Thank the person who said you are pretty, handsome, or intelligent. Thank the person who handed you a cup of coffee at work. Smile at people in the streets. Help those people in need. That will make you realize there are good things in life to look forward to. It makes you believe that humanity still exists. If you are looking to change the world with your skills and talents, being grateful about the bounties that life can bring you is a vital step.

Never underestimate the allure of gratitude and thankfulness. It will provide you success along with happiness and contentment that will endure over time. Gratitude creates a legacy – something to remember you by even after your bones have turned to ashes.

Learn to Say Sorry. Apologizing for your mistakes is a major factor when aiming for a happy and contented lifestyle. It grants you the self-discipline to own up to your mistakes by sincerely asking for forgiveness. Having an apologetic mind can grant a life-long transformation and allows humility and modesty to blossom. These traits, laced with self-discipline, drive a person to success. By listening to the humble voice inside your head, it can bring wonders to your life. It allows you to learn from your mistakes and make up for what you did wrong.

Learn to Forgive. Forgiveness goes hand in hand with love. It does not have to be 'romantic' love, it could also mean love for your family, self, or line of work. Granting forgiveness to yourself and other people clears your mind and refreshes your soul. It promotes love, care, and support that adds to the motivation to strive harder in life. It allows us to keep moving forward and let go of the pain. Songs have been written and poems have been inscribed to show the value of forgiveness. However, it takes a lot of courage and self-discipline to forgive and forget the people who have wronged you. Once you have mastered the ability to understand and comprehend other people's mistakes, you will slowly regain control over your mind and emotions.

Learn to say No. There are a lot of temptations that will derail you on your road to self-discipline. As a mind trick, learn to say "No, thank you," especially when you know it can detract your focus on your goals. Just decline the offer and never look back. Saying "No" to specific activities can be hard at the beginning, more so if it is something you are used to. The trick into walking away from temptation is to believe that you are a completely different person. Think of it this way, there are two people trying to stop their addiction on alcohol. Person A was offered a twenty-percent discount from any merchandise in the liquor store but said, "I am sorry, I am trying to quit." Next, Person B was offered the same, but he answered, "No, thank you. I am not that kind of person."

The difference between these two people is their self-perspective. Person A still believes he is addicted to alcohol, while Person B acknowledges that he has a different personality. Sometimes, our self-concept and our will to change can affect the difficulty of saying no to temptation. So, whenever you feel the need to get derailed, always remember you are not that person. You are a person who is on the road to self-discipline and there is nothing anyone can do to stop you.

Be Confident. It is effective to give yourself a pep talk from time to time. It grants you comfort and it guarantees everything is going to be okay. When you are faced with difficult adversity, create a good assurance to yourself that you can do it. Remind yourself of your skills and capabilities. Convince your mind that good things come out of being perseverant. Always remember, should you commit any mistakes, you can rise back up because you are strong enough to do so. Remind yourself of your inspirations, your family and friends. Tell yourself that they will always be there for you when you fall. You do not have to be afraid anymore.

Plan Good Things. In the journey to be a successful individual, it is important to be open to experience. If you have nothing else to do, plan a trip, go someplace else, try new things, or look for a new hobby. These are great ways to learn a lot from your experiences, something that might come in handy in the future. Planning good things is also an effective way to alleviate stress and reduce pressure, devastation, and anxiety. Consider it as a form of rest and recreation that also helps you learn and gain more knowledge about life.

You know what they say, "Life is not made to be lived in one place." If you travel to new places, you will meet new faces, experience different personalities, get immersed in different cultures, and learn life lessons. For instance, if you plan to travel around the globe, go to the places where Taoism and Buddhism are considered the main religion. In doing so, their elders will be able to teach you the secrets towards a happy life. They might even teach you more tricks to gain self-discipline and self-transformation through meditation. Experience what's like to live simply and peacefully. Let yourself gain realizations and reflections to apply when you come home. Open your mind to new knowledge and you will find yourself on the edge of becoming a master of your mind.

Chapter 5:
The Secrets to Resist Temptation

Acquiring well-established self-discipline is never easy, but neither impossible. To gain full control of the mind, you will need courage, commitment, and persistence to keep moving forward despite the numerous temptations that challenge your perception. Life will always throw you distractions that can detract your focus from your goals. Our goal is to cultivate resistance to your hardest temptations – to act in accordance with your thoughts, and not your impulses or feelings. The main challenge of acquiring well-rounded self-discipline is not how a person interprets a situation but how one controls one's emotional state.

For instance, an alcoholic person is trying to change his behavior. Whenever he is offered a drink, the problem is not how he interprets the temptation rather than how he feels about it. He might feel devastated because he misses the times when he used to get drunk and have fun with his friends. The memories of good times will cause frustration, now that he is being a "kill-joy" to his friends. When the body is desperate to relapse into old habits, a person becomes emotional about pursuing change. One temptation will lead to various reasons why you should sulk towards the dark side. Your mind will argue with you, saying, "This is not you. This does not feel right. Sooner or later, you will not have any friends left." If you let these thoughts intrude your progress towards success, you become a lost cause. These emotions that you emancipate trigger your sadness and desperation to go back to old times. They blur your focus on your long-term goals. These temptations blind you when it comes to self-transformation. Eventually, you will find yourself moping at point blank. These impulses and emotional tendencies should be controlled for unstoppable self-discipline.

I like to symbolize our self-discipline in the form of an iron fist. As we all know, the iron fist is a symbol imbued to people who have withstood the hardest of adversities. The iron fist is known for being steadfast, strong, and committed. It is a symbol of ruthless authority, which is what we need to resist our temptation. Think of it like being Superman, except you are surrounded by Kryptonite. To obtain the iron fist of self-discipline, you need to improve, cope, and adapt to resist opposing powers. Once a person's self-discipline is as strong as the iron fist, no temptation will shy him away from his goals. In this chapter, I will be discussing how to develop the iron fist of self-discipline. But first, let is tackle the types of temptation that can keep you from an unstoppable self-discipline

The Temptations of the Disciplined

The Temptation of The Past.
As you lay down at night, trying to get some sleep, your thoughts allow you to imagine things, remember moments, and go down memory lane. Some moments you remember are timeless, joyful memories that will always serve as an inspiration to your future. However, there are times when you feel the horror of your mistakes. Your mind reminisces the times you failed, the times you were embarrassed, the times you were fooled. The temptation of the past will drive your frustration to its peak, causing fear of another failure. It will make you paranoid about your current situation, afraid of anything that can or cannot

happen, especially when you're trying to accomplish the goals you were not able to before.

The Temptation of The Future.

Another temptation that inhibits your ability to look past your mistakes is your anxiety of the future. It makes you fear the things you do because of their possible outcome. It makes you ask yourself different "What if's" that compromise your ability to think clearly and decide wisely on your challenges. Thinking about the future in a negative manner is a temptation that will make you hit rock bottom. It inhibits your ability to innovate, create, and grow as a person. It allows you to think about all of the setbacks and consequences your journey to transformation will cause. The temptation of the past, along with the temptation of the future, causes demotivation and stagnation in an individual. It hinders a person from keeping an eye on his goals, breaking his spirit of becoming a fully successful individual. Focusing on the past and future gives way to more than just frustration, as the deprivation of emotional self, torture, and depression are known to occur as well.

The Temptation of Procrastination.

One of the worst temptations that cause setbacks is procrastination. When your mind is filled with distractions and enticements, there's a huge probability you will give in. You will remember how amazing it is to finish a whole series of movies rather than doing something productive. You will see your old self; how simple your life was before you decided to venture towards Self-Transformation. Procrastination is a very powerful temptation that has caused lots of ships to burn down and crash in the ocean. It is likened to be a siren's song that distracts the minds of sailors in the middle of the ocean. For young minds, procrastination is the number one enemy towards success. There are literally hundreds of things to dissuade them from productiveness, such as gadgets, friends, gimmicks, and other activities.

The Temptation of Breaking Down

The problems you encounter in life will crush your spirit, pierce your soul and disengage your will to succeed. They will make you doubt your existence in the world, question who you are, your identity, and your belief in yourself. There are challenges that will ward off some friends and family who do not believe in you. But in those moments of loneliness, you will start to think twice about changing for the better. Your mind will try to convince you things are getting worse. Success doesn't always mean money or fame. To millions of people out there, success means happiness and freedom from societal chains. To these people who aim for psychological and emotional success, breaking down is a common factor towards failure. You will think about how tired you are in this penitent. Your heart will start to feel heavy. It will feel like you're making all the wrong choices in life. Once you let the temptation of breaking down get into your soul, your mind and heart start to fall apart. It will clench your spirit and break your vital force. It frightens you take another step because you're afraid of pain, anguish, and frustration to move forward in your life. For me, this is the most difficult challenge to step out from.

The Temptation Between the Truth and The Lie.

In the previous chapter, we discussed integrity as one of the most vital keys to success. During your hardships on the road to self-transformation, you will be tempted to make immoral choices just to make your life easier. Sometimes, challenges force you to tell a lie and exaggerate the truth. These will soon spread into countless lies for the years to come. Once your body and mind start to believe the lies you have been telling people, your real identity is difficult to track. How can you transform yourself into something positive, when you don't know who you really are? You cannot achieve success if your life is built on deception. Eventually, these lies will catch up on to you, causing you a setback that can ruin your life for good. As much as possible, no matter how easy it is to lie, choose to speak -and believe in- the truth. Do not let yourself be consumed by the chain of lies you have created. Find out who you really are. Stand up to your beliefs. Nothing good ever happens to people who pretend to be someone they are not.

You have to admit; we all have been challenged by these temptations. If you remain where you are now, that means you have yielded your strength and gave in to any of these temptations. That's over now. Now that you know what you need to watch out for, here are the most important secrets to resist untimely temptations.

The Secrets Against Temptation

Focus on Your Identity.
Sticking with who you are is important to ward off the temptation between the truth and the lie. It allows you to be who you really are without any hint of treachery. When you focus on your identity, you start to live up to your strengths and acknowledge your weaknesses. You will start to discriminate opportunities from threats. Knowing who you are from the inside out will give you a higher-thinking ability to choose what is right, a trait only a few possess.

You do not have to pretend about anything. You are a unique individual who is way better in something than anybody else in the world. Learn to be satisfied with what you can give, and start to enrich it by learning and by practicing your skills. Pretentiousness causes unhappiness and dissatisfaction. It gives you unrealistic thoughts about your capabilities, increasing your self-expectation, even when you have reached your peak by being your true self. Though playing pretend can get you where you want very easily, soon thereafter, you will start to doubt everything in your life. You will start to realize the real you should be someplace else. *That* is where you should be, instead of pretending to be happy here. Start to live your life the way you want to, not the way others want you to. If you are afraid, they might not accept you, don't be. Your real friends and family will always be there for you no matter what you choose. As the saying goes, "Family is not always about blood. They are the people who care about and love you the most whoever you are." If they cannot accept you for what you can become, and it is not your loss. There will always be people who will accept you, especially on the road towards success and Self-Transformation.

Embrace Your Trigger

Throughout the course of our lives, we have encountered hardships, challenges, embarrassments, and failures, during which we have developed our own cues that trigger our emotionality. There are words, sights, and sounds that remind us of the negativities we have encountered before. Sometimes, these can bring motivation, and enhance our drive to work better and strive harder. However, often times they derail us from being productive for the day. Once these memories trigger sadness, it is very difficult to cope. It makes us idle and unproductive, sulking all day long, ruminating about the past when we should be focusing on the present. To prevent these emotional cues from ruining our day, we need to start embracing our emotional triggers.

The first step you take in healing from your trigger is to forgive yourself for your mistakes. To accept that you were young and knew nothing but to satiate your impulses. Acknowledge that people can change, and so can you. Times are different, you have grown for the better, and now you're trying to be a better person.

Next, you need to face your triggers with an iron fist. When you see something that reminds you of your past, take three deep breaths, and allow yourself to let go of the memory. It may cause pain and sadness, but when you accustom yourself to that feeling, it can no longer hurt you. Rather, it becomes a shield that makes you learn a lesson from your past. Forgive the people who have wronged you and reflect on what you did wrong as well. If it helps, write about it, express everything you never got to say before. Let it be a beacon for change and improvement in your life. Let it make you stronger and bolder to face more challenges in life.

The third step into healing from your emotional trigger is to detach yourself from the memory. Whenever you think of something bad about a situation, try to focus on something positive about it. If none, shift your focus on to something funny, attractive, or delicious. That way, your emotional trigger will not be able to hurt you anymore. Learn to relax your brain in the midst of being in pain, and do something that can ease your feelings about it rather than focusing on your negative feelings.

Embrace Discomfort
One of the things that inhibit a person from moving forward is the discomfort of pushing through. I am sure most of us have encountered the saying, "Get out of your comfort zone." No matter how much people speak about it, only a few have the guts to actually do it. Discomfort is a very advantageous form of learning. It makes you experience and overcome problems you have never dealt with

before. Once you overcome these new issues and challenges, treading with different trials will be a walk in the park. To overcome temptations, you need to seek pain and get used to it. We have discussed earlier that the reason for temptation is not the interpretation of the mind, but feelings from the heart. If you get used to the pain and discomfort of doing something different, then you're one step closer towards Self-Transformation. Not only is discomfort a conduit for growth and development, but it also helps you overcome your fear of failure, anxiety, and depression. Embracing discomfort grants you the ability to be a Strong-Willed individual, in an unstoppable pursuit towards success.

Chapter 6:
Break the Cycle Holding You Back

The most dangerous phrase that holds a person back and results in repeated failure is "Just this once." Just this once, you want to eat chips because you have cravings. Just this once, you want to skip your exercise routine because you feel tired. Just this once, you want to sleep until 10 AM because you do not feel like waking up at five in the morning. Did you know that establishing a good habit takes a person many years to accomplish if he keeps on saying, "Just one more time?" Because of that "last" resort, a person reverts back to the old ways. Because of that one fall, he relapses back to where he came from and starts anew once again.

If you have come so far only to be tempted to roll back your old habits, you better think twice. Do you want your efforts to be worthwhile? Don't you want to have a groundbreaking change as you get older? Don't you want to do something productive in your life? If your answer is yes, you better not get into the temptation of reverting back to your old self.

In this chapter, I will be discussing the importance of positive habits and why bad habits inhibit your abilities to achieve success. First and foremost, what is a habit? A habit is a custom that is ingrained in your mind. All of your decisions and actions solely rely on those habits, like a primary nature. It governs how you act, talk, walk and even interact with people around you. Imagine having bad habits and how it puts you in a disadvantage.

If you have poor emotional and mental habits, you are inclined to be bossier, more insensitive, and greedy in your decisions. You have the predisposition to act on your impulses without thinking about the consequences of your actions. You choose poorly. You get upset over trifles. Imagine having an attitude like that. Do you really think you can achieve success with that kind of thinking?

For instance, you have bad behavioral habits such as being late, absent, and lazy. Top it up by being an alcoholic or a chain smoker. Where do you see yourself in five years?

As a person who's trying to change, there is always a way to break that cycle and create a new one. I believe that nobody's a lost cause. All you need to do is find a little bit of self-discipline in yourself, and all will work from there.

Habits are ingrained in our mind to satisfy short-term goals. If you have bad habits, then your actions will be against your own self-interest. They will cause you to fail over and over again, bringing you back to the depths of your own despair. However, if you have good habits, then your actions and decisions will be in accordance with your long-term goals. They will help you become whom you aspire to be and guide you where you need to be as years pass by.

Stages of A Habit

As we all know, understanding our weaknesses allows us to turn them into strengths. In this segment, we will be discussing the stages of a habit to find out exactly how to put up an intervention for our mind.

Cue
The cue signals the mind about the presence of a resource to do a habit. In weight loss, for example, the cu and e in this scenario are the chips and other unhealthy foods in the refrigerator. They entice the mind easily, given that they are just a few steps away, ready to be eaten.

Craving
The cue brings craving or the raging need to do the behavior. No matter how a part of the mind tries to dissuade the body from doing it, craving takes over and convinces the body to do otherwise.

Routine
When the mind and body have already been convinced that it is okay to give in to the temptation, a person is inclined to do the behavior. The routine stage is also known as compulsive behavior. This is the stage for a person acts on his impulses without thinking.

Reward
This is the ultimate reason a habit is performed over and over again. When the craving has been satiated, the body feels relief, and the mind feels happiness and satisfaction. When the behavior is rewarded, there's a bigger chance the person will do it again.

Break the Routine

Thought-Stopping
Whenever intrusive thoughts take control of the mind, practice thought-stopping. The causes of this concept help a person develop well-rounded self-discipline towards Self-Transformation. Thought-stopping means to literally stop

thinking negative thoughts and redirecting them into something else. This is a cognitive intervention, usually prescribed by psychologists and psychiatrists to interrupt the intrusive thoughts of the depressed and anxious. This works extremely well too in eliminating an obsession, urge, and bad, unwanted habits.

Psychologists believe that in order to perform thought-stopping, you need to consider three simple steps:

- Focus on the present. What are your goals? Where do you see yourself in a year or two? What would it mean for you that your intrusive thoughts hinder you from pursuing your dreams?

- Give yourself a pep talk. Dissuade yourself whenever wanting to do that habit again. What are the disadvantages? How does it affect you personally? How does it affect your goals? Do you really want to be that person again? As much as possible, keep your mind off of the temptation.

- Keep a journal. Whenever something bothers your mind, make sure you keep a journal with you and start writing about it. Writing your thoughts and emotions down can help you think rationally despite the intrusive thoughts. It allows you to decide clearly on what is needed to overcome each temptation that comes into your mind.

- To furnish your ability in thought-stopping, you need to learn how to relax your mind through breathing and reciting a mantra. Clear your head. Recite a chosen mantra ten times while breathing deeply. Do this whenever you feel tempted to resort back to old habits, as it can help you keep your mind off of things, especially the temptations life can bring.

Visualization.

A lot of people remain skeptic about the value of visualization, but what people don't know is that you can turn these images into a reality. The mental picture that flows in your mind becomes imbued with your heart. Thinking about it comforts you. Your goals make you feel like home. So, whenever you feel tempted in any way, once you visualize your goals, it would feel like every trial would just fade away. The feeling of your thoughts running through your veins will be like a 'refresh' that clears your head of the things you need to do and what you need to become. When you visualize your future, you will feel a sudden relief. It will make you realize there is something to look up to. There is a reward for every effort, and all of your hardships mean something to your life.

The visualization of your dreams and aspirations increases your performance at its peak. It makes you believe in yourself, gain confidence and determination to pursue another day without fear. It makes you more innovative and creative, unafraid to generate new ideas towards success. The visualization of your future brings motivation to do -and the self-discipline to avoid- behaviors. Other people think visualization is an old wives' tale told to children to push them to their limits. What they don't is that if you really perform this concept, it can bring wonders to your life you can't even fathom.

Think of A Reason

To break the cycle of your bad habits, you need to think of a reason why you should stop. Whether it is about your health, your physical appearance, your career, even your loved ones, create a reason to dissuade you from ever performing a bad habit again. For example, if your goal is to lose weight, ask yourself, why do you need to lose weight in the first place? List all of the reasons why you want to achieve a beach body: Whom do you want to impress? What do you want to accomplish? What do you want to see in the mirror?

Remind yourself that you are tired of all the bullying and teasing. Remind yourself of the inconvenience of having all that extra weight. How you were not able to climb the peak of the mountain because of your lack of stamina and shortness of breath. How your clothes will not fit you anymore and you need to buy lots of new ones to fill an empty cabinet. Think all of these reasons as a form of improvement and motivation. Let these hardships be a persuasion for you to work harder and never resort to your old ways. Do not take this as a demotivation for not being good enough. Rather, take it as a challenge and convince yourself that you can do it. Other people could. Some reported to having lost 98 pounds in 21 days. Others said they lost more. Now that you have this book, you are more empowered to work hard, especially now that you know the secrets towards unstoppable self-discipline.

Find A Replacement, Workout, Or Sports

As discussed earlier, the main reason why a habit is repeated over and over again is the reward. The most common way to avoid the temptation towards a relapse is to find a replacement with the same effect or parallel to the effect of the bad habit. For example, if your habit is smoking or binge-drinking alcohol, you might want to consider trying new hobbies such as working out or doing sports. These two can also help elicit the satisfaction you get from smoking cigars and drinking alcohol. Workout, along with sports, helps the body release sufficient amounts of endorphins –feel-good hormones- to feel happy and energetic throughout the day.

Unstoppable Day

In your weight loss challenge, if your problem is your craving for oily foods and chips, you can try replacing these with fruits and vegetables. If you're not accustomed to this behavior, it might seem very odd and discomforting at first, but trust me, once your body has endured enough to resist the temptation towards junk foods, it means you have released yourself from the chains of your bad habits.

Another key to making this concept work is restricting all access to bad habits. Remember, out of sight, out of mind. If there is nothing accessible to cue temptation, then the mind is not inclined to crave for that habit ever again.

Share your Goal

Did you know that sharing your goals and principles with your family members and friends can help you stick to your goals? Having people around to support you actually feels good, especially when you are trying to accomplish difficult goals. They will be there to uplift your spirit in your times of hardships. Share your goals with them and they can help you ward off any temptation that comes into your way. Your family and friends will make sure you get the transformation you need by pushing you forward and motivating you to stick to your vision. The best part of sharing your goal is the learning you gain from interacting with your loved ones. Your parents will always have suggestions to help you maintain a good sense of self-discipline towards success. Your friends probably have other experiences regarding your problems. They, too, can help you maintain a stable mindset.

Challenge Yourself

The extinction of your bad habits may consist of the balance between reward and punishment. Have you ever heard of classical conditioning, developed by

Ivan Pavlov? If not, well this is a chance to furnish your self-discipline using a bit of psychological practice. See, Ivan Pavlov discovered that a behavior paired with reward is more likely to be repeated. However, if a behavior is paired with punishment, then the habit is more likely to diminish.

Much like the development of self-discipline, you need to learn when to reward and punish yourself. Challenge yourself for one week to abstain from your old habits. Create a timeline for each day and track your improvements. For every day that you do not do the bad behavior, you reward yourself with something you like (but not a bad habit, obviously). However, if you find yourself violating your promise and feeling on your goals for the day, create your own punishment and stick to it. If you like, you can have some family members and friends help you track your improvements and initiate your reward and punishment system. For example, every time that you commit a bad habit, you will be forced to put $10 or $20.00 in a jar. Or, you will be forced to give up TV privileges. Maybe even dinner.

I remember a few years ago, I had a friend who used to swear all the time. When he wanted to change, I had the idea of making a swear jar. So, whenever he spoke a bad word, he would be forced to put $10.00 into the jar, and he would never get it back. We would spend the money without him and send him pictures of how we used his swear jar money. This pushed him to stop talking whenever he had the urge to swear or say a bad word about someone. Now, he is a motivational speaker to teenagers about suicide and depression. Amazing how self-disciplined works for committed individuals!

Chapter 7:
Getting Work Done Even if You're Lazy

Do you ever have those days when you wake up the morning and want to do nothing except lie down and watch television all day? Do you ever get that feeling of being lost? These days where you have billions of thoughts in your mind but no energy to do anything. It is the feeling of emptiness and discouragement that inhibits your ability to think and be productive for the day. You feel completely numb, not even thinking about the consequences of unproductivity. It is like you could not care less about your future anymore.

Procrastination makes easy things hard, hard things harder.

Mason Cooley

Laziness is characterized by idleness and stagnation. It is the most dangerous habit to develop, especially for someone who aspires to succeed. If you're starting to feel like you need to procrastinate, you better rethink your choices and never give into it. As we have discussed earlier, the reason for obtaining a habit is the reward you get from the behavior. When you procrastinate, you get rewarded for the happiness and joy you feel from watching the TV all day long, or through surfing the Internet. You are inclined to resort to a diet that is detrimental to your health. What's worse, when you procrastinate, there's a tendency that your mind becomes hyperactive in a negative way. It reminds you every mistake you have ever made, of who you were before. It guilts you into becoming a fully-transformed individual.

A lot of people think that laziness is just that – unproductiveness. That there is a reason behind a person's resort to procrastination. In light of this, here are five reasons why a person gives in to the temptation of procrastination.

Demotivation

When a person loses an inspiration to reach for the stars, he becomes idle and unproductive. He thinks, "Why would I be doing this if I can have fun instead?" This usually happens when great adversity strips a dreamer from his soul, like the death of a loved one, a broken heart, or a failed plan. Demotivation occurs when a person forgets who he is and whom he wants to be. Knowing the hardships in life, it will provide various challenges that could test the mindset of an individual. These trials can come in the form of untimely advice to test one's beliefs. It can come from calamities or so-called "signs." Sometimes, people ostracize and disregard something they don't understand, instead of trying to keep up with it. They treat it like garbage. On the road to Self-Transformation, lots of people will tell you how they loved you for who you were before you decided to change. There are people who can dissuade you by providing enticing points such as missing the gimmicks and other happy memories. Some will tell you that you are still pretty young to be doing all those things and that you should be enjoying your life while it lasts, not go rushing yourself to be mature.

But ask yourself whom you want to be in the future, not whom they want you to be right now. Ask yourself: do you want to invest your time doing nothing? Or do you want to be productive, to have long-lasting happiness in the near future? See, there is advice that you should listen to, especially if it is about lifting yourself, changing for the better, and solving your problems. However, there is also advice you should never listen to, especially when it holds you back. The decision is entirely up to you. Only you can live your life, nobody else.

Weariness

When a person starts to lose energy, persistence goes away too. Weariness can influence a person to become unproductive and lazy. It argues with the mind about how the body needs rest, even when it doesn't. It reminds the heart about the difficult trials it has overcome and says it needs some rest to recover, even when you have had enough time to lay low. Don't get me wrong, resting the mind and body is a vital process that allows rejuvenation and alleviation of stress, but sometimes, when the mind becomes greedy of its rewards, it pushes the body to procrastinate.

Emotionality

Some people are highly sensitive to their emotions. They easily get triggered through words, objects, smells, or people. Being emotional can hinder you from reaching your peak. It clouds your mind in the midst of adversity. The mind is a very powerful tool; it can control the heart and the body. It is true that sadness and anxiety have physiological effects. They make a person physically weak, unproductive, and idle. The moment you let your mind think you are sad or anxious about something, you will be unable to perform your duties and your routines well. Nothing will interest you, and your daily routine will cease. You will not be able to work out, eat, sleep, and focus. All of which can have a huge negative impact on your goals.

Fear of Failure

When a person is afraid of trying, he resorts to procrastination. When he overthinks the future in a negative way, he will be demotivated to try harder. The fear of failure, much like the temptation of the future, is one of the hardest challenges to overcome, especially to people who have a flying imagination and an anxious mind. If you keep thinking about the future in a negative manner, it will be like putting your life in a pit you built yourself. It will start to devour your aspirations and dreams, along with your short-term goals. The fear of failure is a very dangerous tread. It makes you imagine things that aren't there, think of situations that can never happen, doubt the totality of your capabilities and it slowly depletes your confidence as a creative human being.

Inattentiveness to Goals

Losing sight of your goal can put you in the pit of procrastination. As the tunnel gets darker, it becomes harder for you to keep track of your dreams. Everything becomes a blur and you suddenly forget the reasons for striving hard. Being inattentive to your goal means that you neglect to remind yourself of whom you want to be. It degrades your persistence and determination to fight for what you believe in. A lost vision is more dangerous than any other temptation. You lose your purpose; you forget your viewpoint and you resort back to old ways.

Stay Away from The Black Hole

Procrastination is like a big black hole. It sucks all life and light it gets in contact with. If you are slowly feeling the emptiness and you want to just sulk in the couch to "enjoy" or "rest," you have come this far to even think about giving in. Once you let yourself get buried in that black hole, it becomes difficult to rise back up.

Unstoppable Day

Procrastination is the art of keeping up with yesterday.

Don Marquis

Indeed, when you let yourself get sucked by its gravity, it will be like resorting to whom you were before rather than putting an effort to build your future self. As an emergency protocol, you need to remember these 10 simple steps to get you out of that couch and avoid the streaming gravity towards laziness.

Think of The Benefits
Before you sit in that couch and turn on the television, stop to think about why you need to accomplish your objectives for the day. Is there a potential income? Do they help you lose weight? Will they make you a better person? If so, you have plenty of reasons to avoid procrastination. Thinking of the benefits can make you focus on your goals and be reminded of your long-term desires.

Think of The Consequences
As you think of the benefits, think about the consequences if you aren't able to meet the deadlines. What do you think will happen if you do not finish your requirements on time? Think about the demerits, the challenges, the penalties. This will not only push you to move, but it also pushes you to work harder.

Visualize
Set your mind on your vision. Look for the piece of paper where you have written and drawn your dreams and aspirations for the future. Remind yourself why you started walking this road in the first place. Remember your dreams. What do you want to do for yourself? Your family? Your career? Your relationship?

Learn to Rest

Taking a break is a very important source of energy and motivation. As we have discussed earlier, laziness is caused by restlessness. On the road to success and Self-Transformation, you need to find a balance between procrastination and respite. If possible, create a schedule for your break time. That way, you can avoid getting in the brink of laziness and be on your way to productiveness.

Do Things One at A Time

In a day, there are various activities to accomplish. Thinking about these objectives can cramp out the brain, which is why you need to create a schedule of your daily tasks so you can do them one by one. Remember to rest for a reasonable number of minutes in between tasks to avoid mental and physical fatigue.

Break Down Tasks

To break down tasks, you need to organize and group your tasks into categories. Manage your tasks done at home, school, and work separately. From these variations, further group the objectives from easiest to the most difficult to accomplish and start from there. Whenever you go to school, take the checklist with you and try to accomplish what you can. Do the same when you get to work and when you go home.

Commit to A Schedule

Once you have created the schedule, you need to push yourself to follow what you have planned. On the road to self-discipline, you need to learn to commit even to the most basic plans. In the beginning, committing and persisting to accomplish your goals is difficult, but once your body is accustomed to it, you will be doing your tasks without even thinking about your schedule. Think about this as 'training' for your future endeavors in school, work, and family. If your attitude remains stagnant, you will never learn to adjust and cope with more difficult adversities. As small and simple as your plans may be, committing to them is a stepping stone towards a more productive and successful life.

Eat Healthily

Eating nutritious food can balance your hormones and chemical structure. It provides 'feel-good' and 'satisfaction' hormones that can help you become more motivated and hard-working, whereas eating junk food and oily foods make the brain sluggish and the body weary. When you eat fruits and vegetables instead of chips and fries, your productivity can increase dramatically and your decision-making and problem-solving abilities are enhanced greatly.

Sleep Well

Getting enough sleep is a way to rejuvenate your body after a long day's work. It helps the mind recharge and reorganizes its contents, leaving it fully refreshed and ready to face the troubles of a new day. Sleep is the stage where the body revitalizes holistically; it resets the effects of stress and hormonal imbalance, reestablishing homeostasis in our physical, mental, and emotional well-being.

Work Out Regularly

Working out regularly can increase the production of endorphins. It decreases the onset of sadness and anxiety, which is why it diminishes a person's chances of feeling emotional. The feel-good hormone prevents overthinking, avoiding stress and mental fatigue. It helps save more energy to be used on more important aspects of life such as working or studying. Instead of moping in bed or on the couch, it is vital to start moving and do some stretching to avoid getting stuck in the gravity of procrastination.

I am sure you can think of other ways to overcome procrastination. However, if you do not stick to your commitment to yourself, every effort you ever elicit towards your goals will be in vain. Instead of looking back down from where you left off, focus on the journey ahead. You have come so far only to let yourself get pulled back once again. Procrastination is yet another challenge. Think about its temporariness: when you start to forget about it, it will gradually disappear from your sight. Your choices are one hundred percent yours. You can either choose to get stuck in the black hole, or you can choose to walk the path of light.

Chapter 8:
Why You Need a Long-Term Morning Routine

"Morning is an important time of day, because how you spend your morning can often tell you what kind of day you are going to have."

Lemony Snicker

Most people disregard the value of mornings as their way of procrastination. Every time we wake up, we feel very frustrated saying, "Ugh, it's morning again!" We have this urge to press the snooze button and go straight back to sleep, thinking that it is okay to miss breakfast before you go to work or school. Instead of waking up at around five or six in the morning to accomplish more daily tasks, we prefer to wake up at seven saying, "I can do it all before ten."

Admit it; it took you years before you discovered the value of rising early. When you were younger, it was possible to delay work and stay up late and skip school. Because it felt better to sleep everything off. It felt like your worries fade away instantly.

But now that you have reached the point in life where you should actually persevere, those late morning habits are difficult to shake away. Now that you have bigger responsibilities, it's time to ban yourself from the snooze button and get yourself an effective morning routine.

Werner Brendon Marcus

Did you know that the most successful people wake up as early as 3:00 AM just to finish their morning routines, and be ready for work? Morning routine plays a role in the definition of a person's success. Not only does it help an individual be more productive, but the morning routine is also another milestone towards self-discipline. Just by not hitting the snooze button, you can feel a lot of improvement in your mindset and your body clock.

Morning is the most important time of day. It defines how you face the problems and trials of your day. It predicts the outcome of your activities, and it plans the schedule of your body and mind. Early mornings allow you to gather your composure before you start with a new day. They inhibit the chance of rushing towards your activities.

Imagine you wake up late. You have no time to cook and eat breakfast. Therefore, you are inclined to eat unhealthy foods from fast-food chains. You have no time to clean and prep yourself properly, which can decrease your confidence when dealing with people. What's worse, with all the cramming and traffic, you will be haggard by the time you get to work.

Setting the tone of your mind and body is a vital key to a successful day. It puts you in a mood that can lessen your frustration, anxiety, and emotionality. This may come as a shock, but early morning routines can make you stronger, holistically speaking. They alleviate stress levels, maintain bodily homeostasis, and improve your overall habit. The question is, "Where do I start?"

Luckily, I have concocted a list of an amazing early morning schedule that can tune you up, ready for anything. First, set your alarm to wake up early. About 4 or 5 AM would be nice. If you can do it at 3 AM, have a go. Once your alarm sets off, get up as fast as you can and never look back on your watch or your bed.

Unstoppable Day

Snoozing the alarm breaks your momentum off to start the day on the right foot. By giving in to this temptation, it will be like accepting your failure and resorting back to laziness. Have a little self-discipline and work your way up from there. Avoid telling yourself, "five more minutes" because it is the most dangerous phrase of all time. From there, you can do these eight routines every morning for a week or two, and you can even improvise.

- Go to the Mirror and Smile at yourself. You might think this is silly but it promotes positivity to flow into your body and mind. Smiling at yourself without any apparent reason for at least 15 seconds allows you to have some charisma that attracts positivity in your day. After doing this, you can observe the difference when you deal with people. You will start to be happier and more approachable towards those around you.

- This day is different. While you are at it, remind yourself that today is another day and it is going to be legendary. Recap what you want to accomplish for this day. Who do you want to be at the end of the day? What do you want to learn? What kind of people do you want to meet? By setting these early goals, you can visualize and attract opportunities to come your way. Plus, it aids courage and strength to face the challenges of a new beginning.

- Make your Bed. Making your bed is the first physical exercise you should do every morning. Not only does it kick-start your blood flowing, but it also marks the first accomplishment of your day. By making your bed, you are acknowledging productiveness instead of procrastination. An activity as simple as that can signal your mind that you are more than a person who dreams. You are a person who is willing to make those dreams a reality.

- Clean a little. A little vacuuming or dusting in the morning is important. If you can do some laundry, then you have accomplished another goal. Cleaning gets rid of idle time. It detracts your focus from laziness and it pushes the body to keep moving forward.

- Meditate. To some, meditation is a mouthful, and a very difficult activity to accomplish. However, you do not need a yoga mat, or to pose like an Indian to meditate. You can just sit on your chair or sit on the bed while you relax your mind. Concentrate your vision into something beautiful, like your dreams. By meditating, you are relaxing your body and mind by focusing it into a safe and happy place. It enhances your motivation and persistence to go forth the day and accomplish your tasks with flying colors.

- Meditation facilitates mindfulness or awareness of the self and the environment. By meditating, you can assess your feelings and your thoughts. So, whenever something negative pops up, you will be ready to give yourself a pep talk or a motivational speech.

- Write a Gratitude Journal.

I love that this morning's sunrise does not define itself by last night's sunset.

Steve Maraboli

Gratitude fosters positivity in so many ways. It emphasizes your skills and lessens your self-doubt. It makes room for self-support and self-regard, increasing confidence and determination to succeed. By keeping a gratitude journal and writing on it every morning, you are reminded of your accomplishments instead of your failures. It reminds you of what you have rather than what you do not.

Unstoppable Day

It makes you thankful for a new day, a new chance to live. It makes you value your time and not waste any single moment.

When writing on your gratitude journal, bask on the blessings that life has offered you. Thank your parents for their love, your friends for their support, even the vendor who sold you coffee yesterday and gave you extra sugar. Appreciating these little things makes you a renowned and transformed individual.

Work Out

Even if you are not aiming to lose weight, it is still essential to work out and sweat a little. We have discussed that exercise helps the body release endorphins and maintain homeostasis. To obtain that warm and happy feeling before you go to work or school, make time to work out for even just half an hour.

Prepare A Nutritious Meal and Prep Yourself

Once you've accomplished these tasks, it is time to prepare the most important meal of the day – breakfast. To avoid stopping at fast food chains to eat some oily and unhealthy meal, why not prepare breakfast on your own? This way, you can control your calories intake and focus on your meal to avoid overeating. At home, you can eat fruits and vegetables, cereals, even enjoy that cup of tea without rushing and bumping into people. For this, you can listen to music or watch the early morning news to stay updated. In any case, watch out for your time or you might be late.

After eating breakfast, take time to prepare yourself to feel good about your appearance and gain confidence while interacting. Having an early morning routine allows you to choose your outfit carefully, and prepare without any glitch, rush, or panic. Then, you can finally leave home and be more determined than ever. You can start fresh at work, and stay calm as you face different adversities or stressors.

"I get up every morning and it's going to be a great day. You never know when it's going to be over so I refuse to have a bad day."

Paul Henderson

Self-Awareness

Wherever you go, whether it is school or work, always remember to keep a good character and own it. Even if it feels wrong or uncomfortable at times to change your attitude and traits, to build a strong sense of control, you need to take a good grip on your impulses and predispositions. Maintaining a great attitude towards your activities helps you boost your self-esteem because it allows you to foster self-awareness. The better a person knows himself, the more inclined he is to know his area of expertise. Apart from that, a person starts to understand himself more – his compulsion, temperament, and tendencies. Every detail he denies and represses becomes a part of his personality. Instead of disregarding his shadow or dark side, he starts to welcome it and train it towards something good.

I would like to share a short story about my cousin who was a bully in high school. See, he had a strong physique. He had a large body and stature. All my life, I have lived with him and watched as he made smaller boys cry in the classroom, and in the streets. Sometimes, he even makes our younger cousins cry, including me. When I was a kid, I was very thin and weak. He would always boss me around, toss me wherever and whenever he wanted it. Every time we play with him, he wanted to be superior. My cousin Bob would do everything to win. Of course, at the time, we only knew him as a bully, feared by most of our

Unstoppable Day

neighbors and playmates. We did not care to dig deep about the hidden reason. See, me and Bob were at the same age. But to my luck, we never became classmates until senior year. During this age, you would expect people to be more mature. But my cousin never changed a thing. He still bullied people in and out of school, had detention, and got suspended from time to time.

One Saturday afternoon, me and my mom happened to pay them a visit at their home. We were neighbors, so it was convenient to go from one house to the other. I was surprised to see him buried in his books, crying in the living room. But when he saw us enter, he quickly dried his eyes, gave me a sharp look and went to his bedroom. My mother asked why he was sobbing and Bob's mom said that he punished him for not doing good enough in Math.

I felt a pact of pity in my stomach but I did not show it to them. I walked towards his room and asked him to open the door. At first, he was hesitant. He threatened me that he will break my arm if I try to open his door. I said, "Okay, then I will wait for you here." After how many minutes, he came out because he had to pee. That was my shot of initiating a small talk.

It was awkward at first. Bob and I never really clicked. But I would bother me at night if I did not ask him. Only to find out that his mother brutally punishes him whenever he does not get a minimum of a B. We all have to admit that Bob is not much in academics. But he was good in martial arts. As he spoke, I realized that he was not aware of his actions toward other people. Bob opened the number of times he has asked for our classmates to tutor him but everyone declined. He felt like he had nobody and he felt like he is nothing.

It was my chance to tell Bob how he has been for almost 6 years. It turns out, he did not mean to push people around like that. He just wanted to gain some friends by being funny. He did not know he was being mean. Maybe it was his outlet of all the pain his mom had inflicted on him. Maybe it was a reflection of what he feels inside. Since that day, Bob tried to change his attitude and characteristics in school. Whenever he has the urge to bully or be mean to someone, he goes to the gym and play sports. After how many months of practice, we were surprised to see him as a different person. Bob started to enroll in Mixed Martial Arts and competed throughout the state for medals and trophies.

See, no matter how difficult for people to change, it is not hopeless. It always starts with self-awareness. In the morning when you wake up, try to get to know yourself better and better each day. Monitor your mood swings, your behavior towards that mood swings. And whenever you feel like having a fit, divert it into something productive instead.

Every morning when you walk or transport to school or work, close your eyes for a moment and think, "Who am I? What am I capable of?" Start to focus on everything around you – the air, your breathing, the sounds, your thoughts. Start to analyze how you feel about it. Get to know the hidden traits of your persona. Do not be afraid of taking the dark side along with the good. To foster a positive attitude towards life, you're going to need all the self-discipline you need to focus that negative energy into something you can be good at. If you are sad, try to write a poem or a song about it. Draw or paint your feelings out as if you are pouring your heart out through art. If you are an angry and irritable person, join the gym, engage in football, mixed martial arts or other sports. Wherever your heart leads you, as long as you let your mind control your impulses, you will discover your unspeakable strength towards your success.

Chapter 9:
How to Multiply Your Time

You might wonder sometimes, "How the hell do people accomplish so many things in just 8 hours?" In that time, only a few can really make something productive. The rest sulk into procrastination.

The secret towards accomplishment is not how you manage your time. It is how you manage yourself. In the first chapters, we discussed the value of self-management in relation to achieving success. In this segment, we will be discussing more about self-management and how to practice it in the long run.

There is actually no way to control time. Every minute will run whether you like it or not. The reason for unproductiveness is not because of how one schedules his time, it is how one conditions the mind and body.

For example, you have a lot of requirements due the next day. On your daily schedule, you have set 8:00 AM to 12:00 noon to do your assignments. You know that 4 hours is more than enough to get things done, but by the clock stroke twelve, you only finished about half. So, what could be the reasons why you were not able to accomplish your tasks?

This time, it was not because of the temptation of procrastination. You know, deep down, that you sat down in front of the computer for the whole 4 hours. You also know that it was not your emotionality because you kept your focus into doing your job. So, how come you did not finish it, even when you know you could have?

The main reason for this is not giving your mind and body what they need. Our thinking minds have their own mood swings too, believe it or not. They define the rate of progress we do in each activity. When a person is unable to condition his mind to think for that particular activity, he is more likely to be unproductive. It will be like your brain is not in the mood to think. Therefore, it slows down your progress, keeping you from finishing your requirements on time.

Much like our emotions, there are also tricks that we could use to fool the mind into doing tasks, even if it is not in the "mood." Let's face it, our minds could suddenly lie low, especially in situations when we really need to think the most. This is what people usually call 'blank-minded' or unable to think perhaps because of information overload, weariness, or stress. But not to worry, in this chapter, we will discuss how you can manage your mind to drive your body towards productiveness and avoid idle time.

Get Your Mind in The Mood

Know your Priorities. First and foremost, you must know your priorities well. Learn to organize your tasks from the most to the least urgent. Overthinking can cause anxiety and stress to an individual, causing the mind to perform according to one's problems and not one's goals. This keeps us from focusing and thinking clearly.

To aid you in this trick, gather a pen and paper and organize the deadlines of your requirements. What do you need to submit later? Tomorrow? The next day? You need to start tracking. Whether or not it is difficult to accomplish, the real key is not its hardship. Rather, your focus is the one driving your mind to

Unstoppable Day

finish the impossible. As you work through your list, check the ones you have finished and move on to the next. Remember to take a good rest before you begin another task, you would not want to strain your brain into fatigue. If you do, you will not be able to perform well.

Learn to Say No. There are times when we are asked to do something or go somewhere with someone. Often, we feel guilty to say no. For this, we need to rethink our priorities and start saying "no" comfortably. Also, when you decline offers and gimmicks, you must request a raincheck politely and make them understand why.

There are also instances in which we are offered a lot of opportunities. Although these are not bad at all, we need to learn how to evaluate our tasks. Yes, it can be flattering to be asked on a job interview or to speak in a seminar, but on your busy schedule, think of what you can accomplish if you say yes to every opportunity that comes knocking on your door. Even if you say you can do it, imagine how it can impact your physical and psychological health.

Stay off the internet and the TV. Unless you are using them for research, you better keep your gadgets turned off for your own good. Have you ever experienced spending hours on Facebook, even if you said it wouldn't be longer than 15 minutes? Social media does that to you. It makes you lose track of time. It entices you to stay for another minute until it becomes 60 more. To prevent any more distractions, turn off your phone, and put it someplace you cannot see it.

Turn your Messenger off. Actually, turn all your messaging apps off. When a friend or a loved one calls, it is very difficult to put down the phone, especially when you are talking about something funny or serious. Deactivate your messenger for a while until you finish what you need for your requirements. The calls and texts you receive can impede your momentum of thoughts in working or doing assignments. It makes you forget the next concepts to write about and the next activities to finish off. So, if you want to stay productive and maximize your time, have your

"me" time away from any temptations. Also, these tricks will allow the mind to focus on more important goals rather than surfing the web or watching a movie. Those memes will be there after you finish. You can re-watch the movies on Netflix anytime you want. You need to solve your problems first.

Post your schedule on a wall. When you are at home, there are a lot of enticements to overcome. Looking at the couch and the bed is one of the worst distractions. So, if you are tempted to sit and turn on the TV, put a schedule near the couch or near the TV. That way, you can guilt yourself into becoming more productive. Reminding yourself over and over about the goals will motivate you to finish all your tasks. At the same time, when you see the checkmarks on your goal, you will soon take pride in your actions. And you will thank yourself for that schedule on the wall.

Put some motivational quotes on a wall. If this sounds corny for you, why not write some messages on the walls. Whenever you want to eat junk food, put a message on the refrigerator that says, "You are going remain a big fat loser if you keep defeating yourself with that habit." Or when you want to watch TV instead, you can put a sticky note that says "Nothing good ever happens when you watch TV. Anyway, there are no good shows to see yet." These messages, although small, can help you lift your hopes up into focusing on what you need to do.

Unstoppable Day

The Death Bed Dilemma. Whenever you doubt whether or not to do those tasks, imagine yourself on your death bed. "Will I regret not doing this for the rest of my life? What if this is the breakthrough that I have been waiting for?" This question works almost every time, especially on important tasks or duties. People think about not doing tons of things and they feel guilty because of the question "What if?" It is better to accomplish things and seize opportunities as they come. If you don't, you will be left asking yourself the most difficult question in the whole world. If you do not at least try, your life will start to be full of regrets. You will never know if that opportunity would have given you the success you deserved.

Wake up earlier. When you need to accomplish more goals, avoid staying up late. It makes the brain wobbly in the morning. Instead, try sleeping early when you are tired and wake up earlier the next day. This will kick-start your energy while you focus on your goals. Plus, it helps you think clearly about your requirements.

Chapter 10:
The Science Behind Why You Procrastinate

In previous chapters, we briefly discussed the main reasons behind a person's procrastination. Who knew that procrastination has an even deeper science of procrastination? In this chapter, I will be discussing the most notorious roots of procrastination that influences people all around the world.

If you feel like everything is hopeless because of your inability to focus on your goals, look around, everybody experiences it as much as you do. The unlucky few have it even harder. See, procrastination has something to do with one's life logic. It is caused by the imbalance of thoughts in your mind that inhibits your ability to feel good about doing things, and actually doing it. It is the manner of convincing yourself where and when you are going to do it without using the word "Later" or "Tomorrow."

These words, among many other phrases such as, "I am not in the mood," are very harmful to achieving your short-term and long-term goals. In life, there are literally millions of heartbreaking and mood-altering reasons not to put effort at all. Today, you are not in a good mood because you are tired of your past activities. Who is to say you will be in a good mood tomorrow morning? What if there is adversity that makes you feel demotivated once again?

Unstoppable Day

These factors must not be tolerated to ensure your productivity as a person. As you work through this list of reasons why people procrastinate, you will see that the power of your mind is the most important tool to get out of this black hole.

Tiredness

Whenever a person feels restless in doing his everyday routine, he tends to lose focus on his long-term goals. Therefore, he procrastinates even more. But this is not the only reason why a person gets stuck in the black hole. Whenever an individual feels tired of everything he is experiencing at the moment, he tends to be demotivated to push through with his goals. There are many factors that contribute to one's tiredness: pain, anguish, and suffering from other aspects of life such as relationships, friendships, or family. Sometimes a person gets tired of putting up with every problem he has, which is why he starts to lose sight of his dreams or long-term goals.

There is no harm in resting from time to time because it adds energy to one's willpower. However, too much rest can cause idleness and stagnation bordering on unproductiveness. There's also no harm in detracting from time to time to solve problems unrelated to one's long-term goals. To focus better on the road towards success, it is essential to break down the building blocks that cause loss of progress.

Anxiety

Anxiety and apprehension regarding the future. People with anxiety usually think negatively about the future. They overthink things that may or may not happen at all. Anxiety leads to procrastination solely because people are terrified of pushing forward towards the road to success. They come up with many reasons not to move forward because of the negativities circling through their minds. They are provided with multiple reasons why chasing their dreams is a bad idea and there is nothing positive about it.

Anxious people are afraid of going out of their comfort zones because of their fear of failure and committing mistakes, although it doesn't stop there. The minds of the anxious are very wide and wild, so to speak. It starts from their fear of failure and branches out to other negativities. Sooner or later, they will claim their pursuit of success will not only affect their emotional growth but also their families and friends. Even when there is no harm at all, an anxious person will always find a loophole to think that something negative is about to happen.

If you're having this problem and you think this is impeding your ability to get in control, there is no shame in seeking help. When you cannot control your anxiety anymore, visit your nearest psychologist and ask for help. He or she can help you reframe your thoughts into something productive and positive. The psychologist can give you various techniques to use whenever you feel like thinking about something negative.

Depression

Depression is also linked to procrastination. Did you know that depression does not only have a psychological effect but also physiological effects as well? When a person is experiencing depression, it can cause demotivation, sadness, and worthlessness. The worst part is that the mind can signal the body it is in pain even though it is not. This phenomenon, also called 'phantom pain', is very common among depressed patients. When the psychological aspect of a person is in pain, it vibrates towards a person's physiological health, resulting in bodily symptoms such as heartache, stomach ache, loose bowel movement, muscle pain, and fatigue. This causes procrastination and laziness because you will believe that you need more time to rest even if you're not tired at all.

Depression is a very lethal illness that kills millions of people every year. If you're feeling the need to procrastinate all the time, you might as well check your mental status. There is no shame in getting help from a psychologist. He can help you get rid of your depression and get on your way to a productive and successful life.

Emotionality

What is the difference between emotionality and depression? Emotionality is simply one's sensitivity to everything one sees, hears, or smells. When a person is emotional, he is easily triggered by the things around him. He gets emotional over things he should not be sad about. Although there's nothing wrong to empathize and sympathize with other people, without balance, it can cause depression and procrastination. Emotionality is a difficult road to tackle. Most people who are highly sensitive will not admit something is wrong. But when you come to think of the consequences, you're putting yourself in grave danger by overthinking and feeling highly sensitive about all the things happening around you.

We have discussed the power of thought-stopping in the previous chapters. It is inherent that you practice this mind trick to avoid hypersensitivity in various situations. It is also important to start rethinking the reasons for your frustration. Learn to give yourself a pep talk whenever you feel sad about something shallow, distract yourself if possible and use it in a productive way. It will make you feel proud of yourself for accomplishing something and the midst of feeling sad or frustrated.

Low Self-Esteem

The lack of self-confidence is one of the most dangerous causes of procrastination. It makes a person doubt his skills, deeming him worthless to even pursue his dream. When a person lacks a positive self-concept, he is inclined to worry more about what is going to happen in the future. He thinks that he cannot do anything right. Therefore, he prefers to sulk in his couch and do nothing because he cannot accomplish anything anyway.

Self-confidence is a person's belief that he can do anything - that he can face the adversities and trials that life throws his way. Without it, he will think of himself as a lost cause that will curb the moment hardships take control of his life. People without a good sense of self-esteem feels the need to be assisted every step of the way. They feel like they cannot accomplish anything on their own. Without support and care from other people, they feel like they cannot go through with anything. This is common among social loafers. If you have been in a team with mates who do not plan to contribute, the lack of confidence is the real issue, not procrastination. They believe that you are good enough to finish the requirements on your own and their efforts are not needed. They lack a positive self-concept because they believe they cannot do anything right. Instead of being mad at these people for being lazy, uplift their spirits by giving them an activity they will enjoy. Much like how you acknowledge yourself. Think of an activity that you know so much about and start from there. Do not lose hope just because you are afraid to try. When you get started on a job or a task, it is unlikely to stop, especially when you keep motivating yourself to move forward.

Guilt

You might be wondering how guilt can lead to procrastination. Well, there are instances when people feel like they do not deserve such success and self-transformation. There are times when people start to become skeptical when they find out that you have been on the road to self-transformation. A person starts to feel guilty when all of his friends and loved ones keep on saying they liked him better before. The lack of people's support and acceptance can cause guilt. Aside from that, when a person feels like he is missing out on the good things in life, he feels like he is not 'living more'. He'd feel guilty about abandoning his friends and not living life to the fullest.

Perfectionism

Having a high sense of perfectionism is very detrimental to one's productivity. This concept is directly linked to anxiety and depression. Everything has to be in place, on time, and everything must be done perfectly. Whenever things do not go as planned, a perfectionist has two options - to double his efforts or to become demotivated.

When he chooses to double his efforts, he has the tendency to overwork his body and mind, causing mental and physical fatigue. When he chooses to be demotivated, he will be less productive on his goals. Either way, both resort to procrastination, which is why it is important to learn the balance between being too perfect and doing things out of compliance sake.

Try not to expect too much out of yourself and from other people. Remember, you are still trying your best to learn from your mistakes. Do not be afraid to commit one more. Mistakes are vital experiences you can use in your journey to your success.

Do everything the best you can but learn to forgive yourself whenever things do not go your way. There are uncontrolled factors that keep a person from achieving his goals. You need to accept these factors and learn to move on. Everything does not have to go as planned. As long as you are on the right track to success, you should not be worried.

If you keep letting yourself obsess on the verge of perfectionism, you will end up with worse problems within yourself. So, as early as now, learn to have that "I am enough" attitude to prevent any more depression, anxiety, and overthinking.

Expectancy and Value of Reward

The likelihood of getting a reward and the value of the prize either motivates or demotivates an individual to work hard. When a person feels like there is little to no possibility to be rewarded for his hard work, he is more likely to procrastinate and look for another line of work or success. If an individual feel like he has no use for the reward, then he is likely to throw away his tasks for good. But if a person feels like the reward is worth it and there is a high probability for him to receive such reward, he will pursue the tasks with burning effort until he reaches his goal.

I cannot blame you for procrastinating given the low expectancy of reward. But the value of doing things with or without reward is timeless. It is all about the wisdom, skill, and knowledge you learn from your experiences. The most common mistake is assessing the rewards way too much. We need to take every opportunity, be it a small reward or not, to learn from our experiences. If we aim to think about the process rather than the reward, we will be more productive and keener on solving various life problems that challenge our vision.

Delay of Reward

The length of time needed to pursue one's goals is also a factor towards procrastination. This is the most common reason for laziness, especially among students - the due date. When a person feels like the reward is still a long way off, he is more likely to concoct reasons not to do it yet. Phrases like, "I will do it next week or tomorrow" are often said because they believe they still have time to procrastinate. This is a very dangerous path to take. When the brain starts to get accustomed to the thought of doing things later, it is very difficult to condition the mind otherwise. The delay of the reward or due date is one of the reasons why students and workers cram their requirements. They did not expect time to fly by so fast. When they reach the final weeks of rushing their tasks, they start to feel tired and restless. Hence, leading to lazier hours. Without knowing it, they are doing their tasks only for compliance sake.

As responsible people, we need to stop thinking about the due date and start accomplishing more given the time. Think of rewarding yourself after you have accomplished your tasks. In that way, you can relax, and take your time in doing your work without hassle or rush.

Chapter 11:
Defeat Procrastinating with Your Mind

In the previous chapter, we discussed that the mind is a powerful tool which defines a person's behavior towards his goals. We have tackled that balance is a vital factor in the accomplishment of tasks and the pursuit of success. In this segment, we will be discussing how you can avoid procrastinating before and during the actual completion of a task or activity.

We can observe most of the time that the greatest pull of laziness starts at the beginning of a goal or a task. It is when the body starts to dissuade the mind, reminding it of the hardships and challenges of pursuing the goal. This is the moment of the truth, whether or not you let yourself stay beneath the gravity of procrastination or try your best to pursue success.

The moment before you start your goals is the most deceptive moment of all time. It is when your anxiety, fear, doubts, and depression kick in to meddle on your concentration. To fight this off, you need these eight simple steps to make sure you get out from the black hole and finally start focusing on your goals.

Forgive Yourself for Past Procrastination
One of the most common reasons why a person becomes demotivated is the feeling of not being competent enough. Some would claim they would eventually procrastinate anyway, so there is no use to be as effortful. To move past that

Unstoppable Day

thinking, you need to learn how to forgive yourself and forget the times you were weak enough to get sucked in by the dark hole.

Remember, in your morning routine, we discussed the need to think that today is a new day. The past is the past and there is so much to accomplish if you believe in yourself. Whenever you are faced with the challenge of staying lazy on the moment of beginning your task, remind yourself that every day you are trying to become a better person. Beating procrastination is the first step towards your success. Have a little faith in yourself that this time you will not bulge in the midst of laziness. Rather, today you will be more effortful, willing to learn in everything you do.

Redefine What Success Means

It is important to keep reminding yourself of what success looks like. Remember the piece of paper I asked you to write your dreams on in detail? It is time to look at it once again and redefine what it means to succeed. Remind yourself of your reasons why you should be doing these tasks instead of procrastinating. Once you do, you will be more motivated to start pursuing your goals.

Remove Short-Term Distractions

We all have a price that triggers our tempest. For some, it is the television. For others, it is their phones and gadgets. To keep focusing on your tasks for the day, you need to keep out of your temptations. I know you know yourself well enough to determine what entices you to stay lazy. For this goal, I want you to stay away from it. If it is possible to work away from home where there are no distractions, do so. If you want to lose weight, go to the gym where you will be more motivated to push yourself and train.

Learn to Break Your Project into Tasks

Earlier, we have discussed the importance of breaking your goals into smaller tasks and work on that list as you finish. When starting on a new goal, do not think of it as a whole. Learn to break it down into smaller objectives so you will not overwhelm your mind. Simplifying your tasks into smaller ones will trick the mind into thinking the goal is easy to accomplish. It makes you forget to think about the hardships you encounter during the process. And as you work on your list and see the check marks, you will be more motivated to finish it all and feel proud at the end of it.

Redefine Your Tasks as Input-Based

The most common mistake is thinking about what you can accomplish. As a mind trick to get you motivated, think of the experiences and learnings you can acquire from the process. Ask yourself, what should I learn from this goal and how can I apply it in the future? By thinking about this, you will be inclined to perform at your peak, disregarding any hint of hardship because you know this will make you a stronger and wiser individual in pursuit of his dreams.

Set Up the Task.

When starting on an activity, make it a habit to set up your task before you do it. This is the stage where you organize your workstation and prepare everything you need before you get started. In doing so, you can maximize your time and avoid any mishaps of looking for misplaced objects or tools. By setting up the task, your mind is slowly conditioned into performing. Therefore, it is less likely to get stuck in the midst of delay or idleness.

Use Motivational Tools

On your workstation, you can use several apps or DIY's to keep you going. For example, you can maximize the use of your gadgets by downloading apps in the store to help you stay motivated on your goals. Be it a scheduling app or a motivational quotes app, these simple ways can aid you to keep pushing forward despite any difficulties. If not, you can search for a mantra on the internet and write it on a piece of paper. Post it on your desk or your laptop and read it over and over again, especially when you feel the need to procrastinate.

Give Yourself a Break

Lastly, it is important to take short breaks from time to time. This is vital in keeping a strong mind and body to reach your goals. However, remember to set up an alarm to avoid idleness and stagnation. Do not let your mind cool down on the activity. When it does, it kicks in an illusion that the whole body is tired and it needs some rest, which is why you need to keep your mind hot and motivated to make sure it does not get stuck in the black hole. If it is possible to set up an alarm, do so. Give yourself 15 minutes of rest every after an objective. Be sure to never exceed that unless you need more time to eat and prepare more tasks. Keep your brain active whenever you can to avoid putting it into the brink of procrastination.

Chapter 12:
The Growth Mindset Think Long-Term

The details of your success written on the piece of paper symbolize your ability to think long-term. In this chapter, I will discuss why it is more important to think of your long-term goals rather than your short-term ventures. On a more important note, I will be discussing how thinking positively about your long-term goals can help you achieve more and develop more within yourself. With this, I am not saying you should only focus on your long-term goals, but rather explaining how thinking long-term will grant more obvious and worthwhile progress to your success.

Thinking about your short-term goals only defines your accomplishment in a matter of hours, days, or months. Although it is essential to acknowledge your progress in this department for motivation, sometimes, it can bring detrimental effects to your cause. There are instances where focusing on your short-term goals too much can make you overconfident on your abilities. You think that you have learned so much that you no longer need to push yourself further. You decrease your efforts because of the anticipation that the reward is already in the bag. When you uplift yourself too much because of your short-term ventures, there is a huge probability you will limit your willingness to learn and gain experience. Sometimes, a person can get too boastful towards his accomplishments that he no longer feels the need to grow and develop towards real success.

Unstoppable Day

Another disadvantage of thinking too much on your short-term goals is your impulsiveness and impatience to gather the long-term reward. When you think too much about what you have produced for yourself, you start to lose sight of the things you need to learn. All that will matter to you are your accomplishments, degrading your ability to push yourself to the limits. You start to rush your accomplishments and lose sight of what lies beneath that so-called reward. Your outputs become less competent and your thinking becomes stagnant and childish.

On the road to success, you must always remember there are a series of short-term goals to accomplish. You must think of these as a form of training or learning to prepare yourself for more difficult challenges. Look at each of your short-term goals as mere milestones on the road to your real success. As much as possible, stop yourself from being blinded by temporary glory for this can inhibit you from ever growing from your nest. You will start to think that you have reached your success even when you barely made it through half. It makes you greedy and lazy in your future endeavors towards success.

Earlier, we talked about the temporariness of problems. Much like short-term success, they are likely to fade the minute another issue comes in play. Real happiness comes when you have crossed the line. Our long-term goals teach us to stay committed and persistent despite the hardships and trials that life can bring. Because once we have reached the end of the line, we can see how worthwhile our efforts are. We can see how far we have come and we start to appreciate the learnings we acquired no matter how difficult they were to obtain. When we reach our true success, no adversity can destroy our happiness because we have gained the skill and wisdom to get through anything in life.

"Failures, setbacks, bad luck, disasters; they are there to serve you, not hold you back. They toughen you up and drive you to improve. Frustration fuels growth. It gives you the energy and resolve to clean yourself up, get organized, fix what you can, and take the next step."

Larry Weidel

How to Think Long-Term

Develop A Realistic Self-Concept

To learn how to think long-term, you need to start knowing yourself from the inside out. Having a clear picture of who you are allows you to think about where you need to grow and what you need to develop. If you have a journal, it is crucial to note down the things you want to change about yourself and why it is key to your success. Think about whom you want to be and why you want things to be like that. Acknowledge yourself as a learning individual who is willing to commit to anything that contributes to his development as a person. Once you have determined what you want to change within yourself, it is time to focus on these betterments while breaking down your short-term goals. Learn to link these hardships into something worthwhile like your growth and your dreams.

For example, you are starting to get tired of the things you do to lose weight. Sometimes, you feel like you cannot go any day more. Think about the temporariness of that dreadfulness. Think what you can become if you overcome your thinking. You will become a more disciplined, determined, and committed person. All of which is essential to fulfilling your dreams in the future.

Mistakes Are A Part of Life

Acknowledge the mistakes you commit in your day-to-day. Whenever you do something wrong, let it be a beacon to learning and self-development. Instead of thinking of yourself as a failure, redirect that frustration into something positive like researching on various ways on how you can improve in that department. In lieu of sulking in your bed or the couch and ruminating on your failures, take this as an inspiration to work harder.

First, you need to accept that you have failed. Stop denying yourself the mistakes that you have made. Rather, accept them as a part of the past, and the past alone. Stop yourself from being anxious about further mistakes. Think of yourself as a constructive learner and your mistakes are only setbacks where you can learn more skills and knowledge from. Never forget your values just because you made the wrong move. Think of your life like you are playing chess. Even when you make the wrong move, it does not mean that you have immediately lost the fight. Turn that wrong into a right by making the most of your experience and doubling your efforts to turn that move into your opponent's checkmate.

Reflect on Your Actions Every Day
Before you go to bed, rethink your actions and see how you feel. You can label your behavior as positive or negative, but you should never let these dissuade you or demotivate you into pushing yourself to grow. Whenever you feel like you did something bad, reflect and learn from your actions. This defines how you will deal with more problems in the long run. When you are able to humble yourself and accept your mistakes, it means you are becoming a more responsible person who is willing to learn from his experiences. It means you are starting to feel responsible for your actions and you are willing to do whatever it takes to utilize your mistakes into something right or productive.

Consciously Practice the Thinking

IF YOU ARE used to thinking about the rewards and setbacks of the short-term, try to control your mind by redirecting it to your long-term on purpose. Instead of thinking short-term, ask yourself what you can learn from these challenges in the long run. How can it affect your dreams? Does it let you grow as a more mature person? You have full control of your brain; you just need to learn how to utilize its efforts to think. You can start by reciting your own mantra every time you feel the need to focus on your short-term goals. Or better yet, give yourself time to meditate every day for at least 15 minutes just to allow yourself to think of your long-term goals. You can soon observe the wonders it can bring to your performance and growth.

Work Your Way from Your Needs

It can be very difficult to accomplish your goals with physical and security needs. This usually happens to people who belong to the lower portion of the financial triangle. How can they reach their success if they cannot even have enough money to buy their primary needs? Well, you will be surprised that some of the most successful people in the world came from the bottom of that triangle. They started out as garbagemen who did not even have primary education. But that did not stop them from reaching their dreams.

As they were dealing with their financial constraints, they never lost sight of their goals. Yes, it took time for them to reach their dreams but their goal never stopped when they solved their financial problems. Truth is, that was never their dream. It was only a setback they needed to solve to stay on track with their long-term goals. So, even when you have primary needs, retain your focus on the things that matter more – your long-term dream. No trial can stop you

Unstoppable Day

from accomplishing success as long as you give yourself the chance to develop self-discipline, commitment, and persistence towards your dreams.

Chapter 13:
Shape Your Future

The road into shaping your future is not a walk in the park. There will always be twists and turns, ups and downs, and tops curves, but this should not stop you from living the dream. One of the most important factors that define a person's journey to success is his support system. In this chapter, I will outline how a stable support system can help you accomplish your dreams.

In the previous chapters, we have tackled the downside of having unsupportive friends and family. They can dissuade you from establishing a concept towards self-transformation and success. Plus, they can cause pain and demotivation that can detract your focus from your goals. But this time, I want you to learn the importance of surrounding yourself with helpful people who can assist you on the road to success.

Alleviate Your Feelings

In our darkest moments, having a good friend or family around is very helpful to help us alleviate our feelings of stress, pain, frustration, anguish, and sadness. They are always willing to lend an ear just so they can listen to our problems and try to solve them with us. If you have at least one person to tell everything to, you are lucky. Nowadays, it is very difficult to find someone trustworthy. Your friends and family will always be there to uplift your spirits no matter how difficult it may be sometimes. They boost our self-confidence because they make us feel that we are the best and we can reach our dreams if we wanted to. Our loved ones alleviate our negative feelings and help us ward off the onset of anxiety and depression. They take care of us whenever we fail and they make sure we get back on our feet to start a new day. When you have friends and family around to listen, it can do wonders to your self-regard and persistence to move past your mistakes.

Our Loved Ones Motivate Us

Whenever we feel like we are about to give up, they never fail in providing us reasons to feel inspired. Our loved ones are always there to get us back up on our knees and continue our venture forward. They would never let us back down because of a setback no matter how hard blown it is. Instead, they ready themselves in reminding us about our dreams and aspirations. They never neglect to tell us how amazing and competent we are. Our loved ones make us strong in their own little ways. By just a simple hug or a sentiment, they can make our blood flowing and our minds thinking on the road to success.

They Push Us to Our Limits

Nobody believes more in our capabilities than our friends and family. They know exactly what we can do, sometimes even more so than ourselves. We are lucky to have the few people who are always there to support our endeavors by pushing us to our limits and assuring us everything is going to be okay. They serve as our foundation because no matter how much we fail or commit mistakes, they will be there for us. They show us that they are willing to help us get back out there even when we fail. Our real friends and family are the only people who accept us for who we are despite how hard-headed we might seem sometimes. All they want to see is for us to keep moving forward despite all the hardships because they know that is where we can learn, grow and develop ourselves.

They Give Timely Advice
When we are with trusted families and friends, it is important to share our future or long-term goals. In that way, they can help you evaluate your priorities and your objectives to have better tasks and timeframe on the road to success. The sayings of our parents and elders are timeless. They never go out of hand. As you venture in your road to success, there will always be words from your parents and friends you will never forget. And when the time comes, you will feel lucky to have listened to their advice.

They Push Us to Be Better People
Your real friends and family will support your decisions, especially when it is for self-discovery and success. Your real friends will always be supportive of your decisions even if it means laying low from your past habits and gimmicks. When they understand your goals and dreams, they will push you towards them rather than inhibiting your growth. They will not try to pull you back to the dark side or criticize your efforts because, as real friends and family, they want nothing but the best for you.

How to Find Better People to Support You
Let's face it, for some people it can be very difficult to have friends and family who can be helpful in achieving their goals. For this reason, you need to look for people whom you can trust. They might be difficult to find, but not impossible. If you live alone, you can join clubs or groups with hobbies that interest you. You can join the book club, chess club, and many more. If you are on the

Unstoppable Day

road to weight loss, you can socialize in the gym and look for worthwhile people to be your friends.

But before you disclose your secrets and dreams to people, you need to assess whether they are trustworthy or not. Do not blurt out your secrets on the first day. Build into it and see if they can accept you or not. You can also stay socially active through sports and traveling. You can meet and get to know other people who can help you develop your skills in the future. Remember that everybody has their own background and beliefs. You can learn a trick or two from the people you meet; you just need to be patient when making friends.

If you are trying to retain your old friends, make them understand what you want in life. If they accept you, then great, you can share your goals with them and ask for help. If not, it could be painful, but you need to move on and start surrounding yourself with more positive people.

For people who have difficult families, it is important to try to reach out to them. Make them see you are trying to change. If they accept you for who you are and what you want to be, you can tag them into your goals and ask for help or advice. On the other hand, if they cannot accept you for your dreams, then you are better off looking for support from someone else. When you start to surround yourself with people who believe in you and choose to see your good side, you can observe the wonders it can bring to your life, especially on the road to success. Not only will you have someone to support you, but you will also have someone to fill your life with positivity and ward off any sign of regret, pain, or frustration that might derail you from your goals.

Chapter 14:
Eat Something You Hate

Finally, on the road to self-discipline, I have one more challenge for you. It is to eat something you hate. You may be wondering how can doing something you do not like make you a better person. Simply put, doing something you hate can make you learn new things out of the ordinary. It pushes you to go out of your comfort zone and try something that will make you see and realize things you never thought you could learn. Do you know why humans are disinhibited to try new things? It is because of their mind's stubbornness. Remember when we were children and we did not like to eat vegetables? The only reason why we cried our eyes out was to avoid their taste. It has been ingrained in our minds that it is not good to taste vegetables. It could be through one bad experience like tasting okra and not wanting its slimy texture or our stubbornness could be from other people's experiences. Some would say they have tried it and they never liked it one bit. But remember, we all have differences. It does not mean you will automatically dislike it as well.

In this final segment of the book, I will teach you to live a little more by eating something you hate. And as you progress, I want you to try something that you hate – any activity. Of course, the main problem for this is that our brains are accustomed to the thought that trying new things can be dangerous to our health. Our brains are used to feeling terrified of doing something they are unfamiliar with because of the consequences. Sometimes, we get disgusted at

Unstoppable Day

the thought of doing certain activities. We get dissuaded by just thinking about the first step. Little do you know that your potential is maximized by trying new things in life. You learn new lessons. You get stronger. You can overcome your phobia. And most importantly, it will make you feel more alive than ever. I am sure that you do not want to live your life with regret. If you do not do these things now, you are left with the most dangerous question, "What if?" But if you tried your best to get through the experience -even if you do not enjoy it-, you will be left with the satisfaction of knowing that the activity or food is not for you.

Now, it is time to dare yourself to eat what you hate. Of course, disregard anything without any nutrient value. Our goal for this is to take things off from your bucket list -and of course, furnish your command on your mind and foster self-discipline and commitment. Luckily, the modernization of technology allows us to try foreign foods without traveling at all, so I want you to pick a foreign food for starters. If you want it to be more accessible, you can choose your most hated fruit or vegetable.

If possible, try it out with a friend. You can make it fun by daring each other to try new food. Plus, you can ask your friends or family to keep track of your progress. Ask them to give you a penalty if you are unable to do the activity.

Once you have chosen a food, I want you to face your fear and just cut the food into little pieces if possible. Of course, have water beside you just in case. Come up with a tactic to make it easier to ingest, like putting flavorings or seasonings. If it smells bad, it is your choice whether to cover your nose or not. What matters is that you experience its taste. Once you have put the food in your mouth, try to enjoy it even if you do not like the taste. After every spoon, reward yourself with nutritious yet delicious food and go again. I know it may sound silly to try things you are unaware of, but you never know if you will ever like it if you do not try.

This challenge goes hand in hand with trying an activity that you do not like. In this way, you can learn more skills and healthy habits that can aid you on the road to success. For your next challenge, I want you to pick an activity you fear or dislike and have some friends and family accompany you. In trying new activities, tread carefully and ask for assistance from experts. You would not want to get injured by trying it without proper knowledge and equipment.

For this activity, I want you to push yourself and accomplish the task. It does not matter if you fail or succeed. What matters is that you develop your willpower and command to push your mind and be open to more experiences. These small things you do to empower yourself can work wonders for your life. Who knows, maybe that one hateful thing you resent doing will push you towards your greatest desires. Maybe that one experience will bring you the hobby of a lifetime. See, you will never know what you can find at the end of the line unless you try.

If you are doubtful, you might as well think of what you can achieve by doing so. What kind of person will you be after the process? How can this affect you in reaching your long-term goals? See, with a little positivity, you can achieve things unknowingly. You can push your mind to stay committed, persistent, and determined. Once you have acknowledged your ability to gain control of your mind, only then can you have unstoppable self-discipline that will lead you straight to your success. You only live once to let these little moments pass.

Unstoppable Day

Remember, no one has conquered success by letting fear stop them at every step of the way.

Conclusion

Turning pro is a mindset. If we are struggling with fear, self-sabotage, procrastination, self-doubt, etc., the problem is, we're thinking like amateurs. Amateurs don't show up. Amateurs crap out. Amateurs let adversity defeat them. The pro thinks differently. He shows up, he does his work, he keeps on truckin', no matter what.

Steven Pressfield

If there is one thing to learn from this book, it is the importance of mind control to overcome all the challenges in life. If you really want to succeed in life, you need to have an unstoppable sense of self-discipline to guide your actions. Without it, you will only keep coming back to your old self – unsuccessful and unwilling to change for the better. In this book, we have discussed the importance of having a well-renowned discipline and how it can affect our other values towards success. Self-discipline is the foundation of all actions towards a person's dream. It guides one's confidence, vision, goals, emotions, and behavior. It governs and defines whether a person will accomplish his goals for the future. It allows a person to obtain helpful habits and morning rituals that can help him or her stay productive despite all the trials in life.

Self-discipline is your weapon against temptation and other forms of enticement. It pushes you to break the cycle that has been holding you back from the road to success. We also established lazy days as inevitable but, with a strong

Unstoppable Day

sense of self-discipline, you can find yourself on your desk, ready to accomplish your tasks for the day.

For many years, procrastination has been a part of your habit, inhibiting all hope for you to unleash your potential and progress towards self-hope. Thankfully, all is about to change now that you know how you can vanquish the enemy and avoid the black hole. Never neglect to have confidence, commitment, and persistence. All of these help you build unstoppable self-discipline that can change your life for the better. Not only will self-discipline push you to your limits and help you learn from your experiences, but it can also help you overcome your fears into becoming the next big thing! The power to control your mind easily lies in your willingness to thrive against all odds and grab every opportunity you can to experience more and more. Nobody can live your life better than you do. No one can control your mind and behavior as much as you. Never disregard the power of self-discipline towards your success because it will always serve as your fuel and your drive to a fully-transformed self.

In reading the lives of great men, I found that the first victory they won was over themselves... self-discipline with all of them came first.

Harry S. Truman

Once you have accepted this challenge, you will be ten steps closer to achieving your goals. Your journey starts now. So, get up, look for a piece of paper, and establish your vision to start.

Relentless Mental Toughness and Optimism

Discover How Champion's and Athletes Develop an Unbeatable Mindset, the Old School Grit of Navy SEALs, and Begin to Take Extreme Ownership of Your Life Today

Chapter 1:
There are Physical Limits but None for the Mind

Mental toughness has been described as a major factor in most of the significant outcomes around the world. It is one of the most used but least understood terms, especially in the sports arena. Mentally tough people deliver more and have a greater commitment to their purpose. This always translates into a top-notch output and timely delivery. Their stress management capabilities help them to remain generally content, and therefore, they are less likely to develop mental health issues. Further, they connect with others easily and handle tough situations tactfully. They are hardly anxious and. They believe that they have the power to control their destiny, and this allows them to remain relatively tolerable to misfortunes. They portray a positive behavior in situations. They are always ready to embrace new opportunities and are always open to learning.

In an era of fast dynamics in the society, therefore, mental toughness is paramount. Leaders, aspiring leaders, or basically success-oriented people, those working in complex and uncertain environments need to be mentally tough. They need to be resilient and ready for the change. We are living in times of great change and uncertainty. It is difficult to spot people in pure pleasure, relaxation, and acquitted refreshment. That "it doesn't matter whether we win or lose" is also too rare a chant in the current times. The world is seemingly highly obsessed about success and the desire to emerge the winner. This applies in all the domains of life including work, education, and sports. Perhaps our drive for success is encompassed by the thought of being the most powerful or intelligent or just being the best. It is a humankind sort of tune to just be at the top or keep improving at the least. As such, usually, the natural mode of selection applies where the fit survives and takes the first position in various lines.

In his book "The Achievement Mindset," Michael Sheard shares insurmountable thought-provoking situations that should be considered by every individual. He poses queries such as "Why some athletes become successful while others fail when faced with misfortunes; how athletes are able to rebound after great failures; what it is that differentiates an athlete who crumbles under pressure from one who thrives through the pressure and overcomes" The answers to these questions, I believe, lie in the successful establishment, implementation, and sustenance of the concept of intellectual strength. The most successful people today realize that it goes far beyond just the basic technicality, but that winning takes on the further dimension referred to as the psychology of winning. The latter integrates a range of varied mental attributes which are often found in intellectual strength skills description.

For a long time in history, the concept of mental toughness has been known to be a big cliché in the sporting arena. Recently, however, the field has attracted the attention of researchers and analysts. Therefore, it has become one of the massively-studied fields with researchers aiming at enquiring into the phenomenon and its relevance to other fields, also trying to highlight it since it is one of the least-understood terms in sports. There are numerous texts devoted to conceptualizing and developing this concept of intellectual sturdiness. The increased flow of interest from an interest of the concept into academic fields indicates its prominence among the pioneers; the coaches, sports psychologists, and the athletes themselves. These groups of people progressively recognize that success cannot be based on raw skill alone, but that psychological factors play a core role. In fact, numerous research results link mental toughness to the excellence of performance and term it as a performance enhancer. However, despite the continuous endorsement of this view among vast populations, there is still a section of the somewhat stubborn audience that is reluctant to embrace the seemingly significant philosophy.

Whenever we face any kind of misfortune or find ourselves in difficult situations, it is believed that our performance is mainly influenced by our ability to balance between internal and external demands, i.e., our negative or positive emotional responses to emergent situations determine the impacts such have on us. This calls for the ability to go beyond the pure technical skill or capability and tap into the power that resides within us to optimize situations and enhance performance. Ever too often, we tend to overlook mental fundamentals when faced with situations that require enhanced performance; that which requires us to act promptly and pushes us out of our comfort zones. Generally, the immediate reaction is usually making adjustments to all levels of our physical routine long before the mental aspect of it could even be considered. The next thing you realize is that you could have done better, yet the result is already out. Even in the field of sports, every athletic contest is usually based on the control of the delicate body-mind connection, yet most often, contestants continue to persist on harder physical training at the expense of psychological training.

Yet individuals who turn their focus into the mental training side have an advantage over those who usually cannot do this. The scientific composition of human beings is designed to direct and regulate its existence from the central nervous system, which is the brain. Regardless of the outstanding technical know-how of an individual, the most certain determining factor of failure or success is most appropriately attributed to psychological factors. How well people develop themselves psychologically and how they apply their skills during high-pressure situations is what really counts. The concept of mental toughness is now used to refer to contestants, especially in sports, who possess superior mental attributes, and it is argued that it is the mental game which differentiates performers as good and very good. Simply put, mental toughness will always set you apart where physical and technical skills are held constant. Importantly, however, improving one's mental performance does not by any chance belittle the significant task of improving physical and technical capability. The point that I'm trying to stress is that an individual with what it takes physically through skills and talent can even emerge a better performer if they train mentally. A person who does not possess similar technical capabilities as others they are competing for the same resource and is maybe slightly weaker in this regard may become a better performer if they develop mental toughness and maintain it. The term fitness is used to refer to the desired condition of being able to reach the highest possible level of performance. In the modern day, however, people need to concentrate on reaching a state of optimal mental fitness as well. Talent alone does not amount to success. There are numerous situations whereby highly talented people have experienced energy burnouts due to mental breakdowns and the considerably less talented people succeeded at high levels due to having mental strength.

Relentless Mental Toughness and Optimism

If you look at today's most job descriptions, you realize that employers are swiftly emphasizing the relevance of having a strong set of soft skills in combination with the hard skills one possesses. In a scenario where two or more candidates possess a similar set of the minimum requirements, the one with success and enthusiastic mindset gets the job. These skills are increasingly relevant for all organizations as they strive to keep ahead of their rivals in their industry. A person with the ability to cope under pressure, to work under minimal supervision, to hit strict deadlines, and to communicate effectively stands a higher chance than the one without such qualities. Strong mental capacity equips one with emotional intelligence, from whence once is able to build strong relationships with others at work, avoid arguments, and be able to handle conflicts from a composed position. Such a person is considered a good employee because despite cases of failure they remain motivated to push on, and even if they come across unreasonable clients, they are sure to handle the situation well by acting like the bigger person. This way they can present an ideal picture of the organization that they work for.

Ideally, there is perhaps no greater thing you can gift yourself than training your mind to be strong and undefeatable. A strong mental capacity brings with it a strong life. You will be able to stand an advantage in any undertaking you engage in. You will be able to be positive because you know regardless of the number of many times life may knock you down you can always collect yourself and move forward. With mental toughness, you will get more much than you lose in life, and you will see failure as an opportunity for you to see better. Mental strength is the element that your opponents fear more than anything. Everyone knows that it is difficult, close to impossible, to defeat someone who never gives up. You decide your future because you know what you've decided to do now. No other person that can decide your fate or fortune for that matter, but you, simply because you can control your mind. Mental strength can be equated to nothing, and that is simply why you will succeed if you set your mind to winning. It does not mean that everything will fall right on your hand for you to use, but because you will make the most out of everything that comes your way. Sometimes, you do not have the energy, and sometimes, everything looks so far out of reach. Sometimes, even others doubt you and your capability. But you should always aim at backing yourself up and show your mental strength. It is mental strength that will determine the direction your life takes after you are tested. Remember that life is a constant learning process, and we learn through mistakes.

The premise of this guide is that if you combine the two types of fitness, technical and mental fitness, you will increase the chances of achieving a top-notch performance every time you indulge in a project or are faced by adversity. You will develop a chance for excellence that would, otherwise, remain untapped and somewhat unattainable. You will be breaking into unique realms of performance enhancement and optimization. Hence establishing and maintaining mental toughness will in the world we live in today determine your success or otherwise a failure. Seek to establish your strengths and weaknesses, so you can improve on your weaknesses every day and use your strengths to conquer every tough condition. Remember that the person who stares back at you in the mirror every time you give it a glance is your greatest obstacle and your greatest strength as well. How well any of these attributes play out is all upon you. The quality of the life you lead is determined by the attribute that you feed most. Feed strength always, and you will be a conqueror always. Feed your

Relentless Mental Toughness and Optimism

obstacle, and you will hardly achieve a thing in your life. Only you can decide what your life is worth.

As a rule of thumb, always remember that the greatest war of all times was not the one fought during the African colonization, neither has that war been fought in the United States or anywhere else in the world. The greatest war is the one fought by your mind. People you meet along the course of your life may always try to dim your hopes and your dreams. It is only the power of your brain that cannot be stopped. Therefore, do not give up! And do not give in!

Chapter 2:
Mindset is Everything

A great author once said that you should feed your mind with success, or it will rot in mediocrity. No one desires mediocrity. The nature of everyone is to move through life with a mission in mind, to govern how they conduct themselves all through in the pursuit of their mission. The path to success is not entirely a path. It is a playfield. You must utilize any chance that comes your way and trample upon anything that brings you down like it was nothing. Most importantly, you have to have a winning mindset. Just like how you approach an interview, one of the most important meetings in one's life, you should approach everything else with a winning mindset.

Some of the failures that you will experience in life are mainly caused by you. While sometimes, luck plays out and you get something in life, you should not approach life from this standpoint. Some people spend their entire life thinking that by luck, they will make it. However, rarely does luck make you succeed without effort. You should believe that you have the ability to conquer in any situation that tests you. Your passion to win must be more than what lies beneath your feet. Any mission that you set out to achieve is accompanied by unreserved defeat. However, you should remember that it is at the moment you are torn down and worn out in the mind that you should take the battle most seriously and fight the hardest.

Relentless Mental Toughness and Optimism

You are human, and you are bound to reaching a critical point in life. It is at this moment when your success begins to take shape. There are myriads of ways that life can get you down, even though we are operating in our purpose. Our choices take us in one way or another into the battles that we face. Yet, there are numerous ways through which we can set goals and achieve them by focusing on each milestone along the way. Ranging from the entrepreneurs who start up a business from scratch to the student who begins his career pathway back in middle school and refuses to give up on his career dream despite how far it may be and even to the army recruit who begins to undertake a combat training and does not lose sight of completing successfully, we are all warriors in our own grounds. To withstand the never-ending struggles, the most helpful substance is the strength of the spirit that we possess to never yield to pressure.

While we are just too human to endure endless struggle, the truth of the matter is that the body will follow what the mind believes in. Even when we have the drive to achieve our purpose, the battle can be overwhelming. At a given point in time, we will all get to a point where we feel like we are losing our way. Everything we have strived to achieve becomes distant as unpredicted blows knock us down to the sands that we once proudly stood upon. At this point, we should remember the golden rule amongst champions that greatness is not handed down, but it is acquired by those willing to fight for it.

Simply put, feed your mind with success!

Purpose has been emphasized all through by every successful person in whichever field they operate in. Purpose is the first thing that demonstrates that you believe in yourself. It is also the first step that gives the direction and makes you want to excel since it means something to you. Failing to do that, you will give up when the going gets tough. You will ask yourself, for instance, why you are working hard to succeed in a job yet you don't even like it. If it is maybe about meeting your bills only, you could opt to take a loan or your savings to settle the bills. But when it is the passion of achieving something higher than that which drives you, then you won't give up on the job no matter what. Everyone has a set of core values which give them a sense of purpose. For instance, you might have a purpose of putting your abilities to test if you have been rejected way too often. Whatever your purpose is directed toward, let it not be about impressing others. You can rest assured that they are the first ones to laugh at your downfall or when you face adversity. Experts have argued time and over again that intrinsic goals outshine extrinsic goals, i.e., once you do something to fulfill an innate desire, it is easy to grind harder than in other cases.

To establish your purpose, it is imperative that you ponder over the question of, for instance, what you value most in your life and in other people, people that inspire you and what you actually like about them, how you think you are different from others and why most people thank you, what your vision about the future is, and if you are actually moving towards that direction.

Self-Awareness
They say that in every aspect of life, the first step to finding success is always to admit that you have a problem, and then it can lead to the improvement journey-and that has proven to be true. Introspection is the superpower that each of us can employ to analyze positions you have been in in the past so that you can march forward knowing what to pick and what to drop. It is the starting point that leads to massive self-improvement. The ancient Greek philosophy

emphasized knowing thyself; a topic that has since then been of great interest to philosophers and psychologists. Research has positioned self-consciousness as a mechanism of self-control. When we focus our attention on us, we compare our behaviors and core values, and we become objective self-evaluators.

Strength is not only about pushing harder. Rather, we need to take a step back from time to time and assess the bigger picture. A former Navy SEAL commander known as Mark Divine argued that self-awareness is your ground to start building the unbeatable mind. Once you know what you are capable of doing and what brings you down, you are much more capable of soaring higher. The best thing about self-awareness is that it equips us with specific techniques to handle situations. For instance, through introspection, you may learn that you are more of a morning person than an evening one. Thus, you decide to make it your do not disturb moment. Even as most successful people would argue, knowledge alone is not enough. You must act on what you have already established. To develop strong self-awareness, start recording a journal, consistently recording your major activities and realizations every day. At some point, say two weeks of recording, find a quiet place, take a deep breath, and reflect about life. This is a great starting point for you to develop an unbeatable mind, being fully aware of yourself.

Goals

All successful people, regardless of their playing fields, attach high significance to picturing themselves as victors in their minds before they actually succeed in reality. They have mastered this significant art and credited it as a core tactic for success. If there is one thing that has been rightfully translated from the sports arena into other domains in life, including business, is the power of visualization. It is exceptionally effective when harnessed and correctly applied. When you set a goal that you want to achieve, it is normal to begin picturing the obstacles that you may face along the way. The problem with most of us is that we often let these obstacles rent space in our head, which inhibits us from moving forward. This is usually the reason why most people are easily content with the ordinary. Do not let this be you. Envision yourself as a victorious person as opposed to letting barriers in your mind hold you back.

Some of the questions you should brainstorm are: What you need to do to achieve the goal, what sacrifices you need to make, and anticipate how you can address any hindrances. Typically, what I mean is that you should ensure your idealized vision shines brighter than anything that may try to make it dull. Most often, picturing yourself as winner increases your chances to win, but without picturing yourself winning you most probably don't win. Spend time thinking about your achievement, understanding as much about it as possible. After setting your goals, allocate sufficient time for each milestone. If you have several doubts, set small goals to motivate you and help you envision yourself as a winner. Achieving various small goals helps build a momentum that you need to get to the big goals.

In Navy SEAL training, for instance, things as small as making your bed in the morning are taken as a significant goal. It offers a sense of pride and sets you for the day ahead.

Team Support
Besides setting goals, you ought to know that nobody can accomplish them alone. We are social beings, and we all need others at various points in our journey. We live as communities, and we find our strength amongst each other.

Relentless Mental Toughness and Optimism

Even as can be borrowed from the biblical teachings, God divinely places people at various points of our lives to ensure that we fulfill his pre-ordained purpose for us. However, it is upon us to activate and use our destiny helpers to gain the most we can from them.

It is the nature of human beings to establish support in relationships. While it may not always be the case, it is good to find someone who has your back always and is always willing to return the favor. Experts argue that everyone should identify other people who are like-minded and willing to support you. It is always easier to push harder with a team that counts on you and supports you through thick and thin. Most of the successful people have accredited the cultivation and alignment of networks of support. You must have the right mindset, define what you need, and align the right people to your journey.

Preparation

Even with goals and a right team, it all boils down to preparation. As a person set out on a journey for self-fulfillment, you are going to face stumbling blocks along the way. Some things that challenge you will even fall in the category best described as difficult. At such times, it is tempting to jump into action and start doing what you think is good. Chances are that instead of making the situation better, you might actually make it worse. Conversely, stepping back to prepare can make a substantial difference. When we do our preparation really thoroughly, we gain confidence to approach any kind of situation. Experts agree that the confidence to perform tasks comes from your work ethic. It is as much about preparation as it is about the mindset.

You are the ultimate designer of your own life, and you make the future by visualizing and actually doing things. You have to become conscious of your visualizations so that you can be armed to handle any hurdle that may come your way. Also, to ensure you are well prepared to face the task ahead of you, you can use simulation. This entails practicing the situation in front of an audience who is your support team, which eliminates the fear of uncertainty. When preparing for an interview, for instance, simulating the situation and answering the likely interview questions in front of, say your friends, beforehand, helps you to identify whether your verbal and non-verbal cues are in place and also gives you the confidence to approach the interview.

Self-Talk

When you are out and about hustling and bustling all day long, it is normal to feel low at times. What you need is this: Take a moment and ponder over what you've told yourself today. Was it critical? Was it kind and helpful? How did this inner discussion make you feel?

Ever too often, we tend to worry about what others think about us, but we seldom think about we speak to ourselves. Yet, you have the capability of speaking life or doom to your life. If you are always hard on yourself, you will never have the zeal to focus on your goals. We can all draw from the experience of a Navy SEAL who is under the training bit of controlling breath under water. In a scenario where the oxygen mask is removed from the mouth, an ordinary Navy SEAL would tell themselves that they are going to die, but a strong person would have to say they can handle it. Talking to oneself positively brings change, but negative thinking brings mental torture. Remind yourself that all pain is temporary and that you are going to pull through.

Focus on Progress, Not Perfection

Relentless Mental Toughness and Optimism

One of the most common things that bring down people is striving for perfection. Wanting to reach the trophy fast but lacking the patience to hone your skills on the path is quite a mistake. We are human, and we are bound to imperfections. It is our different imperfections that make us unique. If perfection is your goal, the outcome will always be a failure. Of course, this does not stop you from setting the bar high. It only reminds you to put your focus on the steps along the way. Incline your mind toward improvement, learning, growth, and understanding.

Once you tie yourself to specific terms, you set yourself up for a win/lose scenario. Conversely, thinking about improvement allows you to measure progress and take pride in it. Although your weakness should not be allowed to occupy the largest bit of your mind, focusing on the weakness is a vital element of your improvement journey. Successful people admit that they spend most of their time focusing on what they have done wrong in the past and debriefing what could have been done better. Most people are torn down by failures, but the strong ones know that failures are teachers that show us what to do next. They present openings that would have otherwise not been realized. Therefore, every time you fail, evaluate to know what went wrong and try to understand how it can be fixed.

Celebrate

Remember that toughness is not all about hard work. You need to take some moments and celebrate even the achievement of minor milestones from time to time. It is such a celebration of the small wins that get you rejuvenated and gives you the strength you need to continue with the journey. Take time to talk and smile with your loved ones out of your busy schedule. This is as important

Werner Brendon Marcus

as the hard work that you have. These moments remind us that our struggle is worth every minute.

Furthermore, part of what creates a tough mind is finding happiness in the simplest of things. Experts argue that happiness is a crucial ingredient for boosting our energy. Several pleasurable moments make us happier than a few big moments. Remember that happiness comes from within. Do what you love. Let your mind be taken away by the music. Talk to friends. We are all human beings, and we want to express ourselves creatively. Do this by showing love to others, and never hesitate to dance.

Chapter 3:
The Mind of a Navy SEAL

You have most probably heard of the Navy SEALs, the leading force known for undertaking the most dangerous and secretive missions in the military arena. Most probably, you have also a glimpse of the training that they go through both in the water and on the dry land. The super-elite team that finished the high-profile terrorist Osama Bin Laden in 2011 is still largely covered with enigma. All Special Forces undergo rigorous training, but the Navy SEALs are considered the most highly trained. It identifies among the public as the most elite force and one you can bet on all-around capabilities.

What's more important whatsoever is the mindset that they possess as they undergo training and even in carrying out their missions in real life. Most of the men on mission dedicate a long time of their life to an upcoming fight, making great personal sacrifices. The pinnacle of SEAL training is referred to as the Hell Week, a period of frequent tests in which all who survive possess a common quality. Even when they are under a test of their lives and are in great pain, they manage to think and step out of their pain, face their fears, and consider how they can help a neighbor who may need their help.

Ideally, what they possess is more than a fist of courage and physical capability. Their hearts are large enough to think about the service of others while putting their own lives on the line and dedicate their lives to a higher purpose.

Seal Commanders and other experts in the field of life coaching and psychology have advanced the knowledge of how you can think like a Navy SEAL and succeed in any of your life's domains. Your daily routine, they say, should be tied to a goal that you work towards achieving, whether you want to get in shape, to eat right, or start up a business in a competitive industry. Navy SEALS usually train their minds and their physique. With the right tools, the so-called regular person can train to have the mind of a SEAL. All these tools amount to setting appropriate goals and getting to achieve them with ease. One requires elements such as mind control and utmost concentration, emotional resilience, proper visualization, and learning how to rest but not quit.

The following are the rules of thumb that one should have to attain the mind of a Navy SEAL:

Never Procrastinate
Have you ever settled down to complete a significant task, but all of a sudden you discovered you were engrossed in the latest song released in your favorite genre? Or you are checking the latest fashion trend? Or perhaps you suddenly realize that there are emails to be responded to, or your ceiling fan needs dusting even though it is only 10 a.m.? The next thing you realize is that it has already come to the end of day, and your most significant task is still unfinished. For most of us, procrastination is a strong force that keeps us from completing the most significant and urgent tasks in our lives. It is a potentially dangerous and mysterious force that causes victims to record poor performance at work, fail in school, or even miss out crucial business opportunities.

Experts relate procrastinators with great visionaries who love to fantasize about the great mansion that they will one day have without actually taking the

Relentless Mental Toughness and Optimism

baby steps involved in setting up and building up the house. What they need is to work like the construction workers who lay one brick after the other, consistently and without giving up until the house is built. With potential distractions at an arm's reach in the digital era, it is very easy to find ways of procrastinating. Do not waste any more time making excuses for the things you have to do. We often tend to put off tasks when there is a challenge at hand and find insignificant activities instead. Remember that the easy way out is to rise up to the challenge and handle every day's important tasks.

Also, remember that it is the small things that matter when you put things into perspective about your future. Some projects or simple tasks may seemingly be trivial that they almost do not matter to you. Take it as a rule of the thumb that every little step along the way matters in reaching the big thing you want. This is perhaps the best motivation you can have to cease procrastinating.

Don't Think of Discipline as a Punishment

Forget motivation. you need discipline! Discipline is a popular but narrowly-understood concept. The most successful people have exercised discipline in all their endeavors. It is vital to everyone, and without it, the world around us would be in chaos. It's about discipline to hold on the course by knowing what you are required to do and making it happen. The battlefield is constantly changing. As a seal in a mission, you are getting gunshots from one direction, and at this point, you are expected to lead your team to pursue the enemy in that direction. You require effective communication and flexibility to make that happen. And so is the case in every domain of life! Priorities are going to evolve and shift from time to time. It is about prioritization and execution. While you may not always be motivated to keep working and responding to emerging demands in life promptly, discipline is going to hold you down for any task.

The ability of a person to have self-restricting values allows them to behave in a controlled manner. Discipline gives shape and stability to an individual, and they extend the same quality to everyone and every organization they interact with. The observance of the well-defined and unwritten rules is the basis of success, without which one would choose to do only what makes them happy, avoiding the challenging tasks and ending up unsuccessful.

The 10-Second Rule

Impulse decision making is natural to human beings. Some impulse decisions may help to keep you out of pressure, but overall, thinking before you act is important to avoid destroying your chance to achieve your goals. More than often decisions made under the heat of the moment cause detrimental impacts in our lives that we could never imagine.

Failure to pay attention to decisions is the commonest reason people find themselves in dangerous situations. Specialists advise that it is imperative to take a few seconds to assess your surroundings every now and then. Take time to study if there is a questionable activity in an environment you just stepped in, if there are suspicious people, if the place is unusually quiet, if you have an uneasy feeling, if an unexpected person is present, or if anything looks out of place.

Ideally, it takes only about 10 seconds to scope your surroundings and spot danger to avoid it. This is a golden lesson everyone can learn from how the Navy SEALs operate. You'd rather spend the 10 seconds before deciding to act, rather than waste your precious time trying to remedy the aftermath of the poor decision.

Relentless Mental Toughness and Optimism

Getting to the Top Takes the Right Drive to Do Things the 99 Percent Others Will Not Do

Perhaps one of the greatest quotes that the SEALs have learned to live by is to let go of the life they planned for them to attain the life that awaits them. There is a fine line between having a vision for your life and letting go of the life you have planned. Learn to differentiate the two. Understand that to let go of what you have planned means to get out of your comfort zone. You must be willing to move out of the ordinary living to discover the oasis of wisdom that awaits you at the top. This is the one thing that most of us lack: the drive to be different. To do what others consider impossible. You must dare to be different!

The one thing that you should know is that the 1 percent has a very different outlook on time from 99 percent. They are always aware that time is limited. They also understand that they have 24 hours a day, just like everyone else, but they have to use their time in the most efficient manner. Conversely, the 99 percent believe that time is infinite, and they just use their time carelessly. They imagine that there is still tomorrow, next week, or even next month. The 99 percent value money over time; hence they try to handle everything by themselves to save on money-even the things which they cannot do so well. They end up wasting their time and energy and still do not receive optimal value for the time. Conversely, the 1 percent value time over money; hence they are not afraid to use the money to buy back time. This they do by paying someone for the services such as cleaning that may consume their time. This way they have time to concentrate on what they can do best and what draws them closer to their milestones.

Ideally, the 99 percent trade time for money while the 1 percent trade money for money. Choose the latter group, which believes in partnering and connecting with people appropriate to establish ideas faster, and most importantly, they believe that they do not have to do everything by themselves. Yes, you will seem crazy. Yes, some will mock you. And most definitely, others will only give you a period of time until you can break down. But dare to maintain your focus and never give in to following the multitude. Know that your path is different! Understand that how you spend your time right now determines your achievements tomorrow. The projects you start today will bear fruits tomorrow. What you learn today will be applicable tomorrow. Learn exactly how to value and spend your time as opposed to spend and squander all your time.

Think About the Long-Term

Long-term thinking is perhaps one of the essential skills one can have. Ever too often, you find people planning tomorrow, a few weeks, or months into the future. While there is nothing wrong with such planning, most people do not remember to think long term. Most of the successful people were long-term thinkers who challenged themselves to unimaginably great missions. They chose to plan about the future rather than being confused by the present.

Some of the reasons why long-term thinkers tend to be successful are that they are often willing to make sacrifices that others cannot make. Instead of feeding on life with a big spoon, for instance, a long-term thinking young worker could opt to save up for an investment for when he is older. Long-term thinking parents also begin saving up college fees for their children once they begin toddler classes to avoid amassing huge loans once it's time for college. The point is, become a good long-term thinker, and be ready to make sacrifices today without expecting fruits in a week or a month's time.

Relentless Mental Toughness and Optimism

Don't Think About Competing Against Others, But Try to Make Progress Yourself

Although life is a competition, it is not a race between you versus others. The real journey of life is the race between you and your unrealized potential. Comparing yourself against others is easy especially in the digital era where they flood our lives with images about their success. There are numerous grounds on which you can compare yourself and against numerous people. This kind of comparison never ends, and you never achieve the real prize of competition. But once you fall for the trap of competing against them, you constantly judge yourself based on their value system. The problem with this is that while you may succeed at it, you only do that which is important for them and not you. At the end of the day, you are still a loser within yourself.

One of the famous mottos that you should all seek to understand is that if any fish compared itself against animals with the ability to climb up a tree, it would forever believe that it is foolish. A SEAL who sets out on a mission to outshine their peers has not succeeded in anything if they do not improve based on their own metrics. Competing only allows you to set goals that fit you best based on what you want to achieve. Comparison against others is always unfair since we presume the best about others and compare it to our worst selves. You are too unique to compete with others fairly. You only have control over your own life and not others. Comparisons take away our joy and add no fulfillment in our lives. Always remember to be aware of your own achievements and unique contributions in this world. Pursue the greater things in life-love, generosity, and empathy- and untie yourself completely from the societal measure of success.

Embrace the Habits Developed Embrace Change

Werner Brendon Marcus

Take it as a general principle that you must create change, or else change will create you. Ever too often, we are resistant to change, and we do not actually realize that change is constant. No matter how much you avoid change, it will, either way, enter your life. A self-initiated change is easier to adapt to since once is ready. Once you realize that you actually have to make certain sacrifices to attain your long-term goals, once you understand that you must be disciplined to succeed, that you should not procrastinate, and that you should make every hour and every minute count, you will have to embrace the change that these success tactics require-and act upon them. Once you sit around and wait to act when the dynamics of life catch you unaware, that is the point at which you make poor decisions, and you cannot control the anxiety that comes with it. To develop an unbeatable mind, you have to be ready to embrace change.

Chapter 4:
Daily Habits that Strengthen the Mind

Unlocking the doors of greatness is not about big gestures. It is much more about taking small steps day by day and being consistent. It is all about pushing a little more every day. To belong to the 1 percent group of people, you must take a deliberate effort to design your life and the habits that you need to develop. One of the greatest philosophers, Aristotle, argued that "we are what we repeatedly do. Excellence then is not an act but a habit." Besides, research has concluded that most of the actions you take every day are not actual decisions but habits. Habits, then, form a way for you to realize your higher purpose. The mindset of the high achievers has always charmed me, simply because of their endless zeal to do what it takes to attain success. They never give up until they are there. And even when they get there, they know that they have to keep up with the habits that led them there, lest they regress. Their failures, their utmost determination in times of difficulties, and the profundity in their priority list is just something to ponder over.

We can all replicate these qualities if we learn to understand and control how we live our daily lives. We must, then, develop the habits of successful people.

Do What Most Successful People Do First Thing in the Morning
Wake up early and get out of bed. The manner in which you begin your day plays a central role in how the rest of the day is going to be spent. Feeling your

morning with success habits will lead to your progress every day. Therefore, wake up earlier than you have to. Waking up early is no easy task, especially when you are not among the fortunate morning people. Most people do agree that they do not like waking up early. However, successful people always take it upon themselves whether they are morning, evening, or an afternoon individual to plan their mornings the night before and actually wake up early to ensure that they do not miss their schedule. Being an early riser has innumerable paybacks to you as an individual. It has some special power to your mind and body. It gives you time for things such as a healthy breakfast, spiritual and mental wellbeing, proper organization of the day, and a better sleeping routine.

First, when you wake up early before the rest of the world around you, there is a peace and quiet environment for you. Then, you have the time to listen to your thoughts, breathe, and relax. Have this moment to reconnect to your spiritual journey, something that kicks you off for the day. Also, you could listen or read some motivational content and simply sit in silence. Such silent moments in the morning increases your brain's efficiency and boosts your overall health as well. Ideally, you are likely to be more productive when you wake up early.

Remember to Make Your Bed Once You Get Out of It.

While it may look so trivial that you may not attach much meaning to it, making your bed prepares you to go change the world. It is always the little things that matter, and making the bed shows your accomplishment of the first goal. It gives you a sense of achievement and leads you to another task, such as working out since you may not have time for this in any other time of the day. Furthermore, bed-making shows that you can manage the little things, without which you cannot do the big things right. Nonetheless, it feels good to come back home to a well-made bed even if everything did not go well out there.

Create the Ideal Daily Routine

Successful people always establish and stick to their ideal daily schedule. If you are able to start your mornings energetically, that's great! However, to keep being energetic, you must have the right daily schedule. Do not rush into fixing a schedule. Rather, make some few tests to see your most productive time and save that time for the most sensitive task. Ensure that you have time for everything you want to do though. Also, insert breaks within your schedule to breathe and rejuvenate your energy. Use breaks to check on loved ones and confirm your to-do list. This way you are able to multitask without over-pressuring your brain.

Experts argue that structure offers a sense of familiarity; which makes sense only to you. It allows you to wake up with a sense of order and organization. It sticks in you that after a particular task, this comes next. It's even easy this way to create time for an emerging or not so frequent task that you have to carry out on a particular day. Ideally, structuring a daily routine increases efficiency in your life. It becomes a footprint which with or without motivation, feels necessary to follow, and helps you build momentum for getting to your long-term goal.

Your typical day is a successful example when effectively scheduled. In the evening, have some time to unwind, and let go of the stressful moments you experienced at work, and prepare for the next morning. Remind yourself that you did the best and that you can make it. Even if you feel overwhelmed, do not beat yourself up since that's something that all successful people experience. Some days are just too much on you, and you almost feel wasted. Do not let it go to your head. Make peace with everything before getting to bed. You are sure to have a peaceful sleep as you look forward to tomorrow.

Exercise Regularly

Your body is your most important asset; hence it has to be maintained properly. Also, it is true that exercise is food for the body and mind. First, it boosts your energy levels, which is something paramount to a healthy lifestyle. It also helps you to release stress and bring calmness to you.

However, do not fall into the temptation of challenging yourself based on other people's ideal time and ways of working out. Establish what your body needs. One of the most common mistakes that people commit is thinking that they have to go to the gym to lift heavy weights until they pass out. NO! Start out small, and build your pace. Include the habit into your daily routine, and rise up to it. If you are able to have your gym session at exactly the same time, the better for you since you can schedule the activity right before and after that session. Over time, however, try to carry heavy stuff to test your abilities. It is such challenging oneself which builds confidence and the drive of competing against oneself. You will be amazed at how much you are capable of. Also, you will eliminate the fear of what seems impossible for you.

Most importantly, make it a pleasurable moment that you look forward to. Experts argue that your body and mind have to be in sync during your work-out sessions for them to add value to you. If running is not your cup of tea, don't run! Also, try to mix different activities to strengthen different body parts. One of the major benefits associated with this regular exercising is are that it helps to tone and strengthen your muscles. You are able to feel and even look better. It also enhances flexibility, and you are able to carry out tasks without too much straining. It also controls weight and reduce the likelihood of contracting diseases, which could reduce your well-being and productivity. Nonetheless, it improves stamina and helps you to use less energy for the same number of tasks.

Eat Healthy

Food is the fuel that keeps your body going. I agree with the saying "We eat to live, but we don't live to eat." A good diet keeps you energetic to maintain your productivity and keeps you healthy. Every little thing that you consumer matters, whether it is a drink or a meal. Healthy eating is one of the most common concepts but yet which few people practice. Most of us are even unable to differentiate between the great and not-so-great types of meal. It is, however, sad that we do not consider diet as a significant part of our daily habits. You would instantly switch into being more mindful into what you consume if you realized just how a good diet influences your daily energy levels.

Although not all of us are able to eat home-cooked meals, this has proven to be among the easiest hacks into healthy feeding. Most of the restaurants out here are so much likely to add value enhancers such as sugars and flavors to meals. After all, they are in business and their offerings have to be marketable! Cooking at home offers you a chance to control use healthy ingredients and culinary methodologies. One traps that we commonly fall into is the attractiveness of the foods and drinks we find in the supermarkets and fast food stores. It often proves hard to resist the temptation of eating chips, burgers, and sodas when you are out there working and are in a hurry. We find them more convenient, sweeter, and better. However, remember that healthy meals do not have to be every meal that you like. Eat something you do not like but which helps to keep your body healthy.

Healthy eating helps to maintain energy levels and keep you away from sudden sugar crashes or energy burnouts. Staying hydrated, for instance, helps you to stay alert in your work, and you are able to get through each day more easily. It also prevents disease and improves your mental health. Learn to make gradual changes that you can stick to in the long-run. Consider consulting your doctor if you are experiencing problems identifying what food is good and healthy for your body type.

Declutter your Living Spaces and Lifestyles

We live in an era where everything in our lives is in abundance. Due to enhanced production and substitute goods in the market, the cost of goods has decreased, and our living standards have improved in one way or another. Ranging from kitchen stuff, bedroom stuff and clothes, we have everything in higher supply. If you are not keen, you find that you reduce your space by filling it with unimportant stuff. It is essential that you create the habit of eliminating all extra stuff that you do not really need to use. Throw away or give out what you do not need to use.

It is easier said than done. We often feel like decluttering is frustrating, and it's almost like we can't afford a perfectly-organized home.

This means to tell you that decluttering should not be difficult. It is enabled when you form the habits that most successful people use to have organized spaces. You should make a plan, and include it in your daily schedule, to take about 15-30 minutes sorting stuff. Do not procrastinate to organize-take it in the same way you would take any other appointment. Ensure that the time you set aside you will have the energy to do so and that you do not have various distractions. Be mindful of what you keep, and start small in your efforts. This helps you feel good about yourself, and it also gives you a sense of pride, which motivates you to keep working on your goal.

Most importantly, understand that decluttering in your life means more than just cleaning and organizing the physical space. Create the habit of eliminating all the life-degrading elements, such as consuming less of social media, toxic relationships, and even the social memberships you never use. This will help you to concentrate on your goal. This is more like applying the 80/2 rule where you identify the 20 valuable things that give you 80 percent of results. Ideally, simplify your life, and only focus on achieving your purpose.

Keep A Journal

Among the best approaches to understanding where you are coming from, where you are now, and where you are headed is to write down your everyday thoughts on various issues. This aids in attaining a proper psychological de-clutter, compile what you have been learning, improve your visualization about goals and ambitions, and boost your general outlook on life. It is easy to see how much you have grown when you maintain a record of the things you have been doing and setting some time apart every day for that.

To start up, note down one thing you feel you achieved, one thing that let you down and one thing you are grateful about. You will realize that you progress gradually over time and even record other big things, goals, and steps you are taking to achieve. Strive not to skip making an entry twice so you can easily follow up.

Meditate and Carry Out Mind-Focus Exercises

Meditation is among the most profound practices, yet very few practices it. Most of us wonder of what importance it is to just sit or lie there silently, and cannot even draw the line between that and sleeping. Yet, research shows that meditation has immeasurable physical and mental benefits. Similarly, we often ignore the fact that mind-focusing improves our attentiveness to details, among the most crucial skills of decision making. Mind-focus activities access your subconscious mind while meditation accesses your unconscious mind. Also true to this knowledge is that most of the decisions we make are guided by the subconscious mind.

The benefits of meditation include sleep improvement, stress and anxiety reduction, relaxation and energy recharge, anger control, thoughts, and visualization improvement as well as discipline. We cannot ignore the results of such physical and mental boost in our everyday life. Meditation helps us to be at peace with others, focus on the moment, and recharge our energies to continue working. Nonetheless, mind-focusing helps us to not miss important details as we go about our daily lives, and we become more efficient and more successful. Therefore, create the habit of taking some moments to train your mind to focus and to evaluate where you are in life.

Chapter 5:
Fragile Mind to Unbeatable Mind

At the end of the day, mental toughness is what creates champions from amongst us. We are progressively expected to be mentally tough in every domain. We have also been made to believe that tougher is better. Despite that, various factors at play make you doubt your ability to have a thick skin. Your biological composition may be making you more temperamental than others, you may have a degree of depression; you make have had a nasty experience in the past that could include any form of abuse, or, most remarkably, you may not know the necessary coping skills.

A fragile mind is extra sensitive to what is happening around it. Even a slight disturbance that would not because harm can be sensed by the fragile mind. With such a mind, freeing yourself from negative thoughts becomes hard. You always amplify a problem than it actually is. Your mind often spins out of control. You make absurd decisions. However, there is hope for you. You can do better. You can learn how to maintain control over your mind. You can develop an unbeatable mind from a fragile mind. With an unbeatable mind, you don't easily give in, you are fearless, you are strong-willed, and you are emotionally resilient. All you have to do is to embrace the following tactics in your journey toward gaining a thick skin.

You Make Decisions Not Suggestions

Whether your company entails people who wander around looking for a leader or you're amongst a confident lot, you always respond to queries with confidence. You have faith in yourself. Believe it or not, you are constantly portraying your sense of confidence to the people that surround you. This reflects in many ways through your verbal and non-verbal communication. How you say everything matters. Confidence is the cornerstone of everything we do in life, and lack of it has direct implications on our overall achievements in life.

Your mind is snarled up. And getting out of the snarl is proving impossible. But anyway, you have to make a decision. So what? The time is now. Have you made up your mind? Besides, you are generally an indecisive person. Decision making just proves hard for you every time. You always doubt your decisions. Once you make up your mind, you start wondering if it was really the right decision. You just know, or maybe you think, it wasn't the right one. You are just overthinking it, and this is one of the greatest inhibitors of quick and effective decision making.

To develop confidence in what you say and what you decide and also to avoid leaving suggestions for other people to decide about its correctness:

- Refrain from self-analysis paralysis, where you over analyze and spend much time than necessary on something as you try to think what could go wrong and where.

- Understand what a bad decision is, but follow "often a good decision now is better than a great decision later" as a golden rule. This applies especially when it is something you can change later.

- Trust your gut, as successful people have always followed their gut feeling when making the most crucial decisions of their lives. Although thinking accesses the logical part of the brain, if there is a feeling that tells you differently from your mind, consider leaning that way.

You Never are Satisfied with Your Achievements Because You Know You Can Do Better and Want More.

One of the commonest mantras by which the successful people made their accomplishments is moving out of the comfort zone and not settling for less than they believed they deserved. As a success-oriented individual, one of the phrases you never want to settle in your mind is that "this is the way it has always been done." In such a fast-paced society like we are living, even a process you think is really short-lived is already outdated. Therefore, there is most certainly a better way of doing things than it is now. Never rest until your full potential is realized. Try to improve things on your own. Have the mind of an achiever. Just because something works doesn't mean it cannot be made better.

Our human nature tends to make us settle for mediocrity every other day. We tolerate people in our lives even though we dislike them, and we accept jobs that do not serve justice to our skills. We often choose to be complacent while the door for opportunities lies right in front of us. It is always easier to remain in a familiar position than to strive for what is desirable and lies ahead. The major reason why people settle in life is that they fear challenges, change, and taking risks. People create an endless list of excuses to justify their satisfaction with some of their mediocre situations. Such people often end up regretting and wishing they had not settled. Understand that there are always better alternatives out there and you are destined for greatness.

Change your way of thinking, raise the bar, and never accept to settle for mediocrity!

Most importantly, realize that striving to do more while you are never grateful about what you have acquired or achieved now is now worthwhile. There is no point of, say, looking for more money, while you never enjoy it. Being grateful is different from settling. You just appreciate what you already have since growth is part of what makes us happy. A great life always begins with a pleasant mind. Nevertheless, never settle for less than you can be!

Failure Isn't Recognized Because You Know There's More Than One Way of Doing something.

Failure is an ideology that instills fear and frustration in the minds of so many people. It has a paralyzing effect that tears one down in a rude shock whenever experienced. Thus, it is perceived as a bad thing. However, a tough mind embraces fear like a long-lost friend. Yes, you invest your efforts, your time, and your money only to lose in whatever you set out to do. Yes, you feel bad. It is human nature to love a happy ending in everything, but it is unfortunate that not all results will give you joy. Keep in mind that a baby falls down several times before they can eventually walk comfortably.

You have all probably found ourselves in a position where you begin to blame your fortune and imagine that a particular path is not for us. This is where we go wrong. People with unbeatable minds do not accept failure, because they know there is always another way of doing something. Failure is not actually

Relentless Mental Toughness and Optimism

falling down. But failure is falling down and insisting on staying down while you have a chance to get up. It is the overcoming of failure that creates success. Even the most successful people have failed in so many instances, but they always get up and reach for their success. Nowhere in the world, however, have we heard of a person who achieved anything by giving up. In life as it is in business, any decision that you make leads to two situations, either failure or success. No matter how talented as an individual you are, you do not make every decision rightfully. What matters is what you decide to do after receiving the results. This decision determines what the rest of your course in the path looks like.

In fact, successful people admit that if you do not acknowledge the value of failure, it is hard for you to appreciate the fruits of success. Failure is your best teacher. It improves your focus, keeps you grounded, and helps you realize your better and eventually best potential. Also, failure helps you to inspire others on the verge of giving up. One of the important prerequisites of the success path is staying grounded and heeding the lessons from failure. The most successful businesses in the world did not attain their status overnight. Every big thing had an innovative and risk-taking entrepreneur behind it, one who never gave up and never lost sight of his goal, one who never stopped to admire his work and think he has made it by accumulating wealth. While his ideas failed to deliver at times, he believed that he had the ability to provide consumers with the highest value of the product or service. Then came a global superpower and also came wealth for the entrepreneur.

You Welcome Pressure and Excel In It, You Control Uncontrollable Situations.

Werner Brendon Marcus

Sometimes, life can give you super high stakes, and you can find it difficult to not crack beneath all the pressure. You have too many things to attend to, and you are trying to juggle too many tasks. Experts argue that those with an unbeatable mind are able to thrive under pressure because they approach high-pressure situations in the state of a challenge rather than in the state of a threat. They use their psychological knowhow to enhance their performance in pressuring situations. We should embrace the skills that successful people use to gain a competitive edge in everything. The difference between crumbling and thriving is basically based on how well and fast we analyze the situation to have a quick plan of our response. Responding to such situations as threats always inhibits performance while taking them as challenges in a positive way leads to better performance.

We are all inevitably going to face misfortunes in life. We are human. And that's okay. We respond to these situations psychologically at the trigger of danger. We can either do what the situation demands by enduring the mental responses such as increased sweating or heartbeat or be overwhelmed by the psychological responses. In the latter, our ability to make proper decisions and respond promptly is hindered. Overthinking in pressuring situations can escalate the idea of the situation in your mind; even what you would normally consider manageable becomes difficult for you. Focusing on the task and doing your best is what leads to a reasonable response. Remember that how your body reacts is guided by your mind. Strive to perform optimally and eliminate any thoughts of negativity.

In fact, the pressure you feel is actually in your mind. It takes a moment for you to decide if the situation makes or breaks you. Always adjust the perspective of the moment, eliminate the pressure, and keep your head above the water. Most importantly, stay committed to your goal and rise above the pressure rather than stay passive and let everything overwhelm you. Never lose the sight of your goal even when you feel like things are going down the drain. Maintain your focus toward the lessons such situations bring along and always strive to stay happy.

You're the First One in and the Last One Out. You Work Harder and Longer. After everyone Quits You Keep Going.

Sometimes, especially when you have very challenging goals, you feel like quitting. It is okay to feel that way. However, you should remind yourself to keep working hard no matter what. Do not entertain the feeling of quitting. Persistence in your goals places your winning stakes higher than those of failure. What you should remember whenever you feel like quitting is that you are doing it for a reason. You can even list down your qualities to stop doubting your ability to pull through. There are definitely going to be those times that you got to remind yourself why it's all worth it.

Also, remember that fear is a lie in your head which makes you blow everything out of proportion. Fear is a motivator for strong minds but very destructive for the fragile mind. But fear never has control over you unless you allow it. Remember, also, that you are human and you could need assistance. Never feel afraid to ask for help once in a while, especially during times when you feel overwhelmed. Also, think about how much you are going to regret your decision once everything is back on track and how you will feel horrible for quitting.

Most importantly, remember to always work hard than every other person. Even if it means taking on a path alone, just keep going. What if the rest are focusing on things that are too shallow? Will you follow their manner of working? Remember to aim at establishing yourself as a brand. Branding takes time and hard work. Get strategic, and always focus on your next move. Think ahead and focus on achieving every milestone. Devote time to develop your skills and capabilities. That extra time and energy that others often use for nonissues, you should use for personal growth and expanding your perspective.

You're Humble All the Time Even in Tough Situations

One of the greatest sayings by the poet Tennyson is that humility is the mother of all virtues. Yet the society constantly endorses entitlement, over-confidence, and unending attention on the self. It has increasingly become competitive, making most people obsessed with their appearances and seeking attention. We can all be somewhat prideful at times. After devoting our time and energy into something we tend to develop confidence about it, and it becomes hard to listen to another point of view.

Experts, however, have emphasized the ways in which being humble can improve our psychological well-being. Maintaining a sense of humility exposes you to an oasis of knowledge that expands your intellectually since you are able to contemplate new ideas from different angles. Objectively detach yourself from your knowledge and ability so that your ego does not control you. Humility prevents prejudice of other people since you do not feel entitled to anything. You are able to tolerate others in their own skin, and also you avoid disappointments.

Nonetheless, humble people always know their limits. Hence, they are able to practice higher self-control. You do not block yourself from learning more, and hence you become more knowledgeable day by day. Always maintain the humility to accept that you don't know yet and give yourself a chance to become wiser and greater!

You Are Accountable for All Your Results and Ideas

It might feel like worrying about accountability is a waste of time. You do not even give it time and think about its value. But as successful people would always believe, accountability is what separates the super elite from the mediocre. Whatever gets measured definitely gets managed. The actual thought and effort of carrying out your work from beginning to end are pretty hard-hitting. You find that year after year, you are still spinning the wheels, but you are still facing the same predicament.

One of the major reasons you are not reaching your goals is a lack of accountability. You do not cast blames or point fingers whenever things go wrong in your life. Even though the actions of another may have placed you in a difficult position in your life, refrain from the idea of sitting around just because someone caused you some sort of suffering. Remember, at the end of the day, it is about you and you alone.

Being accountable begins looking in the mirror and accepting who you have become, as you think of the way forward. Accountability keeps you engaged while the road to reaching your goals brings distractions and takes you off-course. It enhances your level of responsibility, and you are able to close all loopholes that may inhibit your chances of success. You will take good care of yourself, and your performance will enhance.

Chapter 6:
Must Know the 40% Rule

The 40 percent rule is a Navy Seals' concept that when we think we are done; it is time we are actually only 40 percent done. It aims at showing us that we have much more ability than we think we do. It helps to explain phenomena such as why almost all the people who start a marathon race actually finish it. Practically, these people are armed with the thought that even when they think it is over, it is actually not over yet.

The 40-percent rule has been applied by the most successful people on their path to goal achievement. They are armed with the idea that they can achieve more than their current achievements. Most of us want to be successful and are willing to do anything, provided it is legal, to achieve success. We often have the energy to start something, anything. But most often, starting is not the problem. Perseverance is what makes us get our prize. All people who achieve and even exceed their expected levels understand that it is often our minds, not our bodies that create obstacles in our path.

The 40-percent rule is a game changer when it comes to triumph. It is an aggressive game plan which shapes you into what you need to achieve what you aspire in the future. The main message that the 40-percent rule sends out is about not giving up when something feels uncomfortable. We often tend to hold ourselves by thinking that we are not capable of. Our insecurities are our

Relentless Mental Toughness and Optimism

greatest enemies. These may have been made profound by the people around us, who may always be pointing them out and criticizing us. For instance, a low performer in the classroom may be criticized and discouraged, especially by the teacher. However, what keeps you in the battle is the purpose that you have.

The 40-percent rule teaches you to rise above your insecurities and the sense of self-doubt. Your insecurities are especially manifest during your time of suffering. You forget that you are great and even you forget all the milestones you have crossed. However, when you focus on the better version of yourself that you want to achieve, you are able to look beyond the perceived limitations. The small things that you do consistently are what results in great things. Little by the little enrolment of habits in your life eventually leads to immense makeovers. Once you are able to start a journey, just know that you can finish it.

Furthermore, in our day to day lives, we often limit the things we can do. We have what we believe we can. For instance, you believe that you can only manage running 200 meters, and if you tried to pass that level, it would not be possible. Do you actually know that the 200 meters in your head are just but 40 percent of the number of meters that you can run? Have you tried to challenge yourself to do more than you do on a daily basis? The 40-percent rule is all about adding small efforts day by day, which keeps adding your percentage. Whenever you think you are tired and that your body or your mind cannot do more-stop to think again.

The great stories of people whose world has at some point have fallen apart and they managed to overcome them can inspire us into applying the 40-percent rule in our lives. Leave alone those who have endured entirely long periods of suffering but eventually pulled through. Think about a marathoner who endures the pain and turmoil in their journey but still makes a point of completing the race. Research has it that 99 percent of people who begin a marathon race in the US normally finishes the race. That is quite surprising considering their struggle to get there.

If we were keen to examine the mind setup of such a marathoner, we would surely draw substantial lessons from their approach of issues. It is obvious that they feel a sense of accomplishment after the race even though they do not try to cover-up how challenging their road to get there normally is. A sports physician once referred to the marathon as a durability event that subjects the body and mind to tremendous stress. During this event, marathoners focus on being present in the moment, and they strive to ignore self-consciousness, which may draw them too much into whatever is going on in their bodies. If they focused their attention on how tired they are or how they have been hit by a hurdle on their way, they might start worrying, and anxiety may inhibit their ability to continue. Most importantly, the power of positivity keeps the marathoners going, since any sense of negativity or defeat may lead to slowing down or dropping out. This way, they are able to realize their full potential of completing the race, more so with minimal injuries. They have mental toughness coping skills that eventually pay off.

Using the marathoners' tips, we can be able to employ the 40-percent rule in our lives: We see that it is the mental focus that helps the marathoners go through a period of about four and a half hours in the zone until they cross the finish line. Believe it or not, you get what you attract. Believe that you can make it and you are already halfway there. Keep doubting yourself, and even the far you have gone in your journey is vanity. While we are used to the idea that to get what we want it has to be hard, we should try to not focus on the ways of reducing the perceived unavoidable suffering. Instead, we should go with the crazy mantra that suffering does not have to be part of the equation. It is really amazing how the whole system works; the things we want to come to us can be achieved with ease and joy. Getting into the space of allowing the law of attraction takes time. We have to shift our energy and start acting in a way that supports our journey rather than hindering it.

Give Things a Chance to Be Easy

Whenever we are facing sort of adversity, we try to figure out the best fitting solution. Whenever numerous solutions fail to work, we dig even further with the hope that things will get better. Our minds tell us that we cannot fall back until the solution is achieved. However, the more we dig for the solution, the more we become frustrated and start building a negative momentum. The unpleasant feelings persist in eluding us that we start doubting ourselves and wondering why the universe does not respond to our energy. All this while, however, we are asking for the universe to respond to the wrong energy.

Here's the thing. If you want things to manifest more easily, you must be willing to take a step back, breathe, and let things be. Do not continue down the drain with your frustrations, anxiety, and all the shitty feelings. The time you take to breathe, you align your energy with the road you are taking. Therefore, if you are relentlessly searching for information from the internet, and all of a sudden, you are bombarded with the countless sets of information until you can't tell one from another, get off the internet and use that time to do something else. With your mind lighter, you may be able to come up with a perfect search item that will land you right into what you would have spent hours of searching without bearing fruit. Most often when you step back and relax, something that you have been overlooking along the way will pop up. Your energy is aligned, and you are ready to carry on. Even if you were doing sit-ups, and you thought you are limited to doing 10 times, yet you know you should do at least 50 in a day, take your 5 minutes off, and start all over again. You will find that, with time, you are comfortable doing around 60 sit-ups in a day.

Concede That What You Want Is Not the End

Whatever you think that you want now is only a small fraction of what you are truly capable of. Truth be told, your current desires are based on your vibrations and belief of the current moment. People who lack the energy to continue and quit would grow a little bolder if they knew about the law of attraction. But by and large, most of these things tend to be muted. And that's okay. You don't begin imagining making about 40 grand a month when you are barely striving to get a dime in a month in your new venture.

Our main challenge is being overly attached to particular manifestations in our lives and directing all our energy into this. While the whole idea of stepping back and letting this seems like a good idea, our mind considers it as an enemy to the manifestation of our thoughts. Whilst it makes sense logically to feel connected with what we want to achieve since we can feel its absence, our energy blocks the channels of receiving, through which we can possibly get even better stuff.

The idea here is that you should pay attention to the present and trust that the universe knows exactly what you want. Then, it will be easier to align your energy into achieving more. Just know that when you get your vibe up, you will meet along the way things that make you feel just as good as the pleasant feelings you are currently cultivating. Acknowledge in yourself that what you want is not just what is filling your mind right now. What you truly seek goes much deeper. Most importantly, be willing to concede that you can't even conceive of all the scenarios that would offer you the exact state that you want, and that you would be ready to welcome them if they show up. Just do not be tied by the make-up of your mind that tells you what it feels you should do.

Stop Seeing the Suffering but the Value in It

The society has taught us that to become successful, you have to toil and suffer and work really hard. This is quite unfortunate for the people whose minds begin focusing on the suffering part of their journey the moment they commence it. This paradigm is, in fact, embedded in the minds of many people, especially with all the evidence of people who have achieved great results through suffering and hard work.

It is quite unfortunate to actually believe that hard work and suffering make us worthy of the success we get at the final end. We set our minds to be all manners of miserable for a certain period to get whatever it is that we want. However, we should learn to truly embrace the idea of energetic alignment rather than having pre-determined series of painful endeavors. We should train our minds to accept this and allow things to be easy.

The most disquieting belief that most people possess is that some outside force keeps tabs on all of us and that it will eventually reward us when it decides that our suffering is enough, and it has proven our worth of attaining what we want. After all, we have been made to believe that you must be willing to strain and sacrifice to succeed. With this in mind, the idea that leads our actions is trying to reduce the inevitable suffering, rather than the empowering idea that suffering does not have to be part of the journey. Now start putting things in your mind like what you want may be easy and fun to get there. Think about those activities that give you results with less effort and those which feel good and that to be happy, it is not a must that you pass through a bunch of things that make you unhappy. Start aligning your energy right now to what you can do to make things easier and stop the suffering.

Take it as a general principle that you cannot keep engaging in the suffering waiting to drop them when easier stuff shows up. The universe never defies your vibration. You will actually suffer and lose all your energy when you focus on your suffering. You cannot realize your full potential until you are able to align your mind with what really matters. Things cannot change until you decide in your mind that you will from this point adopt a new perspective to life- that it does not have to be painful and torturous. The energy of allowing things to be will allow you to do more, achieve more, and enjoy the process.

Chapter 7:
Develop the Confidence to Lead

"Be confident" is perhaps one of life's most significant pieces of advice that will make no sense when you've never done something. You already have seen confident people, and you know what they look like, the benefits they reap from being confident, and you also think you would be better with confidence. Most often, we tend to be intimidated by that one confident person who seems to believe in themselves. We tend to look at confidence as a value that one is born with, once we how seemingly flawlessly one presents them. It is easy to even think confident people know exactly how to deal with situations they are engaging with for the first time with ease. But that is usually not the case. For how could they know how it will be before attempting something?

The truth is we are all uncertain about doing something for the first time or taking on a journey, maybe to achieve a long-term goal for a long time. We can all screw up when doing that thing. But whatever it is that differentiates between someone with confidence from one that is not is the attitude. We let our fears and insecurities make us less confident. More so, the mere fact of having never done something that others seem good at makes us think that it as a thing for the lucky few. A confident person does not care how many people have tried down that road and failed and does not listen to noises from the side. They pursue their journey resting on the understanding that they may fail in their experience but also knowing that whatever happens will be alright. Their positive outlook on issues aligns them to their very best mental state to master that situation.

In its simplest form, confidence is the aspect of understanding what you do and the value it adds in whatever field and reflecting this to the audience that may be watching you. There is a thin line between confidence and egotism, whereby the latter can also be referred to as over confidence-and which makes you practically believe that you are better than anybody else hence you start misusing your talent and knowledge to look down on others. Also, there is a sharp contrast between confidence and low self-esteem, whereby the latter makes you think that you are less valuable and cannot achieve things that others do. Imagine that feeling-having the self-approval that you can actually do anything that you set your mind sets out to do. That you actually can stand out amongst a crowd without trying to think that you are better than anyone else.

All confident people were not born like that. They most likely made a deliberate decision to stop fears and insecurities from controlling their lives. They saw the better light of changing the behaviors, thoughts, and even decisions that used to hold them stuck in a cocoon of self-doubt. Things that you can do mentally to start building your confidence:

Being confident is a matter of your mindset. It is just about the way you think. It means having positive thoughts and being confident. Confident people feel a sense of belonging and appreciate others. They often tend to be successful in life because they are confident enough to take on challenges and are always finding positive solutions. Rather than spending their energy on negative thoughts, confident people use their energy to pursue healthy quests.

Relentless Mental Toughness and Optimism

If possible, healthy confidence building should have taken place earlier on in life-in one's childhood, but a majority of people discover that they should build their confidence levels later on in life in their pursuit of the life they desire. To have the confidence to lead, you have to push through your self-limiting thoughts and beliefs. It is a natural thing to have really huge aspirations as a child, but as you grow up, these aspirations tend to fade off. There are natural inclinations of squashing big dreams. We start letting the society impose on us its own beliefs of our capabilities and weaknesses. To break this off, you have to test your ability by embracing opportunities in life and handling pressure effectively.

Also, develop a sense of curiosity. This will allow you to approach each new experience as fun. Human beings are naturally born explorers, but the confident ones who dare to try new things out become the founders of how we do things. The simplest illustration of how you should treat a new experience is by looking at a playing child. They happily look forward to new involvements because they have not familiarized with the notion of disappointment. To the young child, it is always a chance to learn something new and not a door to disappointment.

Talk to yourself. This is one of the critical mantras that may seem crazy but which actually work. Research has it that we say around up to 1000 words to ourselves every minute. Why not make this count? Talking positively to yourself makes you smarter, improves your memory, and enables you to focus. This is actually one of the aspects that the Navy SEALs are trained on. Speaking positively to themselves helps them overrule fears and deal with anxiety properly. Remember that how you talk to yourself influences the brain's response to it.

In addition, there are tactical actions you should take to improve how you feel about yourself, and consequently what you believe you are worth.

Start by doing what it is that you want to be confident in. Confidence, at the end of the day, is built through experience. Confidence is not an item that you can buy or even borrow. Building it demands action. You have to take solutions every day that will help you start having faith in yourself and being confident. Also, keep doing what you fear, and every step you take brings you closer to what you aspire.

Exercise: The benefits of working out cannot be understated when it comes to confidence building. Once you exercise, your body releases endorphins which leave you feeling pretty good about yourself. Also, exercising keeps your body in shape. More importantly, exercising gives you tangible proof that you have done something constructive, and every inch of your body is programmed to endorse that response. If you keep at it and make it your daily habit, exercising results in a healthier body and the results cannot be hidden. It tones you and makes you just look good.

Learn how to dress better: Dressing works magic in how we feel ourselves as we walk and as we interact with others in our day to day activities. Ever looked at yourself in the mirror and gave yourself the first approval before waiting for anyone else to tell you how smart you look? Try that, and you will not be disappointed. One of the common mistakes that we make as humans is that we dress to impress people, and we actually expect compliments while not everyone may actually like your dress code. Once someone points out an error in our dressing code, we become frustrated, and feelings of low self-esteem dominate us. Therefore, we should learn to dress our bodies according to our

Relentless Mental Toughness and Optimism

wishes since we are all unique in our own beautiful way. This way you will not be turned down by any mean comments out there.

Also, realize that how you look is in sync with how your audience views you. More so, confidence is attained by presenting your best self. Therefore, learn power poses. Our minds can be influenced by what our body is doing. Research has it, for instance, that with outstretched arms, you feel more confident by increasing your testosterone levels. How you position your body directs your mind to feel a particular way, and other thoughts flow from that position. How you carry yourself around also says a lot about yourself to others. Be sure to let them know about your self-confidence and that you are in-charge. Learn to walk with your head up and shoulders back since this is the way the world will approach you.

Keep improving your knowledge through research. In an era where almost every piece of knowledge has been brought close to us, we would not have a reason as to why we would take advantage of our devices to improve our know-how. Before you approach someone or something, have a thorough search about it from the internet. A core trap here lies in differentiating between the valid information and the fake since it is all on the internet. Embrace the reading material. Embrace research. E-books are readily available from accredited booksellers and authors. Those, you can be assured, can give you a glimpse of knowledge into whatever field you are seeking. When approaching an interview, for instance, you build your confidence through thorough research about the industry that the company you are interviewing with belongs. You also learn how to behave and respond to questions, and this boosts your confidence and your chances for landing your dream job because you are most likely going to nail the interview and impress your hiring authority.

Below is a checklist of things that confident people do not do:

1. They do not settle for the less than they deserve. While self-limiting thoughts make most people settle for mediocrity, confident people continue to pursue greater challenges and testing their limits even when it feels like they've done too much. They have a vision for what they want and do not let their fears hold them back.

2. They do not look down on others even though they clearly stand out: They do not need to make negative comments about others to build themselves up, something that most of the less confident people do. Instead, they allow themselves to be inspired by successful people.

3. They do not avoid connecting with others. Most often, staying disconnected is a sign of low esteem. You fear to put yourself out there where other people may judge you or even see you fail. The confident people recognize the value of being in a community of people they share ideas and even partnerships.

4. They do not compromise on their values. Having personal guiding principles provides a framework for all that you do in life and being aligned with these principles ensures you do not compromise yourself based on external or internal pressures.

5. They do not avoid calling out for help when they need it. Lack of self-confidence makes you feel lower when you seek help from others. Confident people, however, understand that seeking help is a sign of strength and not weakness. You develop confidence, and you do not stay there stuck with a problem that you clearly cannot figure out.

Relentless Mental Toughness and Optimism

6. They do not try changing their personality. They understand that being confident develops from feeling good in your own skin. They also understand that authenticity and uniqueness count in success. They accept themselves and do not compare themselves with others, which is a great thief of self-confidence.

7. They never assume that they are done building their confidence. They understand that confidence requires an enduring vow to rise above feelings of self-doubt. This is because, in everyone's course of life, there are periods of testing one's strength.

8. They do not try to win the approval of others by pleasing them. They never succumb to the need to please people. They go about their lives without the fear of disappointing others when they do not fit their interests. They never compromise on their goals or needs to make others like them.

9. Confident people do not let fear hold them back. They understand that fear is a component of success. They focus on heeding the valuable lessons of failure and never take it as an excuse for quitting. Less confident people will quit at the first instance of failure since their low esteem shows them that they did all they could.

Most importantly, confident people believe in winning. They believe in saying YES to opportunities and also saying NO to where appropriate.

Chapter 8:
Techniques from Navy SEALs

It is interesting to learn how the participants in the Olympics handle the pressure of competition when they know they are being watched by the entire world. More so, it is interesting to learn how the Navy SEALs develop the mental toughness to overcome deadly situations. It is also interesting to learn that these two most envied groups of people apply more or less similar tactics in life. Most interesting is to know that the techniques used by Navy SEALs can offer what you need to have an unbeatable mind.

When facing adversities and our lives being threatened, our minds offer us a powerful protection mechanism. It has an automation system which allows us to act before we can come up with conscious decisions. Some of the actions we take during these times may not be the best for us. Navy SEALs are constantly facing life-threatening situations. What keeps them going is the ability to conquer their fear and respond to frightening situations appropriately. They are able to utilize their mindset to make more conscious decisions during these situations.

The following is a checklist of the techniques we can all learn from how Navy SEALs build mental toughness.

Setting Goals

Relentless Mental Toughness and Optimism

Goal setting has been established as one of the most effective techniques that keep you going and focused even when you are facing difficulty, and every inch of your body feels like quitting. It allows you to see the brighter part of the future, and it prevents you from melting down by the heat of the moment. We constantly hear the concept of goal setting, but most often, we connect it to organizations, businesses, or project teams. We imagine that there has to be something big one is aiming. That is where we go wrong.

Goal setting entails all the things, minor and major, that you are looking forward to achieving. You can have a goal for a day, a week, a month or even years. And what do you do after achieving those? You set others. The SEALs are advised to have goals at every single time. Be it in their workouts or working until lunch, they are asked to have something they look forward to achieving. The main thing is to keep improving; hence you must set new goals after achieving the old ones. Be sure to monitor your progress to ensure it aligns with your goal's expectations.

Visualization

Visualization is as important as goal setting. Setting goals is being practical, and visualization is being tactical. It is a strategy you use to anticipate any challenges and get ready to face them. Visualization helps to keep you on your toes since it presents the bigger picture. You see yourself succeeding through all challenges and ultimately accomplishing your goal. The reason we are encouraged to see the bigger picture from both the negative and positive dimensions is that visualizing an ideal situation does not motivate you to put in the required work for you to succeed.

Visualization is a key success factor for the SEALs. Analysis has it that the SEALs spend a considerable portion of their morning time imagining every disaster and error that might occur during the day ahead. This helps them to tie any chance of risk to an appropriate response. They see themselves accomplishing any mission that they are assigned. Typically, by visualizing, you conquer in your mind even before you get to the ground. In every goal that you set, remember to visualize yourself winning so that you are able to ignore critics and eliminate thoughts of self-doubt. You will not have to think about what to do when you are already in a mess. Your mind will guide you on how to stay focused and motivated.

Positive Self-Talk

As mentioned earlier, it is estimated that a person says from 300 to 1000 words to themselves per minute. If there is a comment the SEALs would have to make about this, they would say that those words need to be positive. Tell yourself that you can do it when you give it your best shot. The SEALs always tell themselves this during their several stressful situations. They look at challenges from a unique perspective and convince themselves that bad things are temporary and that they are going to overcome them. They also say to themselves that all things have a cause, and it is not their fault that things happen the way they do. Their goal is to keep pushing until the end of the tunnel where the light is.

One of the things you need to really realize for your life to change is that every moment is temporary, both good and bad. Your gloomiest moments are momentary. Hence you should not give up on yourself when it is raining in your life. Likewise, the liveliest moments are temporary; hence you've got to live in the moment when the rays of sunshine still warm your heart.

Relentless Mental Toughness and Optimism

Pessimists do not see anything good when they are in a stressful position. They lose their trust in everyone and everything, and they keep telling themselves that it is their own fault for not having been able to do something correctly. Do not entertain negative self-talk. Kick such ideas out of your head and give space to the positive self-talks that come from an optimistic point of view.

Reciting a Mantra

One of the common habits of the SEALs is forming their own chant that they recite whenever someone tries to show them that they should quit or once the voice in their head is negative. They use this over and over again to condition their brain into thinking that the only option is to keep going. One of the most powerful mantras is that "A man is only beaten in two ways; if he dies off or if he gives up." This conditions their mind into keeping going even if the going gets tough. After all, it is much easier to develop mental toughness when your mind chant is conducive to that development.

Some ideas for mental toughness mantras include that "quitting is not an option," or "Only me can get myself out of the race, and I won't let me."

Simulations

In simple terms, take your visualization and positive thinking to the next level like the experts do it! Simulation entails practically indulging in a situation as close as possible to the real-life situation you are anticipating. Simulations are usually the order of the day during the Navy Seals' training. They try to develop replicas of the situation they are approaching, which helps them shape their training into dealing with what they are to face. They always simulate an upcoming situation and create various conditions they might encounter.

Start acting like the SEALs. Do not sit around and say that when the real time comes, you will rise to face the situation.

How will you manage to stand and deliver a speech in front of a multitude when all you've done is the theoretical part of public speaking skills? To raise your chances of nailing the speech when the actual day comes, try standing in front of small audiences and keep overcoming your fear and correcting mistakes you do while in public. There is a big difference between a person who just does their research to learn the best ways to behave in a situation and one who actually simulates the situation to test it practically.

For instance, a job candidate approaching an interview stands a far much better position when after researching what is expected of them, stands in front of a friend or two who interview them. An interview question, for instance, answered the 50th time is far much better than being said for the first time. Have your friend (s) correct and challenge you from an objective standpoint, so you can identify your strengths and weaknesses and be ready to face the real situation.

Break Down Your Challenge into A Step by Step Process

Breaking down a challenge is compared to the popular chant "eat the elephant." An elephant is considered the biggest animal in the jungle. Eating it literally would take you a long time. But with the goal being finishing eating it at the final end, the only logical step for you to take would be to take one bite at a time. You may not finish it in an hour, a day, a week, or even a month. What is really important is that you are taking a bite after another.

The real secret here is about the breakdown of an intimidating task. The SEALs and the best athletes have always applied this principle to tackle the challenge step by step. They study it to come up with a good way of dissecting it into manageable pieces. Trying to tackle a crucial task all at once may leave loopholes from where the enemy can attack. Basically, the idea is to take your challenge step by step. Set achievable objectives and milestones. As long as you have the desirable deliverables, you are able to tell if the small bite counts towards meeting your standards. Avoid considering the whole as it might confuse and even discourage you.

Focusing on What's Right in Front of You

So, you have broken down your goal or challenge into tiny steps. But then what? It is a huge goal that is probably going to take you long, consuming a lot of your time, effort, and other resources. One of the successful tactics of the SEALs is to first divide a task into tiny steps to keep their mind from wondering how far the finish line is from where they're at, and then to focus on what is right in front of you. Literally put, for instance, a SEAL will most likely focus on crossing the bridge some few miles away, and it is until they cross that that they begin to focus on the next phase.

After all, it is hard to get your mind to actually accept that you have to stay tough for the whole year, but you can easily convince yourself about staying tough for a day.

Raise the Stake:

Commonly referred to as upping the Ante, raising stake means to increase the level of the potential reward of doing something or the risk of not accomplishing it. This determines your level of involvement in a particular situation. When you are actively pursuing a goal, raise the stakes to ensure that you persist until you succeed. You are much more likely to persevere when there is a lot to gain or to lose when you finish a task.

The SEALs have always operated with high stakes, hence the zeal they have for any mission that they undertake. They usually have at stake things such as "If I quit the battle, I will be letting my whole country down," or "If I quit before the mission is over, my family will never respect me again, and I will be setting a bad example to my children." They realize that their individual role counts in the whole group and they stay faithful to their commitment by raising the stakes. Ideally, tricking your mind into believing that there is a lot at stake is likely to keep you going till the end of any mission or journey.

Bouncing Back Quickly After the Unexpected Befalls

To survive the daily life-threatening situations and look forward to the following day with hope and strength, the SEALs are trained to be mentally tough. A vital component of this is a quick come back from the challenge of the unexpected. The SEALs have, therefore, learned not to waste time arguing with themselves on what is actually happening and whose fault it is among the team that there was an unforeseen stumbling block.

For instance, if a team is asked to rescue a person from a situation, they are given the exact outlook of the scene and even the dangerous weapons they might encounter. However, getting to the scene, they might actually find walls that they were not informed about. While a common person, particularly a complainer would start looking for a person to blame or even give up on the mission, the most logical thing that the SEALs take is to acknowledge that it's actually happening, accepting and adapting to it, then acting on it.

Relentless Mental Toughness and Optimism

Learn to behave and think like the SEALs. You are already in a mess from something unexpected. But so, what? Do not just give up. Focus on how to take on the challenge.

Work Towards Emotional Balance and Control

The benefits of emotional control cannot be understated when it comes to being mentally tough. It is far much easier to focus your mind on relaxing in a stressful situation when you are emotionally stable than when you're not. The SEALs have a simple solution to emotional control. They believe in breathing in for 4 seconds, breathing out for 4 seconds, and doing the same again. Generally, people that are not in proper control of their emotions always get uncontrollably upset when something does not happen as projected. Such people alienate from others, be it friends or family with petty manners.

On the other hand, people who are in control of their emotions are just mentally tough. Hence, they are able to prevent outside circumstances from affecting them. They have developed a thick skin that does not easily crack.

You can be sure that there are going to be countless times when things in life will be out of your control. Being emotionally stable gives you the mental toughness to maintain your course with what you had in mind from the beginning.

Identify Where you Belong

The SEALs, though strong individually and whom it all took a personal decision to engage in a mission, work in a group. They work in a community of people they resonate with and who are focused on accomplishing a goal. It is okay to establish your personal goals, but it is also imperative having a team that you resonate with, who shares your interests and ideas, and who have your best interest at heart. The only vital aspect is to draw a line between what is to be shared with others and what should remain personal.

Feeling necessary is food for the soul. It replenishes your energy and keeps you on track. Alone you can walk fast, but together you can go very far. As humans, we crave meaning by associating with others and sharing our values and vision.

Essentially, in every goal that you seek to accomplish, it takes utmost mental toughness to:

- Overcome setbacks and obstacles
- Ignore critics and mean comments
- Remain motivated even when it feels like all hope is gone
- Constantly take appropriate action
- Connect with people you resonate with
- Develop emotional control

Chapter 9:
Mental Training of the Top 1%

As earlier mentioned, the top 1 percent people do not just work hard to get to the top, they must be smart too! If you belong to the 1 percent, you read, listen, and inquire because you are yearning for more from life. You are not like the rest. You are not inclined to taking the easy or path in life or one that feels safe. You know that you can do it, and you actually want to serve as a mirror to people who may be looking up to you. No matter the position you are at in life, there is always a level higher than that. Your treasure awaits you at the peak of the mountain. To get to that level, you must have a relentless self-drive, take the initiative, and refrain from moving with the crowd.

We all know a lot about goals already. Goals are a central reason for the success of the top achievers. They have been the powerhouse behind the building of billion-dollar firms, global superpower inventions, and even why sports superstars have been globally recognized as achievers and received global medals. But it all boils down to how brave you are willing to know your path and stick to it regardless of how the rest of the people behave towards it. It is about the push you have to work hard at all times. Most importantly, it is about the mental capacity that we all need to maintain on our paths and striving to act as an achiever already even though we are not there yet.

We all recognize successful people by their qualities and achievements that set them apart from the rest. We all understand that it is good, and it feels really good to be the best. But what good is that if we do not have the requisite capability and effort to get to that level? There are particular successful thinking habits that often differentiate the top 1 percent from everyone else, the 99 percent others. Research has it that the 99 percent tend to focus their attention on the wrong things, they do not take enough action to fuel their goals, and they prioritize short term comfort over long-term success. Conversely, the top 1 percent people have a mental capacity of managing themselves appropriately and using the resources at their disposal more wisely.

The following are ideas you can use to have the mental capacity of the top 1 percent as opposed to belonging to the 99 percent.

Regularly Review Your Goals

We have already covered so much about setting goals and their role in our life journeys. Now we want to understand why a regular review of goals is paramount for us. The reason why any project, especially in the business field is implemented and followed up with a proper monitoring process is to ensure that everything is moving in the right direction, in what it was intended to. Evaluation is also done to identify the areas that need improvement.

If you are fully committed to your work and taking all appropriate actions, and you feel like your goal is not being achieved, or maybe you have not received results you expected, goal reviewing is what you need. Experts suggest that goals should be reviewed as much as weekly. You may realize that you need a little adjustment to your plans to achieve a particular outcome. It also gives you an honest outlook about your efforts and also inspires you to keep going.

Relentless Mental Toughness and Optimism

Remember it is all about working hard and smart. You don't want to go all the way until you reach your destination and realize that there is a better route that could have gotten you there, with less effort. Also, you don't want to get mediocre results and realize there is something you could have adjusted along the middle of the road and achieved more success.

Identify A Niche Through Which You Can Create Value.

Simply put; focus on being the only one rather than being the best. While the average person thinks about how to become the best in a particular field, a top achiever focuses on identifying the gap in that particular field and creating some unique value. Such a person always looks for ways to complement others who aggressively compete over the same resource by providing them a unique perspective. Articulate what you are good at, and ensure to add value to society. You need not just start competing without knowing what you are really offering. Sustainable and long-term progress comes from starting out on the right trail. Instead of committing to simply getting ahead and being the best, identify a niche or a 'sweet spot' and pursue that.

Remember to take as a rule of thumb that your uniqueness is what creates value and sells you out. Learn about your strengths, what you are good at and what you are not so good at, and advance from that point. Figure out what works for you and align that with your skill. Develop your own style and follow that.

Attack the Day Very Early in The Morning

We have already covered the benefits of waking up early in the morning. There are various factors that determine whether one is an early riser or late to get to bed. Some of these are variations in lifestyles and natural influences. Yet, it is proven time and over again that the top achievers tend to be very early risers. That one person you probably spot through your window jogging outside while you are struggling to wake up most probably has some secrets to success.

While research shows that evening people are often more creative, our modern society has just naturally inclined to cater to early risers. When the 99 percent others are trying to figure out what to do with their day and fixing tasks, 1 percent of people are already busy into their schedule. There is great enthusiasm brought by waking up early which tunes you into the day ahead. Early risers make the most of the early hours.

Complement Your Knowledge with Action

All other success factors held constant, the top 1 percent of people realize that every piece of knowledge should be followed by a plan that is persistently and aggressively pursued. One of the benefits of taking actions and practically testing your knowledge is that you obtain more control over your journey's direction. You get a chance to advance your skills, experience, and qualifications.

Remember that experience is the best teacher. You are your own driver, and you ought to realize that you should be the mastermind of change. Also, remember that you become unique by being creative to come up with a unique selling point. You attain this level by actually testing your knowledge. Merge your talent and skills to make yourself more marketable. We all need something extra for us to be unique in the information-driven society where everyone has unlimited access to information.

Create Your System

Be assured that the top 1 percent looks for systems to implement. They put the right systems in place, and this sets them to the path of achieving goals. Just as Simon Sinek would say, "Imagine a system where everyone would wake up every day motivated to get to work and finish the day feeling complete by the work they've done, feeling that they have contributed to something better than themselves. The top achievers mostly wake up ready to share everything they have with the world because they realize that it is so aligned with what they care about. It takes a little bit of retrospection to develop your own system.

Identify what is important to you, the times that you are the happiest and even if not for the money, how you would spend your every day. Create and implement a healthy feeding and exercising scheme to achieve mental health and fitness.

Have Priorities

The experts agree that having too many primaries is similar to having none. You cannot be a teacher, artist, yoga expert, and a house painter. Be articulate enough to cut down your priorities and remain with the ones that really matter to you.

The concept of prioritizing is by far and large the reason why some people are always moving but getting nowhere; it is the reason why most people may not be as successful as they may want to be. Most often, such people do not clearly define their priorities. Hence, they lack have motivation. Priorities define a person and give one the reason to do stuff. Prioritizing on one area that you deem best allows you to focus your energy and incline into winning and not giving up. It allows you to measure how good you are at something and it determines where you focus most of your energy and resources. Hence, while most people try to tackle too many things at once, be like the top 1 percent achievers who are pros at prioritizing.

Network

No such thing as too many friends. The more people you know, the more connections you have and definitely the more chances of acquiring knowledge and opportunities. The top 1 percent achievers consider networking a necessity in their journey. More so, knowing the right people is a powerful tool for reaching the top 1 percent.

Most people shy away from the thought of having to grow the number of people they know. Yet networking is one of the greatest pieces of advice you'll find in the professional environment. Factors such as educational achievement, experience, and skills held constant, a job seeker who has connections is much more likely to land a job easier and quicker than one who does not. Networking applies in our personal lives. Ideally, the more people we know that are right, the easier it is to achieve something.

The top 1 percent achievers stand out by excelling at networking, informs people how they are doing in life in an intriguing manner. If someone is new to them, they offer some additional information which makes their first encounter memorable.

Comprehend Your Flaws and Specialties

The top 1 percent achievers understand and differentiate between what they can do and what they cannot do. They utilize their strengths to cover up for their weaknesses as they try to improve on the weaknesses over time. While most people may look at them like flawless beings, people at the top have realized their weaknesses, but they have deliberately chosen to not dwell on it.

Relentless Mental Toughness and Optimism

Early in your career, for instance, your boss may seem to be flawless in everything, but if you listened to them on a personal level, you would understand that everyone has weaknesses. It is only a matter of how you treat your weaknesses. It can control you, but you have the potential to control it.

Realize that you cannot be competent at everything. Once you realize this, you focus more on your strength to become more productive and happier. You will cease engaging in activities that you know you may not impact much and you will stay away from frustration. Most importantly, realize that strength is not only something you are good at but something that makes you feels strong as well. Therefore, embrace your fortes and steer clear of your weaknesses.

Focus on The Long-Term
While it is good to take your journey step by step, it is also good to focus on the bigger picture. A top secret for the top 1 percent achievers is delaying their gratification until they have gotten to the top. While the other 99 percent satisfies their short-term cravings, the top 1 percent always keeps their eyes on the grand prize. Neither efforts nor courage are enough without a long-time prize that you wait. For without the long-term vision, your energy often is directed to the less important functions. Even as you set minor goals and milestones in life, it is good to picture where you want to get.

Focus on Finding Solutions to Your Challenges
They key accomplishing most of your life's crucial goals is constantly finding solutions to your challenges. There are two different ways, however, in which we approach problems in life. While most of the people have a problem-based approach and keep wondering why the problem emerged, the top 1 percent of people are solution oriented; hence they focus on identifying possible solutions.

While the problem-oriented approach helps us to avoid similar problems in the future, we should first focus on finding a solution for the challenge at hand and deal with the cause later.

The problem-focused approach often has negative influences on a person's motivation. Having this mindset helps you live your everyday life purposefully. Whenever we know we are to face a challenging task or have an activity-filled day ahead, we can decide to approach such situations from a positive or a negative viewpoint.

Understand that how well you find solutions to your challenges determines how you move past the various hurdles that life may present. It sets you apart from the crowd that may decide to just sit around in the excuse of a challenge that they are facing.

Chapter 10:
How to Actually Break Bad Habits

Do you struggle with too much TV or social media while you shouldn't be engaged with either? Or eating too many burgers and sodas while you know the truth- that these have detrimental impacts on your health? Bad habits may seemingly be harmless activities or indecisions that are easy to overlook. Any activity qualifies to be called a habit when individuals cannot stop doing them. They develop over time to be fully integrated within our system that we cannot stay without doing it. To us, it even feels normal even if some voice in our head may tell us that what we are doing is probably not good for us. Sometimes, we feel too lazy and become too ignorant to find out the detrimental impacts of the habit in our lives.

But do not be deceived. Bad habits can potentially harm your entire life and prevent you from realizing your optimal purpose. Maybe, you have a habit that you struggle getting rid of. The truth of the matter is that you still have the power to fix your bad habits no matter how much they are engrained into our systems. Even though it is not easy, it is definitely possible. It is up to you to confront and attack that character before it destroys you. It is never too late to take a reverse gear and start living a more purposeful and healthier life.

Every change begins with an understanding of the system. You embark on the journey to change your habits by first gaining an understanding of how habits work. Research has it that every habit has a system through which it develops and becomes commonplace in our lives that we do them without resistance and without thinking. Typically, habitual behaviors go unnoticed because one does not need to analyze what they are about to do. Also, they are hard to break because of the behavioral patterns that become completely imprinted.

All habits work in a system of cues and rewards. The cue is also referred to as the trigger that induces the brain to get into the thing it does in a routine form. There are internal cues which are based on your emotional state and external cues which occurs when you see something, and it reminds you that you should be doing a certain thing. Further, the routine is now the action that we do as a habit; that which your mind actually allows you to take. Finally, the reward is typically what we get from performing the routine. Each habit has a reward which signals our brain that we actually need to take action. Therefore, the process of breaking a bad habit has all to do with studying the cues and rewards and knowing how to best go around them. The following is an easy way of breaking a bad habit:

First is to eliminate the cue, which works especially if the cue does not have to be seen every day. For instance, if your cue is meeting friends in a pub, and then you end up taking alcoholic drinks (routine) and get the fulfilling feeling that alcohol gives you (reward), you should seek to block the cue by choosing a different meeting spot. While alcoholic drinks are often taken for pleasure and relaxation, you may realize that consuming it every other day inhibits your thinking and derails you in your work. Therefore, you have to take the first step of blocking the cue.

However, if the cue cannot be avoided, such as having a mobile phone and Wi-Fi which sends the signal to your mind that you actually need to check your social media accounts, you should take the step of making the routine difficult. Use the concept of the 20-percent rule to manage your activation energy. This concept plays around with your mind since it is often so hard to start trying harder for something that you are used to having so easily. For instance, to reduce the amount of time you spend on social media, you can disable the functioning of social media apps in your mobile devices and leave your social media accounts deactivated. The effort of having to reactivate your accounts when you want to access social media will keep you off from them.

The other step you can take to dismantle the system of a habit is by making the reward unsatisfying. This is probably tricky to do, but it is definitely possible. It refers to the concept of identifying something that gives you a higher level of satisfaction or reward than the bad habit does, yet with less dangerous effects on you. Consider this. It is the feeling of sweetness that one has after eating an ice-cream which makes them crave for it. But once you identify something different, say milk, which gives you a good feeling yet you know it is more beneficial to your health, you will be able to override the seemingly pleasant feeling you have from taking ice-cream. More so, the following are the tips you should consider to make a change in your habits:

If behavior can be controlled, then it is a habit. It is contrasted with addiction, which is very hard to stop. With strong willpower, one is able to subdue the bad habits.

Pre-Commit to Change

Change can be scary. In a way, we all enjoy the comfort and stability associated with sameness. We only realize its effects once this has taken us down a road of complacency, and we become irrelevant. First, understand that change is a must, and if you do not initiate it, change will overwhelm. You will realize when it is too late down the road that you actually needed to change to achieve a certain goal. Then, your life will be a mess.

Conversely, pre-committing to change ensures that you are ready to handle the developing new you. You are ready to do what it takes to achieve the desired you. To break off the bad habit that is inherent in your system, be honest with yourself to understand that you really need change, and you will be ready to embrace it. If you have pre-committed yourself, for instance, to stop being on social media too much, you should uninstall the applications on all your devices. Also, if you have decided to stop sitting a lot without exercising, you should identify a way, for instance, walking a manageable distance that you used to drive home.

Assign Yourself a Challenge, Say 30-Day Challenge.

Have you ever promised yourself to stick to a personal goal, but then your intention fell ineffective a few days later? I suppose yes.

There is still hope for you. A 30-day challenge can help you out. It is an excellent strategy that has been used successfully to develop good new habits or break old bad ones. This challenge is as specific and timely as possible; hence it is measurable and easy to stick with. Rather than telling your mind that you do not have to stay online for five hours a day for the rest of your life, make it a challenge to have at most, say, 20 minutes on social media per day for thirty days.

Relentless Mental Toughness and Optimism

Whenever you want to break an old habit, a spark of excitement may keep you going. You will even acquire the tools needed for you to forego that habit. Say, a skipping rope that will help you exercise. However, you are only excited for the first few days until you realize that you were not actually getting rewarded for the overwhelming long-term goal that you set. If you do not want to give up shortly after starting, embark on the 30-day challenge. You may be surprised that your challenge will form into a habit. If it becomes a new habit, make sure to add another habit onto it to prevent it from becoming boring. Experts have it that developing about 12 challenges in a year is pretty simple and manageable.

Attach a Tangible Reason to Your Desired Change

'Why you are seeking a change' is a question that may have to ask yourself before you even plan on how you are to change. Is it that you want more money? Is it that you want to achieve a life goal and you have identified a habit that may be hindering you? Is it that you want to live a healthy lifestyle and your habits such as eating unhealthy and lack of exercise hinder you?

What motivates you in acquiring the desired change is attaching a goal to it. Realize that you may never progress if your habit still holds you down. Every successful person had to make a choice at some point that they needed to make every day count in their journey to achieving their goals. Even the world's most renowned athletes knew that to be globally celebrated of their success they had to practice physical and mental exercises every day. You wouldn't find such a person stuck on the internet for five hours a day. Also, you wouldn't find them taking junks for the better part of the day. Therefore, attaching change to a goal is far much better than blindly going about it.

Start Small

Whenever you realize that you are constantly struggling to achieve your goals, one of the contributing factors is that your mind has it that the goals are too big to accomplish.

We often talk of the much-needed change but do not realize that it all boils down to an individual to effect the change. We may accept the value that change will add to our lives, but we do not actually strategize to know the way to get there. For instance, it is unreasonable for an ice-cream lover to think that they would shut down their bad habit all at once. It happens through the way of small steps to get you there. A person who does not read and has realized that to be knowledgeable and achieve their goals in life they have to start reading cannot embark on reading 3 books in a month. Even people who are not used to the gym do not go lifting the heavyweights. You can always start as small as it may seem, even reading just 5 pages a day. You will realize eventually that you increase the time you set aside for reading, and you begin to make it there. They begin small, and eventually, they build the momentum that is needed to adapt to the new lifestyle.

Track Change:
One of the best success driving habits is tracking down and measuring your success. You definitely need to measure and track down the progress you are making regarding your habits. A habit tracker is basically a to-do list of the items you are trying to stop or embrace. You tick off or make a record of what you are trying to measure.

A tracker helps you to realize where you need some new mechanism of affecting your change. It helps to show the activities that give you the best results. It also motivates you to realize that the baby steps you are making are actually adding up to some good change. More so, it helps to keep you focused on avoiding breaking the chain. Most people fail to achieve the desired change because they forget why they started and the reward they looked forward to getting. Once you do not track and measure, you are most likely to focus on your failures and see the negative side of things. You will most probably focus on the reward you are foregoing more than the goal you are focused towards.

It is important to track the results from each step, say a daily entry of the progress. If you are embarking on reading books, record the number of pages that you read each day. You will realize that you have created a pattern in a few weeks. A tracker can help you look back and take pride in the progress of the work you have managed in the past. It also strengthens the momentum by having to activate the new task daily, and eventually, your mind never feels like the task is uncommon.

Change Your Identity

We already have it that every change begins from the mind. You tell your mind what to believe in and what not to believe in. We identify with what we tell our minds we are. Therefore, one of the essential steps of breaking a bad habit is changing our identity. We no longer identify ourselves as say, smokers or obese. We break that identity in our minds. Whenever you are performing a habit, there is a voice in your mind which tells you that you identify with the habit. Also, when we want to change a habit, we are literally losing a part of us. Therefore, we should cease to identify ourselves with action and set our minds free. For instance, you no longer call yourself lazy. Rather, you consider yourself a person who has unproductive habits. Also, try to instill positive identities in your mind. For instance, start calling yourself a strong and healthy person before you embark on the gym training and healthy feeding. Start associating yourself with wisdom before you start reading books to become more knowledgeable.

Start Changing Your Bad Habits Today.

Let's recap. A habit forms through a pattern of behavior that becomes innately part of our daily lives. A habit that forms in us can be either good or bad. It begins with a mental trigger that develops a routine of action and leads to a reward. Habits are also hard to stop, but they can definitely be stopped.

All you have to do is apply the above techniques and move away from procrastination. Start today because tomorrow comes and you will have already made the first baby step. Procrastination is a delay habit that can destroy your life purposes. When you start today and avoid taking tasks to tomorrow while you have the potential to do it today, you are able to do other things without the guilt of having pending issues. Also, it takes you a step closer to your end goal.

Mind every single choice you make no matter how small it may be. We often make minor decisions that may unknowingly change our course. In fact, this takes us back to the system through which a habit form. Any choice has the potential of getting us closer to where we want to be or getting us off our course. Each of them starts with a decision that we consciously or unconsciously make. Therefore, we should be mindful of every decision that we take along our way every day.

Chapter 11:
The Difference between Winners and Losers

Human beings are intrinsically driven towards competition. It is our ultimate source of pride. Contemporary society especially conditions us to be competitive. In every field of our lives, those who make it are those who possess the winning attitude and characteristics. Also, society has made being a winner the symbol of success. It neither tolerates failure nor does it make it an option. We all compete for various resources in life. And then, there are winners, and there are losers. The truth of the matter is that we all have the potential to become winners. The top achievers are aggressive people who put in work and dedicate all their energy into becoming successful. Who wouldn't admire to lead a happy and successful life? Who wouldn't want to get rich and travel the world and achieve their ultimate satisfaction levels? If you are fed up with losing or you simply want to win more, you have to put in the work. You have to differentiate between what makes a loser and what makes a winner.

As a starter, what you need to know is that a winner is always part of the answer and a loser is always part of the problem. You contribute towards the end of the course that you take. You want to be a winner; you are going to have to contribute immensely towards that. Also, being a loser, you knowingly and unknowingly contribute to becoming one.

The following is a checklist of differences between winners and losers. It shows the things that winners do and do not do.

Do Not Crumble Under Pressure:
In all honesty, life presents its own pressures in ways we cannot prevent at times. It all depends on how we handle that pressure and make it work for our own good. Having had a taste of both sides, I can tell you with confidence that top achievers do not crumble under pressure, but the losers are easily crushed by pressure. Even your most valuable skills do no matter if you cannot perform when you are required to perform the best during competitive pressure. Experts argue that how we perform under pressure is a reflection of our mental capacity to respond to the situation. It is our human response to stress that allows us to meet the demands of the pressuring moment that differentiates between winners and losers.

Simply stated, winners approach pressure in a challenge state while losers approach pressure in a threat state. Most often, the threat state blocks our ability to perform efficiently and focus on the positive side. The challenged state, on the other side, activates the part of our brain that is able to calm our nerves down and take an accurate and efficient decision. Take a look back at a single time when you failed in something. Say, for instance, an interview. You may realize that you actually felt worried about the situation and that you were highly uncertain prior to the situation. Most often, the fear to fail makes us overthink the situation, and it even hinders us from presenting our best selves. An interview, in this case, is considered one of the high-pressure situations where every word you say and every move you make is being observed by your potential boss. They study you to see if you are a good match for the values and needs of their company. A simple error makes you lose your chance for the job

Relentless Mental Toughness and Optimism

even if you have the skills it takes. In these situations, the confident candidate who handles the situation articulately acquires the job while others fail.

Now that we know that how you handle pressure determines whether you fail or you win, it is paramount that you break the habit of overthinking situations and performing poorly, and adopt the "never bowing in to pressure" attitude. When you enter a high-pressure situation, activate your ability to focus on the task. Do not waste your time and energy thinking about how you'll perform. When you become too anxious about the pressure you are facing, you are much more likely to perform in a way that is contrary to your goals and strategies. The good news is that we can all train our minds to see the positive side of the challenge and successfully pursue it.

Do Not Have A Negative Self-Image.

Self-image is basically the mental picture we have of ourselves in mind. It is about who you perceive yourself to be, and it stems from the ideas and beliefs we have about ourselves. The image you have about yourself influences how you carry yourself around every day. How you feel and think is tied down to your self-image. Interestingly, it also influences how other people see you because it reflects in your body language and general demeanor. The thing is, the winners have a positive self-image, and the losers have a negative self-image. Winners are never stopped by how others think about them, the kind of social status they have, or even the events in the past that might have tampered with their self-esteem, including peers that might have teased them about being different in a certain way or being ugly or being a weakling. Winners rise above such things and train their mind to think the best about themselves.

Your mental state is in peril if you are full of negative self-image. Just because in your lineage no one ever excelled in mathematics, you start thinking you were just born that way. Just because no one ever became an athlete, you start thinking it is a family thing, and you can never win in athletics. You let such thoughts hinder you from pursuing the path that may have brought you success in the long-run. You spend your entire life believing that you cannot make it and you give excuses about your abilities not being enough. You automatically anticipate the worst, and you often blame yourself if you mess up once. Failure becomes your biggest enemy because you think you have to be perfect. You magnify the negative parts of a situation and dismiss the positive sides since you have a negative self-image which becomes the basis of your thoughts and actions. Then at the final end, you become a loser.

Be like the winners. Believe that you can actually make it. We were all created equal, just that our paths are different. However, we can all be successful in our unique way. Start looking at yourself as someone worthy of the good things in life. That mindset is enough to take you through your journey of being successful.

Do Not Play to Lose

The biggest secret of personal success is to identify your calling and play to it. The great question for success is, whatsoever, do you have the winning or the losing mindset. One thing that is common among the most renowned achievers is that they never play to lose. They never let the fact that they could lose get in their way.

It is one thing to establish your zone of genius, and it is another to operate in it. Things are not always easy. Believing that you have the capability to achieve

Relentless Mental Toughness and Optimism

is easy to say but not to achieve. One day you are on top of the world, and on another day, you are overwhelmed by a wave of doubt in your abilities. The fear of failure and not having what it takes may make us lead our lives half-heartedly. However, the most successful people do not entertain such thoughts. They never let such factors undermine their motivation to perform. They have their mind focused on the grand prize they are to realize from working hard and smart.

It is the motivational focus in life that influences how we approach life's demands. Promotion-focused people are always eager to play and win. They see their goals and paths as a way of advancing. Further, they focus on the rewards they get when they achieve their goals. Such people play to win because to them, the worst thing they know about is a chance not taken to advance. Also, they work quickly since they want to get things done as opposed to lazing around. Further, they focus on the long-term benefit that they sacrifice the short-term pleasure and step onto the time-limited painful step.

Importantly also, winners do not engage in stuff that requires them to be different from the person they believe they are. They have to ask themselves if what they are doing requires them to change their personality. They have to know if it is right for them, and they have to know if it is sustainable. Further, they always do due diligence since they believe the reality, they owe themselves is that it is going to work out. Most importantly, the winners know that their inner life determines their outer circle. They know that it is all in mind to concentrate on failure or success.

Therefore, do it like a winner and always play to win.

Are Always Committed

Werner Brendon Marcus

Most people claim to have an understanding of the importance of setting goals in their lives to get to that better life that they desire. But in the actual fact, most of these people have no goals for themselves. This is particularly true for people who are not involved in some sort of commercial undertaking that endorses the setting of goals. Even more surprising, science has it that above 90 percent of the people who set goals do not achieve them. We have all at some points in our lives set goals that have not been achieved. We experience a setback, and it wears down our willingness to stay committed to the goal. Considering that most people who set goals often target the easily achievable goals, it is surprising that other people are able to accomplish highly in their lives.

But the reason why successful people become more successful while the losers deteriorate further into the losing end is clear. They are passionate about their goals, and they stay committed to the end. Whenever obstacles pop up in their lives, they are totally sold out to reaching their goal, and they never lose sight of it. When it comes to goals, the winners realize the significance of commitment. The difference between simply desiring something and being committed to achieving it is also clear. When you are committed, you do not entertain excuses-you are only focused on results. Commitment influences how you think and act. You always try harder and do not consider quitting an option.

Be like the winners; pursue your goals relentlessly despite what may come along. Take a quick moment, and check into yourself. If you are not really committed to achieving your goal, it doesn't matter how appealing or challenging it is-you are just not going to achieve it.

To stay committed to your goal, lean on a trusted coach, avoid multitasking, and track your progress. It doesn't matter how much talented you are, or you believe you are rather, seeking expert guidance makes a big impact in achieving your goals. The winners surround themselves with winners, those who will support their journey. Also, they are patient and take one thing at a time, since cooking from too many pots at a go can be detrimental to their success. Handling too many tasks may diminish your commitment, and make you split your focus, and, therefore, lower the quality of your work. If a number of them fail, you may spend too much time correcting others, and this reduces your commitment levels. Typically, commitment gives you a footprint of how to handle things when times get tough. Commit today and enjoy being a winner tomorrow!

Do Not Dream Small.

One of the most popular sayings that we consider cliché is "aim for the sun and land at the moon." Now, we know that the sun stands at a much higher altitude than the moon. A right mindset and necessary actions can definitely push you to reach the moon if not the sun. The moon, after all, is a high position that can shine down light to everyone else. Typically, the good thing about dreaming big is that even if you fall short you will still have gained a lot. We only limit ourselves, yet the sky is the limit. What successful people do not do is that they do not limit themselves. They trust their ability to achieve anything. They look up to other successful people and know that if someone else, with the same 24 hours in a day has achieved, they can also achieve.

Never let the position you are at today hinder you from deciding where you are headed. You might be in a hopeless position in your career, for instance, such that this dampens your ambition in life. Your mind may tell you to be conservative about your dreams to have a smaller blow should your dream fall short. While setting big goals does not exactly mean you'll achieve them, failure to set them definitely means that you have nothing to achieve. Winners maximize on the time they have to gain the possible positive experiences. Truth be told; life has no rehearsal, and life is short! Do not settle for mediocrity. Understand that big things do come true when one has the courage to pursue them.

Imagine someone whose dream is to be the next top athlete. Such a high goal pushes you to heights you may not reach otherwise. They require a lot of hard work and achievement. You may not make it there but definitely a lot of good will come out of it. While there are plenty lots of benefits from leaving an ordinary life where complacency is entertained, and compliance is not executed, there is nothing quite like being a dreamer and having wild visions of a life you aspire to leave.

Winners envision success well enough that they are able to feel it since as the universe has it; whatever we can imagine we can become. Losers never want to imagine goals that may disrupt their common life. Be a winner, and set yourself aside from the losers.

Chapter 12:
Guaranteed Strategies to Build Mental Toughness

With all said, it all boils down to mental toughness. It has been described as the ability to bounce back from failure and respond articulately to adversity and to work relentlessly toward your life's purpose. In other words, it is the inherent state of mind which propels people to keeping toward the future they desire.

Now, intellectual strength shapes the foundation for success in the long run. People who have made it in life are associated with a particular personality trait that makes them persevere and remain passionate about their long-term goals. For instance, mentally-tough people are known for withstanding temptation. They also overcome fear and go on to do what they need to do. What they have deliberated as valuable to their life purpose, the remarkable top achievers consistently and uninterruptedly keep doing it. These qualities require mental toughness. It is no coincidence, therefore, that those are the qualities of the successful people.

To develop mental toughness and consequently become more successful, here are the things you need to consider and do:

Have a Mindset of Total Control?
Believing that you are in control of your life to be able to own up to your successes and failures responsible is among the crucial mind-strengthening

habits. Be responsible for your own self and nothing will move you out of focus. You won't waste energy worrying about what might or might not happen to you. Instead, you will invest in making things happen. Direct your energy into realizing your end goal and reaping the fruits of success.

While most of us tend to believe that luck will play out to get us what we need in life, the mentally tough people like to be responsible for their own life. They identify what works best for them and where they are talented in. As long as they have made the first step, they believe that nothing is unachievable. Such people do not listen to the noise of the world surrounding them discouraging them from losing the sight of their vision or from losing balance over their lives.

However, the difference between being in total control and actually dwelling on things that do not align with your destiny is clear.

Do Not Dwell on Things You Do Not Have the Ability to Impact

There is so much obscurity in the concept of having control over one's life that tends to make us fail in achieving it. There are factors that come in shaping us as individuals and also shaping our future. Some of these are completely out of your control. Trying to control them to bend to your desires will only frustrate you and diminish your energy. It takes a lot of courage to admit that that's the reality we live in, and there's no way around it. Once you realize that there are certain things beyond your control in a life that is where you draw the line.

We tend to spend too much time worrying about the affairs that are totally out of our capability. Obviously, concentrating what goes around in the world has profound effects on our lives. It triggers our emotional responses to our lives. We start doubting our abilities to achieve. We start seeing ourselves as less talented. But that is all in our minds. How we respond to things that are beyond us is entirely in our minds. We have the ability to control ourselves and nothing else.

The mentally tough people always take time to breathe and relax whenever they encounter situations beyond their control.

Consider the Past as Valuable Training and Nothing More

For a majority of people, they understand that dwelling on past events, especially failure and mistakes, is much likely to ruin our present and our future by holding us back from going forth. However, most of us are tied down by allowing thoughts about our past to dominate our minds.

Yet, one of the most powerful ingredients of the successful people is taking time to analyze what they should take from the past and what should not bother them. To them, the past can only be used to train them to become better versions of themselves but not to hinder them from approaching the present and future with confidence. We waste our worthy time feeling sorry for ourselves for things that happened long ago. But the truth is we all have the capacity to become mentally stronger by letting the past go and taking only the useful lessons with us. As mentioned earlier, being retrospective allows you to analyze the past and know what you picked from a situation and that can be applied in the future. This also applies when approaching challenges in life. Having a solution-based approach to problems often helps you focus on the present and the future rather than past experiences. It allows you to see the challenge as an opportunity to learn something you did not know.

You become stronger by having many lessons and values you can apply in life.

Celebrate Another Person's Success

The society has become so cruel that the shining of another person is considered as a diminishing of another person's light. People consider success as a zero-sum game which when one gains something it automatically makes another person lose that thing.

But that is not how a mentally tough person is. They know that resentment will only add them mental baggage which will consequently reduce their productiveness in other areas. They also understand that resentment does not stop other people from shining. Therefore, once a person they know wins at something, they are happy for them. If a friend won a tough interview, they are happy for them. In fact, they draw closer to have a taste of what success feels like and to gain the tactics that such people employed.

Remember that another person's win does not reduce your chances to win. You should help them celebrate and take the motivation that such a win give. In fact, once of cliché sayings that we should consider very relevant in our lives is that birds of a feather flock together. Associate with people who have big winnings. Celebrate success wherever you find it, and you will condition your mind on having more of such success in your life.

More so, mentally tough people do not criticize others because they know that everyone has something to offer. They refrain from passing unfair judgment because they need not need pull others down to feel good about themselves. They understand that everyone has their path in life and they celebrate the unique talents of others.

Cease to Complain

Relentless Mental Toughness and Optimism

We have heard time and over again that we attract what we always think. Your words and thoughts have power over you. If you are always complaining, then you have a negative attitude towards life, and this weighs you down. Most people have the tendency of complaining over even the pettiest things including traffic delays, the weather and a queue at the store. They think that complaining will make them feel better, but they fail to understand the power that complaining has over their lives.

The mentally tough people do not waste time complaining. They know the inner peace that comes from not complaining. They allow others to be and become generally happier. This improves their clarity of mind, and they are able to go about their daily lives better. Be like the mentally tough. Do not talk about the situation that is wrong. Instead, concentrate on how you can make your life better. Also, do not listen to other people complain to you. Be kind and help them improve by showing them the limitations of complaining.

Focus on Impressing Only Yourself

Among the greatest accomplishments in life is the ability to be yourself when the world is constantly trying to mold you into a different form. There is a lot of pressure from the society which influences how we live and interact with others. This has the potential to make you lose yourself and want to live your life by the standards set by others. There is a chance that you follow what others want you to be or remain true to your purpose. Realize that successful people do not compare themselves with others since they know that this is a limiting aspect in their lives. They do not waste their time trying to wonder whether or not they measure up. Instead, they funnel that energy into creating a better version of themselves.

If you want to realize your ultimate purpose, it all starts with being yourself and doing what makes you happy. You should know what is right to do and what not to do. You should know yourself and your limits, and then live a more rewarding life without being pushed from side to side. Even when you want to focus on helping others and celebrating another people's success, you have to start by being yourself and pleasing yourself. When you work to impress others, and it turns out that they do not appreciate your efforts, you become frustrated, and you keep trying to conform to their values to please them. Once they invalidate something, you try to look for one that they will definitely acknowledge. At the end of the day, what you are doing does not add value to your personal being. You cannot have control over what you say, do, wear, eat or even work. It is easy to spend your entire life wasting your energy on things that will never lead you to your ultimate life's purpose. We are all different in our special way and it is only by embracing our uniqueness that we are able to succeed in our own unique way. The world's best athlete might not have been able to reach their success if they wanted to please the world's best entrepreneur, who was busy pursuing their goal.

Count Your Blessings

Take a moment every day to appreciate what you have. This will keep you from worrying about what you do not have and will most definitely make you happier. You will also stop comparing yourself with others over what they have that you do not.

Be grateful every time for what you have, as you await what you desire. When you keep appreciating what you have every day, you will be motivated to work harder and achieve more. It is not always about making a huge achievement at once. It is also about the little things that count. Even single drops of water can fill a tank over a long time. Appreciating what you have will also align your energy into being happy and positive always. You will find out that there's a lot to be grateful about. Feeling good about you is a powerful mental recharge.

Furthermore, counting your blessings will make you go through tough times more easily. We all encounter difficult times in our lives, and it feels like we are the worst-case scenario. If all you chose to see is the problem of the moment, how do you expect better times? How do you expect to be happy? You have to deliberately seek to find at least one thing you can feel blessed about no matter what your day entails. Before you realize it, your list of blessings will grow and you will grow along with it. Conversely, focusing only on what you have not achieved fills your spirit with sadness. Therefore, you should focus on your blessings to radiate your life.

Do Not Wait for An Apology to Forgive

One of the toughest things in the world to do is to forgive someone who has caused you pain and suffering. Most probably, we have all been in situations that called for forgiveness-asking for it and giving it. Daily interactions with fellow humans are difficult since we all have conflicting ideas, interests, and wants. We are by default, therefore, bound to have conflicts, misunderstandings, strain, and division. We find it hard to forgive because we are all, by nature, self-centered. We want anyone who wounds us to accept fault for what they did, ask for forgiveness, and even so, we still want to make them feel indebted to us.

Mentally tough people, however, know how that forgiveness is a brave action that they forgive even people who never apologize. Negative occurrences are from the past mess with your happiness today, and they take from you so much energy. Abhorrence and rage are just parasites in your life that you had better get rid of. The negative emotion attached to anger triggers a response in you that has devastating impacts on your health and wellbeing. Forgiveness reduces blood pressure, eliminates anxiety, and improves our sleep quality. Consequently, this improves our decision making, and our lives become more high quality. Forgiveness qualifies as an attribute for the strong. Be a strong person and forgive.

Some of the things that you ought to understand to help you in forgiving people are that imperfection is part of human nature, forgiveness improves your life even if not theirs, it is not in your place to judge people and also there is karma to repay people for their actions. Move on with your life and leave what already happened in the past.

Finally, Be Mindful of How You Regard the Word "Quit"

We all feel like throwing in the towel from time to time. No matter how prepared you are for a journey in life, things happen and throw us in a dilemma as we wonder whether or not quitting is the right choice. People quit for different reasons, including running projects that end up as a mere mess or at times because they feel like they are safer not pushing forward.

However, you should always consider some things when you want to quit: What is making you quit? You find that most of the time we feel like quitting because of the negative energy we have fed our minds with. Once you understand why you really want to quit, consider if it a good reason, what perseverance would bring to you, if you are likely to regret the action, and most importantly, why you started what you are about to quit in the first place. Once you train yourself to take these steps, you will go harder about your goals, and you will hardly quit anything. You will be like the Navy SEALS or the marathoners. They hardly quit once they are set out on a mission or a competition. We all celebrate their success eventually, and they lead a fulfilled life.

Now we know the things that separate those who are good from those who are great. We understand why mental toughness is such a huge factor that it overrides the potential of talent. We understand that building our capacities to handle adversity is so much about removing the harmful habits that consume our energy and hinder us from achieving our purpose in life. Now, it is time to go out there to create goals and make our dreams happen.

Conclusion

In conclusion, this guide describes the concept of mental toughness, its relevance in our lives, and how we can develop mental toughness. Mental toughness is a popular concept yet which only a few understood. For a long time in history, mental toughness has been thought of as a thing for the sports people or the Navy SEALs. Recently, however, it has become relevant in various fields as researchers and coaches attempt to offer people the crucial tactics that these most successful people have in common, and that has helped them to achieve this success. This guide takes us through what it means to refrain from putting about our limitations in mind. It directs us how to be as relentless about our goals as ever. It shows us how to persevere and never think of the word "quit" as an option in our journey to achieving our goals. It differentiates between winners and losers to help us see what makes two people, gifted uniquely but on the same playing field achieve different results, whereby one succeeds and one fails. It shows us how we can develop daily success habits and also how we can break from bad habits and create good habits. It gives us techniques from the Navy SEALs that we can embrace to become mentally tough and pull through every situation that tries to beat us down in life.

The reason why the Navy SEALs is the most admired army is that among other armed forces, the SEALs undergo the toughest training, and they also undertake the most dangerous missions. It is interesting how these troops carry out their dangerous missions to completion with all the challenges that they face.

Relentless Mental Toughness and Optimism

They never quit. They focus on the end of the mission and not the mistakes or misfortunes that have happened in the past. They are ever prepared to face challenges, and even when the unexpected occurs, they do not stop to wonder whose fault it was that the misfortune befell them. It is all about their mindset. They have a positive mindset which sees challenges as opportunities from which they can learn. Also, they are able to approach challenges from a solution-based perspective and not as a threat. They employ various principles to know how to best handle a situation. Most importantly, the SEALs funnel their energy towards their mission and focus on the prize at the final end. Another admired group is that of the marathoners. Research has it that almost all marathoners who begin a race keep at it to completion. They are able to rise above several hurdles that they face along the way because they focus on the bigger picture: the finish line. Essentially, therefore, this guide shows us how to enhance our performance with a simple mindset switch.

Among the points that the book emphasizes is that there are physical limits but none for the mind. Every time we are faced with a situation such as adversity, our performance is always influenced by our ability to balance between internal and external demands placed on us. We often emphasize on physical training or simply highlight our talent at something, but we ignore the mental training that is more paramount than anything else. Every other factor held constant during a contest, a person with the right mindset has a high chance of defeating one with the wrong mindset. We are human, and we are bound to experience critical points in life that make us want to quit our goals unless we feed our minds with success. Purpose, self-awareness, goals, visualizing success, team support, preparation, positive self-talk, focusing on progress, not perfection and celebrating the small winnings are some of the most ingredients prerequisites for success. We achieve this by showing our minds that this is the way to do it. Without a strong will power, we cannot manage these other tactics.

From the mind of a Navy SEAL part, we learn to never procrastinate, to think of discipline not as a punishment, to consider the 10 second rule when making decisions, to be ready to do what the 1 percent people will do that the 99 percent others will not, to consider the long-term, to make progress on ourselves and not dwell on competing against others, and to always maintain these habits in every undertaking that we engage in. Further, the daily habits that strengthen the minds include waking up early, making the bed, create an ideal daily routine for us, to exercise regularly, to eat healthy, to DE-clutter our living spaces and our lifestyles, to keep a journal, and to meditate and conduct mind focus exercises.

To develop an unbeatable mind as opposed to a fragile mind, we ought to learn to make decisions not suggestions, to always know that we can achieve more, to not dwell on failure since we know there are various ways of do things, to welcome pressure and excel in it, to work harder even when everyone else is quitting, to remain humble in tough situations, and to remain accountable of our ideas and results. An important concept also discussed is the 40 percent rule, in which we should know that whenever we think we are done, we are actually only 40 percent done hence keep on with the grind. To achieve the 40 percent rule, we should give things a chance to be easy as opposed to having a quick and negative response to situations, concede that what we want is not the best we can achieve, and stop seeing the suffering but the value in it.

Relentless Mental Toughness and Optimism

Further, the significance of confidence cannot be underrated when it comes to developing mental toughness. We should develop the confidence to lead and stand out among the crowd. To start building our confidence, we should develop a sense of curiosity, talk positively to ourselves, start doing what we want to be confident in, exercise, learn how to dress and carry ourselves around better, and improve our knowledge at every chance that we have. Also, we are reminded that setting goals keep us tied to our purpose, and we should always recite a mantra that strengthens our willpower. Also, to face a challenge, we should simulate an exactly similar situation, break down the challenge step by step, focus on what lies right ahead of us before we move to the next step, raise the stakes, bounce back quickly from the unexpected, achieve emotional control and identify where we belong.

We are also advised to follow the mental training of the top 1 percent; it is the group of people that comprises of achievers and who do things that others find difficult to do. To belong to this group, we ought to prioritize, regularly review our goals, and identify a niche where we can create value, complement our knowledge with action, create our own system, network, understand our strengths and weaknesses, focus on the bigger picture, and focus on finding solutions to our challenges. Most importantly, the strategies we all need to build mental toughness include having the mindset of total control, not dwelling on things we do not have the ability to control, considering the past as a valuable training, celebrating other people's success, stopping to complain, focusing on impressing ourselves and not others, counting our blessings and forgiving even when someone has not asked for an apology.

www.ingramcontent.com/pod-product-compliance
Lightning Source LLC
Chambersburg PA
CBHW031056080526
44587CB00011B/713